MODERN HARYAṆA

History and Culture, 1803-1966

K.C. YADAV

MANOHAR
2002

First published 2002

Hardbound: ISBN 81-7304-371-X
Paperback: ISBN 81-7304-440-6

Published by
Ajay Kumar Jain for
Manohar Publishers & Distributors
4753/23 Ansari Road, Daryaganj
New Delhi 110002

Typeset by
A J Software Publishing Co. Pvt. Ltd.
305 Durga Chambers
1333 D.B. Gupta Road
Karol Bagh, New Delhi 110005

Printed at
Print Perfect
A-23 Mayapuri, Phase II
New Delhi 110064

MODERN HARYANA
History and Culture, 1803-1966

To my mother
whose love and care
made my life what
it is.

Contents

PART THREE: CULTURE

PART FOUR

Preface

I am happy to offer to the readers this work on the variegated and multimorphous history of Haryana. It covers the modern period, from 1803 when the British occupied this region through 1966 when it became a full-fledged state.* I have tried here to take care of almost every aspect of life of the people—political, economic, social, religious, and cultural—in a comprehensive manner, though it would be presumptuous on my part to claim that anything like a final word has been said on the subject.

My purpose in doing this work is none other than to know the truth—the simple truth, to be precise—about the history of the people of Haryana which has, for some obvious reasons, remained untold so far. For if not supplied, this desideratum might harm us in two ways: (i) the neglected people would remain uninformed about themselves—their roots and tradition, their economy and polity, their culture and life; and (ii) the Indian colourful tapestry the threads of which represent the various shades of life and culture in various regions encompassed in it would look incomplete without the threads from the little, 'big' state.

More often, local biases and prejudices creep in regional studies which tend to distort our findings. I have taken every possible care to keep such things away from the present study. How far have I succeeded in the venture only the discernible readers will be able to say!

A large number of persons and institutions have helped me in doing this work. I am especially grateful to my friends, Shri R.C. Rao, Dr. S.S. Nehra, Dr. M.L. Ranga, Shri B.K. Muztar, Prof. Sheotaj Singh, and Dr. Y.P. Bajaj; to my students, Dr. Rameshwar Das, Dr. K.L. Miglani and J.K. Abhir; and to my wife Shashipriya and sons, Neeraj and Nitin, and daughter-in-law Shraddha Yadav for their help in ways more than one.

I am also grateful to the following institutions: the Kurukshetra University Library, Kurukshetra; Haryana State Archives, Panchkula;

*Its companion volume covering the period 1966-2000 is under preparation.

Haryana Civil Secretariat Library, Chandigarh; Dwarka Das Library, Chandigarh; National Archives of India, New Delhi; Jawaharlal Nehru Memorial Museum and Library, New Delhi for their kind help and cooperation.

And finally my thanks are due to Shri R.C. Jain and Ajay Kumar Jain, Manohar Publishers & Distributors, for handling so well the production and publication of the book.

K.C. YADAV

Part One

GENERAL

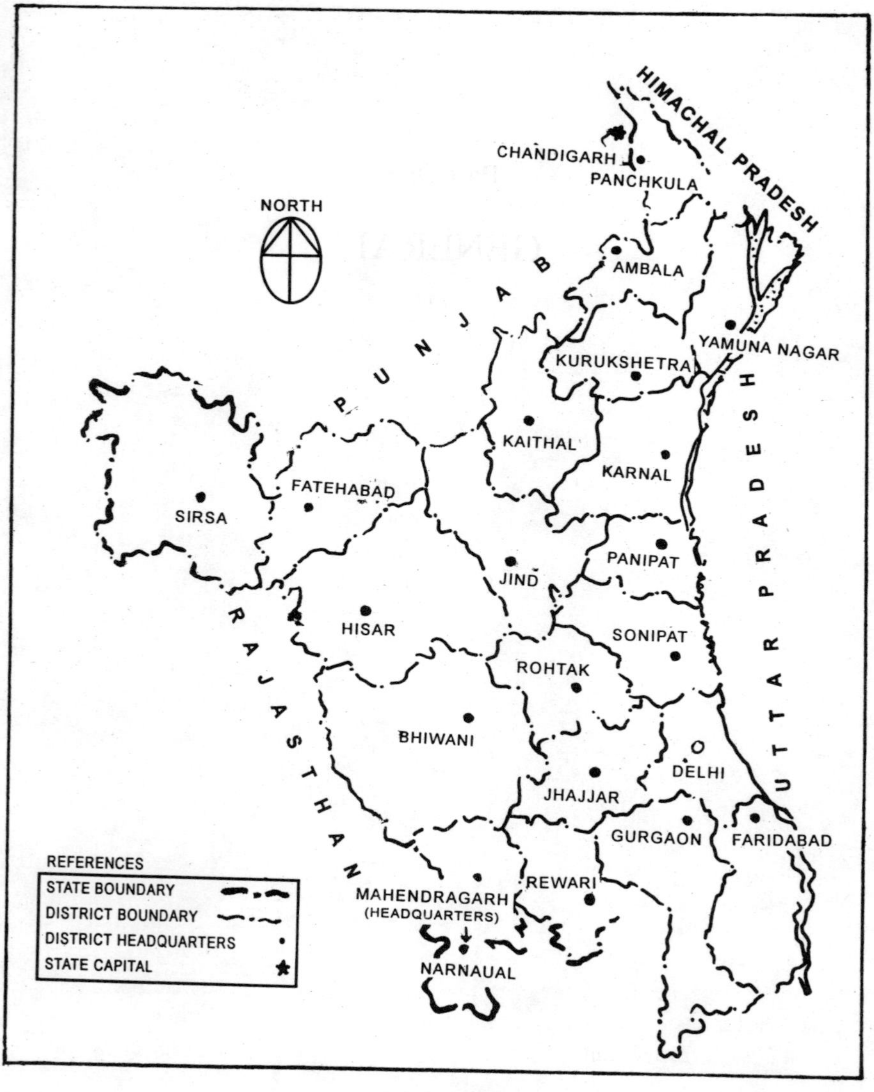

MODERN HARYANA

1

Haryana: The Land and People

THE LAND

Location

Haryana, a small state with a big name, is situated in the north-western part of India (Lat. 27^0 39' and 30^0 55.5' N; long. 74^0 27.8' and 77^0 36.5'E). It sprawls across 44,212 sq. km., and has, according to 1991 census, 16,463,648 people living in its 94 towns and 7,064 villages. It is bounded by Himachal Pradesh and Punjab in the north, by Punjab in the west, by Rajasthan in the south and by Uttar Pradesh in the east. Delhi, the national capital, sits majestically on its lap down below on the south-eastern side.[1]

The Nomenclature

Though the state has appeared on the politico-administrative map of India only recently—1 November 1966, to be precise—it has been in existence as a distinct socio-cultural entity since time immemorial—of course with its names and boundaries changing, as in the case of other states, like Punjab, West Bengal and Uttar Pradesh, to name a few only—many a time. Its present name, Haryana, say the knowledgeables, was given to it some time in the early medieval times.[2] By whom? Regrettably, we do not know. Nor do we know what precisely is the meaning of the word Haryana. Different people have offered different explanations. One scholar has attributed the name to Raja Harishachandra, who is said to have come from Oudh at some undefined period, and peopled the tract. Hence it came to be called after him.[3] Another scholar believed that Haryana actually stemmed from the word *Hari*, that is, Parashurama, associated with a tradition of great slaughter of Kshatriyas here on 21 different occasions.[4] Another view is that the name has come from *haribana*, a wild plant with which the area was formerly said to be overgrown.[5] Another view, which is fairly popular, is that the name is derived from Lord Krishna (*Hari*) who used to pass through this region in a plane (*Yana*), while going to Dwarka from Braja. The two words *Hari* + *Yana*, put together made Haryana.[6] According to Maharaj Krishna, a local scholar, this region was previously inhabited by robbers and dacoits and the name 'Haryana' actually came from the act of robbery (*harana*) on the part of these people.[7] Dharinidhar, another local scholar, says that the word actually stemmed from *Haribanaka*, connected with the worship of *Hari*, i.e. Lord Indra. Since the tract was earlier very dry, its people always worshipped Indra (*Hari*) for rain; and as such it came to be called *Hari-Ka-Bana* (forest) or *Haribanaka*.[8] Grish Chandra Avasthi, a noted Sanskritist, traces its origin in *Rigveda*, where the word *Hariyana*, he says, is used as a qualifying adjective with the name of a king Varuraja. This king, according to him, ruled over this tract; and as such, the region came to be known as Haryana after him.[9] Acharya Bhagwan Dev believes that the name has been derived from Hara, Lord Mahadeva, who was worshipped, and is being worshipped even today, by the people of this area.[10] Mahapandita Rahul Sankrityayana was of the opinion that the word 'Haryana' was a corrupt form of *Haridhanakya*, a term often used for this region in the ancient literature.[11] Bhagvatadatta, a traditional scholar of ancient Indian history, held the view that the word had come from the *Dasharna* (a place having ten forts), which has been used for this region in the *Mahabharata*.[12] Dr. Hari Ram Gupta, the Punjab historian, believed that this region being the earliest home of the Aryas was called the *Aryana* or the abode of the Aryas, like Ludhiana, the region of the Lodis and Bhattiana, the home of the Bhattis. The *Aryana* in due course of time, said he, became Haryana.[13] Dr. Buddha Prakash, another eminent historian, said that since this region was inhabited by the Abhiras during the post-Mahabharata period, it came to be called after their name: *Abhirayana* = *Ahirayana* = *Hirayana* = *Haryana*.[14] Dr. Vasudeva Sharan Agrawala agreed with Buddha Prakash.[15]

Unfortunately, all these views are based on guesses and speculations; none of the learned authors has tried to give historical evidence in support of his contention. Personally, I believe that the region derives its names from its *harayali* (greenery). Here we find such a wonderful flora that soon after the first shower, the entire tract becomes, so to speak, a lush green forest. And it was probably due to this that the region came to be called *Harita-Aryanyaka* during the early medieval times.[16] This supposition is also corroborated by a twelfth century inscription of

Aranoraja, a Chauhana king of Ajmer, where this region is mentioned as *Haritanaka*.[17] As time passed, the *Haritanaka* assumed different forms—*Haritanaka* = *Haritana*[18] = *Haribanaka*[19] = *Hariyanaka*[20] = *Haryana*.

Geo-Physical Divisions

Geo-physically, Haryana falls into two broad natural divisions: (i) the Sub-Himalayan Tract, and (ii) the Indo-Gangetic plain, which run in south-eastern direction, almost parallel to each other. The Sub-Himalayan tract which forms a sort of girdle in the north-eastern parts of Panchkula district consists of two types of hills, the higher hills and the lower hills. The former are made of two ridges, running throughout the district from the north-west to south-east, with numerous spurs branching out in all directions. These hills are known as Morni and Tipra ranges. In conformation and character, these hills belong to the outer ranges of the lower Himalayas. There are many beautiful valleys in the tract but excepting Kalka and Pinjore, none is adequately habited.[21]

The Indo-Gangetic plain, the second broad natural division, is in the true sense the backbone of the state. It is a vast, level plain standing nearly on the water-parting between the basins of the river Indus and the Ganga. In view of variations in the deposits, this extensive plain is divided into five subdivisions.The first subdivision, called *Babbar,* forms a fringe zone along the outer margin of the Shiwaliks. This has big deposits of alluvial sands brought and deposited by rivers and streams coming down the northern mountains. The subdivision is very slopy. The second subdivision, the *Khadar*, occupies the levels lower to the *Babbar* near the river/stream channels. Owing to its low level, it is very much prone to floodings which occur almost every now and then. Its deposits are mainly composed of sand, silt, mud and clay of recent times. The third subdivision, the *Bangar*,[22] is composed of the alluvium of about 1 to 2 million years. Owing to its higher elevation, the subdivision is not flooded by rivers/streams. The soil is, at places, not very good, because of calcareous concretions (*Kankar*) and saline and alkaline efflorescences (*reh* or *kallar*) formations.[23] The fourth subdivision, the sandy tract, comprises the districts of Hisar, Sirsa, Bhiwani and Mahendragarh, where wind blown sand stands piled up in the form of sand dunes at several places. The only parts useful for cultivation in the sandy tracts are the ones called '*tals*', where, due to some reason or the other, sand does not collect.[24] The fifth subdivision comprises the southern region where a number of hills stand out against the horizon and break the natural regularity of the plains. These hills are considered to be of the pre-Cambrian age and are popularly called Arrawalis, 'perhaps one of the world's oldest mountain ranges of significant size'.[25]

Rivers and Streams

Except for the Yamuna, there is no perennial river in Haryana. The Yamuna rises in the Tehri (U.P.) hills and, traversing through its rough, tough mountainous course, enters the state in Ambala district. Then it flows on through Kurukshetra, Karnal, Sonepat and Faridabad below Delhi, forming the boundary between Haryana and Uttar Pradesh for over 230 km. and then finally enters the latter state just past Hasanpur in Faridabad district. The Western Yamuna Canal taken out from it at Tajewala provides irrigation to the thirsty plains of Yamunanagar, Karnal, Hisar and Jind; and the Agra Canal to some part of Faridabad.[26]

The Yamuna was not an important river in the good old days: we get only three references to it in the *Rigveda* and that, too, in a passing manner in its praise.[27] This was probably owing to the fact that the Yamuna was then a small river. Its course was also different from what it is today: Raikes has suggested that in earlier times it flowed westward and was captured by the Indus system. In the later times (probably during the Brahmana period), the river changed its course to the present one. Owing to some changes near its source it received greater volume of water and became perennial.[28]

The state has many non-perennial rivulets/streams. Of these, the Saraswati[29] is most important. In the most of its course, the Saraswati has no defined bed; it is only after the Chutang, another small stream, joins it at Bhaini that it acquires a continuous channel and is worthy of being called a stream. Its floods, however, rarely extend to any distance. Passing through Kurukshetra, it ultimately joins the Ghaggar in the Patiala district and dries up with it near Bhatner in Rajasthan. Earlier, traversing through almost its present course in Haryana and then in the old bed of the Hakra, it met the western sea. It gave affluence and prosperity to our region. And this explains why the river is described in the *Rigveda* as 'the foremost of rivers' (*naditama*), 'the mother of rivers' (*Sindhumata*),[30] 'the holy of the holies',[31] 'the best of mothers',[32] and even 'the best of goddesses'.[33] But this position could not continue for long. Some seismic disturbances, which occured at the end of the Vedic Age, changed the entire character of the river: it was reduced to the stature of a small monsoonish stream.[34]

Along with the Saraswati flows another rivulet—the Drishadvati, which was, like the former, a highly important river in ancient times. According to old literature, it gave affluence to the thirsty lands of Haryana. It is a small stream now which takes its birth in the Sirmur hills, and after moving in the western direction up to Nahan, takes a turn towards south and moves on until it enters the Haryana state in Ambala district. Then it joins the present Western Yamuna Canal with its Hansi-Hisar branch.[35]

Another important rivulet is the Ghaggar.[36] It rises in the outer-Himalayan ranges between the Yamuna and the Sutlej. Entering the plains as a rapid and variable mountain torrent, it passes near Ambala and after south-westerly course of about 110 km., chiefly through the Patiala district of the Punjab, where it is joined by the united streams of the Saraswati, Markanda and other numerous hill torrents which cross the Ambala district between the Yamuna and the Sutlej, it bends to the west through Hisar district and goes to the Bikaner division of Rajasthan where it is finally lost after traversing some 450 kms. In earlier times, it conveyed a much larger volume of water than what it does at present. It was perhaps the Sarayu of the *Rigveda*.[37]

There is another rivulet near the Ghaggar—the Markanda.[38] It also rises in the outer Himalayan ranges and, like the Saraswati, flows across the Ambala, Kurukshetra, and Karnal districts as a rainy stream, unless it empties itself of its surplus water into the Sanisa Jhil where it joins the Saraswati. It was perhaps Hariyupa in the ancient times.[39]

Besides these, there are the following other small streams in the northern region which flow during the rainy season: the Chitang (Apaya), the Rakshi (Raka), the Sinivali (Some, Sombh), the Brahaddiva (Bilaspur rivulet), the Kaushiki (Hiranayavati) and the Ambumati (Amsumati).[40]

In the southern region there are four main streams: the Sahibi, the Dohan, the Kasavati and the Indori. The Sahibi[41] is a powerful stream. It rises in the Arravali hills in Rajasthan about 150 km. north of Jaipur. Gathering volumes from a hundred petty tributaries, it enters Rewari district above Kot Qasim. From here it flows due north through parts of Rewari, Pataudi and Jhajjar tehsils and parts of Gurgaon district till it joins the Najafgarh Jhil and falls into the Yamuna through a channel. Bhargava identifies the Sahibi with the *rasa* of the *Rigveda*, and believes that it was a big, perennial river in ancient times.[42]

Another rivulet, the Dohan, also originates from the Jaipur hills. It flows in the Rajasthan territory some 29 km. before entering the

Mahendergarh district where it is eventually lost. If the rains are exceptionally heavy and the volume of water increases greatly, then it moves further to join the Sahibi near Bilochpur. The two, then, fall into the Najafgarh Jhil. It is believed that Dohan was perhaps the *Vadhusara* of the ancient times.[43]

There is yet another rivulet not far away from the Dohan—the Kasavati. It also originates in the Jaipur hills. It enters the Mahendergarh district at Chaudhari-Ka-Nangal and after passing through the Narnaul, Mahendergarh and Rewari tehsils for about 50 km., it joins the Sahibi near Kasri. The stream, says Bhargava, was called Krishna in ancient times.[44]

Another important rivulet in the southern region is the Indori. It rises near the old ruined city and fort of Indore, perched on the Mewat hills, west of the town of Nuh, in district Gurgaon. After some run, it joins the Sahibi.[45]

All the streams mentioned above flow, as already indicated, with usually enough water in the rainy season. However, they dry up in the hot season and indeed seldom last beyond October. They usually cause great damage to extensive areas during the rainy season. But that is just one side of the story. They also add a great deal to the state's prosperity: they bring a lot of rich clay with them and leave it behind at the places they pass through. As a result, the farmers get luxuriant crops of wheat, gram and sugarcane on their fields. Besides, the subsoil water level also rises along the beds of these rivulets which is helpful to the farmers in getting irrigational water for their crops.[46]

CLIMATE

Climatically, Haryana is no different from other northern states. It has three seasons in a year: the cool season, from November to February; the hot season, from March to early June; and the rainy season, from June to October.[47] During the first season, the state remains under the influence of cool, outblowing land winds. Fortunately, the Himalayan mountain walls protect it, as it does the rest of India, from the icy-blasts from Central Asia. Hence the low temperature (the mean January temperature at Hisar is 56^0 F.) The general anticyclonic conditions of winter months are sometimes interrupted by the feeble cyclones which give a little rain to the region. Summer months experience hot weather with dry desiccating hot wind (*loo*) and occasional dust-storm. The climax of the season is reached in May and June when the region is hot like a furnace. About the middle of July the monsoon clouds begin to appear and the humidity increases rapidly till a thunderstorm announces the advent of the rains. About 80 per cent of the overall rainfall in Haryana falls between July and September. There is a pronounced rainfall peak in the months of July, August and September.[48]

MINERALS

Though Haryana has not been geologically investigated thoroughly, some surveys conducted so far reveal that about 5.6 per cent area of the state contains a large number of minerals of which at least some can be commercially exploited.[49] For instance, iron ores of low to medium grade in Dhanauta-Dhanchola, Antri-Chhapra-Kamania and Shola areas in Mahendragarh are estimated to be around eight million tonnes. It is reported that copper ores are also available in some quantity near Mothuka and Ghatasher villages in the district. The copper reefs ontcropping in these villages are the continuation of the famous deposits of Khetri. Extensive deposits of limestone, mica, etc., occur about Golwa, Durga-Ka-Nangal near Narnaul. Muscovite occurs at various places, especially at Ghatasher, Sirili, Panchanauta and Masnauta in Narnaul tehsil. True asbestos, sheef-like small fibrous concentrations in bundles of tremolite, has been reported near Nazir-Ka-Bagh near Narnaul. There is a plausible occurrence of Barytes near Bail and Masnauta, Garnet around Sirili ridge, Mukaudpur, Islampur, etc. Marble of good quality is found in the Antri Beharipur area and slate near Kund.[50] Medium quality sand stone is found in district Kaithal, Gurgaon and Panchkula,[51] Saltpetre in Rohtak and Hisar, Potassium nitrate (*Shora*) in Kurukshetra and Karnal,[52] and *Kankar* and limestone almost everywhere throughout the state.[53]

THE FLORA

Haryana has been rich in its flora all through its long history. The ancient and medieval sources speak of the presence of thick, green forests in the region. However, because of pressure of population on land, these have considerably thinned in the modern times. At present the total area covered by forests is 3.4 per cent only.[54]

A large variety of flora is found in the forests and elsewhere which can be divided into two broad categories; (i) flora of the Shivalik ranges and (ii) flora of the plains. In the former category we have miscellaneous scrubs inter-mixed with *chil*, *chal*, *sandan*, *siris*, *kachnar*, *khair*, *am*, *biul*, *jaman,* etc. In the plains we have the common trees, like, *neem*, *pipal*, *bar*, *siris*, *shisham*, *am*, etc., where there is plenty of water and *khejri*, *farans*, *kikar*, etc., where the soil is sandy and rain insufficient.[55]

The state has almost all the plants and herbs growing here which are found in northern India. It is, however, exceptionally rich in its grasses, like *dub*, *dila*, *bathu*, etc., which are considered the best fodder for the cattle and medicinal herbs.[56]

The Fauna

Like flora, the state is also fairly rich in its fauna.[57] In olden times, lions and tigers were not uncommon in the hilly tracts and forests of Ambala and parts of Karnal. The *nardak* in the latter district was especially a favourite spot for the Mughal emperors to hunt lions and tigers in. But now the two species seem to have extricated.[58] Likewise, the panther which was quite frequently seen in earlier times is at present an extinct species. Now, in the jungle, we find only jungle cat, fox, jackal, deer, neelgai, rabbit, etc. The domestic animals are: cow, buffalo, goat, sheep, donkey, horse, pig, dog, etc. Almost all the varieties of reptiles found in northern region are seen here too.[59]

Yadav and Maleyvar have spotted 161 species of birds in the state which come under 47 families and 16 orders.[60] Of these, the important and common birds are: debchick, darter, pond heron, cattle egret, black ibis, flamingo, teal, common pochard kite, shikra, Indian whitebacked vulture, grey partridge, common quail, Indian pea-fowl, sparrow, crane, cuckoo, crow, myna, bulbul, jungle babbler, baya, movi, etc.[61]

The above survey shows that Haryana in terms of its area and population is a small state. In natural resources, its position is not very good either: it is rich in flora and fauna, but not in mineral resources. Except for the Yamuna, there is no perennial river here. The soil is fertile and given enough water, can yield good produce.

THE PEOPLE

A general notion presists that Haryana does not have a distinct, separate socio-cultural identity of its own. When placed at the bar of history, however, this otherwise popular belief does not stand scrutiny. The mirror commanded to hide the truth betrays the reality: a distinct

Haryanavi identity, crafted by the Haryana people during the course of thousands of years of their history, is clearly there.

Ancient Period

When exactly did this process of identity formation begin? Specifically, who were the people who started the work? And how? These, and some other such questions, are no doubt pertinent here but, regrettably, we are not in a position to provide anything more than this by way of their answers that this historic phenomenon was started about 20 to 30 thousand years ago by the so-called stone age man. The archaeologists have found some tools of stone used by him in some parts of Gurgaon (Arravali hills) and Panchkula (Shivalik ranges). This early man of Haryana, it is surmised, belonged to the begritos race. He led an exceedingly simple life; knew no cultivation; and fed himself with natural fruits, nuts and roots and flesh of small animals. He knew of no fabrics and covered his body, in bad weather, with bark of trees and animal skins.[62]

The population in this period was quite sparse: in exact terms perhaps the density should have been 'less than a person per square kilometre where the carrying capacity of land was ordinary, and a little over this where the conditions were favourable'.[63] The possibility of their having formed some sort of social institutions, too, cannot be ruled out.[64]

This stage of the early settlers of Haryana continued for several thousand years. About third millennium BC the society was, however, transformed by a new discovery—farming.[65] A pertinent question may, however, arise here: about the authorship of this revolutionary discovery. Was it done by the indigenous settlers of Haryana? Or by some one else who came from outside? Fortunately, archaeological evidence supplies useful clues that some chalcolithic people who were settled in Rajasthan moved into this region[66] through the valley of the Drishadvati around 2500 BC. They introduced farming here.[67] The indigenous population does not seem to have offered opposition to the newcomers. There was in fact no need to do so: their population, as indicated earlier, was sparse and land was available in large measure. Instead, they seem to have befriended with the superior 'intruders' and learnt many a lesson from them to improve their economy and social life.[68]

As a result, sedantry life came in vogue and villages came up. The lot of the people improved. Indeed the cultivation of crops and the herding of food-animals provided a total production which exceeded the individual subsistence requirement for a year. This is proved by archaeological finds from the area. Take, for instance, fine pottery beautifully painted with motif in geometric or naturalistic styles in bichrome, black and white[69] curves which is by all means the work of professional potter, who, it can be surmised, was paid out of surplus foodstuffs. How much this applied to other crafts, such as weaving, stone cutting, wood carving, shellwork, brickmaking which were common enough at the time, we cannot say with certainty. We can be sure enough, however, that the 'appearance of these crafts in full array was a measure of the consequent success of agriculture and domestification'. Beyond this we are hard put to create the society of these early people of Haryana whom the archaeologists designate as 'Siswals'.[70]

Around 2300 BC, a very significant socio-cultural upheaval took place in this region. This was owing to the advent of a new people, the so-called Harappans. There is no controversy regarding the original habitat of these people—they immigrated from the north-western region, now in Punjab (both Indian and Pakistani). One thing is, however, still shrouded in mystery: why did these people leave their hearths and homes and come here? The answer may not affect us much, because, for our purpose this is sufficient that they came here and settled down.

The newcomer Harappans were city-dwellers; and no sooner did they land here than there ushered in an urban revolution leading to the emergence of a complex society of specialized tradesmen, skilled and unskilled labourers and workers.[71] Archaeological excavations conducted here so far give us interesting details about the settlements of these people, their economy and way of life. One of these interesting details is that the Harappans did not drive out the old settlers of this region, but let them live here side by side—the Harappans living in cities and the Siswals in villages. In the smaller towns, however, the two 'peoples' lived together.[72]

The above situation does not seem to have lasted long. After a while the cities which were populous centres of trade and craft broke the tribal isolation by attracting the citizenry and the village folks. Now there came the process of social assimilation—the city-dwelling Harappans belonging to the Dravida group of the anthropological type of the Southern Europoid Minor Race mixed up with the old indigenous inhabitants and gave birth to a new ethnic community—the Haryanavis, who created a distinct Haryanavi culture of their own.[73]

The 'Siswal-Harappan' community continued to live in the region peacefully with ample social security owing to their superior economy. But sometime around the later half of the second millennium BC, a new people using the Painted Grey Ware—the Aryans—arrived on the scene and disturbed the placid waters. The newcomers had shifted from the north-western region owing to factors not easily accountable.

It is popularly believed that the Aryans drove out old inhabitants and occupied the region. The archaeological excavations and explorations conducted here so far do not support this contention. The population of the Siswal-Harappan Ethnic Type was sparse: according to a rough estimate, in the open areas restricted by surrounding mountains or dense forests their density might have been something near two persons to the square mile and in the open places the number could have been a little larger, about ten persons to the square mile. In the second place, the PGW immigration was also not on very large scale (See Table 1). And since quite extensive cultivable land was available, there was no clash between the two races. They lived sparately in peace. At some sites both the Siswal-Harappans and P.G. Ware men are found living side by side. There is no evidence of clash or killing of one by the other at this place. This negates the current theory that Aryans annihilated the original inhabitants or drove them out and occupied their lands. At least in our region this did not happen. Rather the correct position seems to be that there 'were peaceful contacts in which migrating hands mixed up with the indigenous population; the result was a synthesis of cultures'.

TABLE 1: ANCIENT SETTLEMENTS IN HARYANA[74]

Valley	Siswal-Harappans	PGW men (Aryans)	Both at one site
The Ghaggar Valley			
The Main bed	4	3	1
Tangri bed	2	8	–
The Saraswati Valley			
The Markanda bed	4	14	1
The Main bed	12	36	3
The Drishadvati bed	40	20	7
The Yamuna Valley			
The Western course	20	1	–
The Middle course	7	2	1
The Khadar	–	16	–
The Sahabi Valley			
The Dohan bed	4	–	–
The Main bed	9	3	–
The Indri-Ujjina Drain	7	3	–

A question may, however, arise here: How could the tribes such as those of Aryans overshadow such materially well-off, urbanized people in such a way that soon after we find a very superior position assigned to the Aryans? In the present state of our knowledge, it is difficult to give an exact answer to this baffling query. However, the explanation provided by a Soviet scholar, Y.V. Gankovsky seems to be a little satisfying. According to him, in the mid-second millennium BC, a serious internal crisis overtook the northern region—including Haryana. This was owing to the whetting of social contradictions as a result of the expansion of slavery, debt, incongruity between the level of development or productive forces, and exploitation and probably authoritarianism on the part of the socio-political superstructure which crowned the edifice of the Siswal-Harappan civilization.[75] This crisis seems ultimately to have resulted in the fall of these great people.

The Aryans, on the other hand, were dynamic; they were liberal and assimilative. They were industrious and hard-working and had hardly any social contradictions in their life. As a result, they made rapid progress in every field of life. The development of productive forces, e.g. the emergence of iron and iron tools, helped the new people 'to husband new, uninhabited areas, improved irrigational cultivation and advanced different kinds of handicraft and farming'.[76]

This had, however, serious social implications and brought about social change after some time. There was 'an increase in the social surplus in the hands of the clan aristocracy, chieftains and priests. Barter and armed conflicts added to the property and social inequality.' And thus came the classes, which may be styled as *varnas*.

After the Bharata war, however, the *varna* system seems to have undergone radical changes. The very basis of this system, i.e. equality of man at the time of birth and acquisition of social status by dint of merit in later life was done away with. Now Brahmanas assumed great power and their injunctions became socio-religious authority which none could dare to challenge. In the new scheme of things, birth decided the *varna* of a man; and here the caste came into vogue. The Shudras began to be treated with contempt in this age. They were not allowed to read or recite the scriptures; nor were they entitled to any social privilege except for rendering service to the *dwijas* (the twice-born). The meaningless, but expensive and rigid, rituals made the simple life of yesteryears very complicated. The caste became a part of religion, i.e. *dharma*. And exploitation by Brahmanas became the order of the day.

In this situation, Jainism and Buddhism which came to this region in the sixth century BC, struggled to effect some change. But owing to different factors, which are outside the scope of this survey to be discussed, the reforming orders achieved precious little and after some time they became almost an extinct force.

In the new political atmosphere, the Brahmanas again came to occupy the pride of place. Their wishes became laws which governed the socio-religious life of the people. The social stratification as decided by them came to be accepted without any word of challenge being uttered from any quarters. In the new system, most of the tribes became castes (popularly called *jatis*) which were arbitrarily placed in the newly-created social hierarchy as it suited the Brahmanas and the elite in power. To place the system on a permanent footing, an elaborate code governing the modes of social and religious behaviour of different *jatis* was devised. Now *varna* became a theoretical proposition, the *jati* doing the real social stratification of the society.

A pertinent question may arise here: how many *jatis* were there in Haryana during this period? No precise answer to this question can be provided in the present state of our knowledge. Nevertheless, a guess can be hazarded. The Brahmanas were a caste now. The Kshatriya tribes who had immigrated after the collapse of the Kurus,[77] turned into the following *jatis*: the Abhiras (modern Ahirs), Iatior[78] (modern Jats), Yautiya[79] (later Yaudheyas), Rohas[80] (modern Rohil Jats), Prajunas[81] (later Arjunyas—Joon Jats), the Agras (later Agrawalas)[82] and the Kuninds[83] (Kundu Jats). The Vaishyas and the service-classes—the weavers, potters, cobblers, etc.—were also transformed into permanent castes. There were, in any case, more than a dozen castes at this juncture.[84] But this number was not static. The people forced by their circumstances, broke the rigid code of social behaviour every now and then. As a result, they became outcasts who added to the extant number of castes.

The political developments of the post-Mauryan period which further changed the picture deserve a little more explanation. When the Mauryan Empire collapsed in the third century BC, a number of new people came in Haryana. They were the Greeks, Shakas, Scythians, Parthians, Huns and Kushanas. They came in pretty large numbers and in most of the cases settled down here almost permanently. After a short while, these peoples were highly impressed by the Hindu culture and expressed keen desire to mix and mingle with its preservers. But could they do so? This was a baffling question, but its solution was easier than another question, i.e. if they could, then where would they be placed in the social hierarchy? To be sure, being ruling races they had to be placed somewhere at the top. But not all of them: the upper stratum were taken into the *dvija* fold and in times to come formed several separate Brahmana and Kshatriya castes or say sub-castes which we come across today. Persons belonging to the lower strata of these races got into the Vaishya and Shudra ranks.[85]

Medieval Times

In the medieval times, a great change took place owing to the coming of the Muslims. Although the Muslims touched Haryana in the tenth century for the first time, their real socio-religious impact came to be felt in a substantial manner in the beginning of the thirteenth century when Qutubuddin Aibak established Turkish Empire over here (1206). A new revolutionary religion, Islam, created a stir in the extant social system. Its adherents, unlike the earlier immigrants, did not join Hindu ranks but kept up their independent entity as a socio-religious force. As a result, the Haryana society, as it happend elsewhere, was divided into two vertical socio-religious divisions—Hindus and Muslims. But that was not all. A large number of Hindus, in due course of time, embraced the new faith which divided the Muslim populace horizontally, for the new converts changed their religion, but retained their *jatis*.[86] In other words, now there were Jats, Rajputs, Meos, and others among the Muslims, too.

In 1763, another new faith came. This was of the Sikhs. Formed into military bands, the bellicose Sikhs took advantage of the situation created by the Third Battle of Panipat (1761), and driving out the Afghan officials from upper Haryana, they occupied it. They established about three dozen small estates in the region in the present districts of Ambala, Kurukshetra, Yamunanagar and Karnal. A large number of followers of these chiefs out-migrated from their original habitats and settled here.[87]

Modern Times

In the beginning of the nineteenth century—1803, to be precise—the Britishers came here and with them came yet another faith—the Christianity. To begin with, a small number of followers of Christ (mostly holding official positions), settled here in big towns. They were all Englishmen who lived here as temporary immigrants. But after some time, a new lot of their countrymen came. They were missionaries. The newcomers made great efforts to convert 'heathens' to their faith. Their

TABLE 2: MUSLIM POPULATION THAT LEFT HARYANA IN 1947[88]

District	Total population that left Haryana
Hisar	3,90,600
Rohtak	2,10,500
Gurgaon	90,900
Karnal	3,85,200
Ambala	1,30,800
Jind State	40,300
Mahendragarh	39,400

efforts bore fruits and a small fragment of the Hindu and Muslim population, especially those belonging to the lower castes, embraced Christianity. Ambala, Karnal and Delhi were the chief centres where conversions took place. In the villages, the number of the converts was negligible, however.[89]

The British rule provided settled life in the region: there was order all around. Secondly, as compared to the drier lands of adjoining Rajasthan, Haryana tract afforded better economic conditions to the general populace. As a result, a sort of continual immigration of people is witnessed in the nineteenth century from the Rajasthan side. The Bagri Jats, Bishnois, Pachhadas and some Bhattis of Hisar and Sirsa, several Rajput and Ahir clans of Mahendragarh and some Jats of Jhajjar tehsil (district Rohtak) are these immigrants.[90]

In the present century, uprecedented movement of population took place in 1947: a large number of Muslims left the state (Table 2) and an equally large number of people came in from Punjab (Pakistan) to settle for the most part in the towns of Haryana (Table 3). Thanks to the efforts of great national leaders like Gandhiji, a number of Muslim Meos of district Gurgaon (33.5 per cent of entire population) stayed back (only 10.2 per cent of them left for Pakistan.)

TABLE 3: 'PUNJABIS' SETTLED IN HARYANA[91]

District	No. of settlers
Ambala	1,94,403
Karnal	3,25,173
Rohtak	1,41,695
Hisar	1,55,995
Gurgaon	60,794
Mahendragarh	29,100

The people who came here from Punjab (Pakistan) were, without any exception, all Hindus and Sikhs. They usually took to trade and commerce, ran industries and joined professions. They were, by necessity, dynamic, hardworking and industrious and made good their losses suffered in Pakistan sooner than expected. In one respect, however, they remained unchanged. Unlike other 'comers' to Haryana in the past, these people resisted to take to the process of Haryanization. They practised exclusiveness, spoke their own language, and continued to retain their own mannerism. They called themselves 'Punjabis' with a certain touch of pride and superiority. Surprisingly, this exclusiveness of these people has not withered completely even after over five long decades of their settlement in the Haryana region. And apparently there are no signs of its being replaced in the near future. Will it, then, one might ask, go on for good? Perhaps not. For history tells us that many a time several people tried to remain like that in the past also. But they were obliged by historical forces and factors to change and become Haryanavis. Sooner or later, these people would perhaps do the same too.

This is in brief the story of how the people of Haryana have become what they are today after passing through complex historical processes over countless centuries and acquiring through them the best in different races and religions, castes and cultures, economies and politics. This explanation would, I think, go a long way in helping us to understand the people, the events and the forces in their lives that kept them going throughout history.

NOTES

1. See K.C. Yadav, 'Haryana: The land and people', *Haryana Research Journal* (hereafter *HRJ*), vol. I, no. 2, 1966, pp. 1-16.
2. K.C. Yadav, *Haryana: Itihas Evam Sanskriti* (hereafter *Haryana*), vol. 1, pp. 5-7.
3. *Hisar District Gazetteer*, p. 18.
4. Ibid.
5. Ibid.
6. Jhabarmal et al. (eds.), *Babu Balmukund Gupta Smaraka Grantha*, p. 1.
7. *Tarikh-i-Zila Rohtak*, p. 4.
8. Dharnidhar, *Akhandaprakasha*, p. 5.
9. Girishchandra Avasthi, *Vedadharatala*, p. 779.
10. Bhagwan Dev, *Virabhumi Haryana*, p. 38.
11. Quoted by S.L. Yadav, *Haryana Pradesh-Ka-Lokasahitya*, p. 38.
12. Quoted by Bhagvan Dev, op. cit., p. 38.

13. This view was expressed by him in the course of a discussion with the present writer.
14. *HRJ*, vol. I, no. I, 1966, p. 1.
15. S.L. Yadav, op. cit., p. 59.
16. This view is also held by Sir J.N. Sarkar, *Fall of the Mughal Empire*, vol. IV, p. 237. The point is further corroborated in *The Imperial Gazetteer of India*, vol. XIII, p. 54. Also see A. Seton in Foreign Political Consultation, no. 34, 22 July 1809 (National Archives of India); F. Wilson, *Punjab Notes and Queries*, no. 547, vol. 1, p. 67.
17. *Indian Antiquary*, vol. XX, p. 133.
18. *Epigraphia Indica*, vol. XIII, pp. 23-6.
19. Dharnidhar, op. cit., p. 7.
20. *JRAS of Bengal*, vol. XIII, pp. 104-10.
21. For details see K.C. Yadav, *Haryana: History, Economy, Social Life and Culture through the Ages*, pp. 15-16.
22. Ibid.
23. Ibid.
24. Ibid.
25. Ibid.; *Delhi District Gazetteer* (1975), pp. 12-13.
26. For details see *HRJ*, vol. I, no. 2, 1966, p. 4; *Ambala District Gazetteer*, pp. 11-13; *Karnal District Gazetteer*, pp. 4-5; *Rohtak District Gazetteer*, p. 6; *Gurgaon District Gazetteer*, p. 3.
27. The three passing references to the Yamuna are found in the *Rig*., v. 52, 17; VII, 18, 19; X, 75, 5.
28. See *Ambala District Gazetteer*, pp. 6-8; *Karnal District Gazetteer*, p. 4; *Settlement Report*, *Sirsa*, para 5; *HRJ*, vol. I, no. 2, 1966, p. 5.
29. *Rig*. II, 41, 16.
30. Ibid., VII, 36.6.
31. Ibid., VII, 95, 2.
32. Ibid., II, 41, 16.
33. Ibid.
34. See P.L. Bhargava, *India in the Vedic Age*, pp. 63-4.
35. For details see M.L. Bhargava, *The Geography of Rig Vedic India*, pp. 53-61.
36. *HRJ*, vol. I, no. 2, 1966, p. 5.
37. See M.L. Bhargava, op. cit., pp. 96-7.
38. *Ambala District Gazetteer*, p. 6.
39. M.L. Bhargava, op. cit., pp. 62-4.
40. For details see ibid., pp. 58-61, 67, 70.
41. For details see *Gurgaon District Gazetteer*, pp. 5-6; *Rohtak District Gazetteer*, pp. 6-8.
42. M.L. Bhargava, op. cit., pp. 45-7.
43. Ibid.
44. Ibid.

45. *Gurgaon District Gazetteer*, pp. 4-5.
46. See *HRJ*, vol. I, no. 2., 1966, pp. 59-66
47. Ibid.
48. Ibid.
49. Ibid.
50. The account, if not otherwise mentioned, is based on R.C. Kanwar, V. Gupta ('Economic Resources of the Mahendragarh District'), *HRJ*, vol. I, no. 1, 1966, pp. 59-66.
51. *Gurgaon District Gazetteer*, p. 9.
52. Ibid., *HRJ*, vol. I, no. 1, 1966, pp. 59-66; *Karnal District Gazetteer*, pp. 10-12.
53. *Ambala District Gazetteer*, pp. 14-15.
54. *Statistical Abstracts*: *Haryana: 1968-75*, p. 37.
55. *Ambala District Gazetteer*, pp. 84-5, *Rohtak District Gazetteer*, pp. 10-14, *Phulkian States Gazetteer*, pp. 7-41;*Karnal District Gazetteer*, pp. 16-20; *Hisar District Gazetteer*, pp. 9-13.
56. Ibid.
57. Ibid.
58. Ibid.
59. J.S. Yadav, R.P. Maleyvar, 'The Birds of Haryana', *Journal of Haryana Studies* (hereafter *JHS*), vol. X, no. 1, 1978, pp. 37-51.
60. Ibid.
61. Ibid.
62. Ibid, vol. XIII, 1981, pp. 31-41.
63. The account is based on historians' demographic estimates of such societies. See, for instance, a valuable study by V. Gordon Childe, 'The Urban Revolution', *Town Planning Review*, vol. XXI, no. I, pp. 3-17.
64. *JHS*, vol., XIII, 1981, pp. 31-41.
65. For detailed information on this point see S.P. Sen (ed.), *Sources of the History of India*, vol. II, pp. 109-17.
66. This sort of movements were very common among the early farming communities. Since the people did not know anything like measuring their plots or rotation of crops, their plots soon became exhausted. As a result, their yields declined. In this situation, the owners abandoned those plots and cleared other patches of virgin soil. When all handy plots had been in turn cropped to exhaustion, the whole group packed up, deserted the village and started the cycle afresh somewhere else.
67. To these people 'the Drishadvati valley probably had greater attraction as is indicated by the discovery of nine sites as against only two each in the other valleys (of the Saraswati and the Ghaggar). The distribution of the ware in the parts of Hisar, Rohtak and Jind districts of Haryana contiguous to Northern Rajasthan suggests that Kalibangan I colonisers had immigrated from North Rajasthan'. Suraj Bhan, *Excavations at Mitathal (1968) and other Explorations in the Sutlej-Yamuna Divide*, p. 117.

68. This is attested by the evidence of archaeologists and anthropologists who have given these people to have belonged to the Negro-Austroloid major race. See V.Y. Gankovsky, *The Peoples of Pakistan*, p. 24.
69. See Silak Ram, 'Archaeology of Rohtak and Hisar Districts', unpublished Ph.D. thesis, Kurukshetra University, p. 91.
70. They have been so called after a type-site of this name—Siswal (26 km. west of Hisar) where they were met with for the first time. For details see Suraj Bhan, 'Siswal: A Pre-Harappan Site in the Drishadvati Valley', *Puratattva*, vol. V, pp. 44-6.
71. *Banawali*, A Haryana Govt. Publication, pp. 15-16.
72. For details see *JHS*, vol. VIII, nos. 1-2, 1976, pp. 1-11.
73. This is a mere guess, however.
74. Suraj Bhan, op. cit., pp. 121-6.
75. V. Gankovsky, op. cit., p. 44.
76. Ibid.
77. See Buddha Prakash, *Haryana Through the Ages*, pp. 11-12.
78. *Mahabharata* (VIII, 44, 11) calls these people Jartas or Jartikas. According to Dr Buddha Prakash (*Haryana*, pp. 11-12) they came from the valley of Jazartes around Tashkent.
79. Ibid. They came from outside India.
80. Ibid.
81. Ibid.
82. Ibid.
83. Ibid.
84. Several present-day castes trace their historical origin from this period.
85. It is difficult to find the traces of these tribes in the present population.
86. See *JHS*, vol. XIII, 1981, pp. 31-41.
87. Ibid.
88. Ibid.
89. Ibid.
90. Ibid.
91. Ibid.

Part Two

HISTORY

2

The Sources

The sources of the history of Haryana relating to the modern period can broadly be divided, for the convenience of study, as follows:

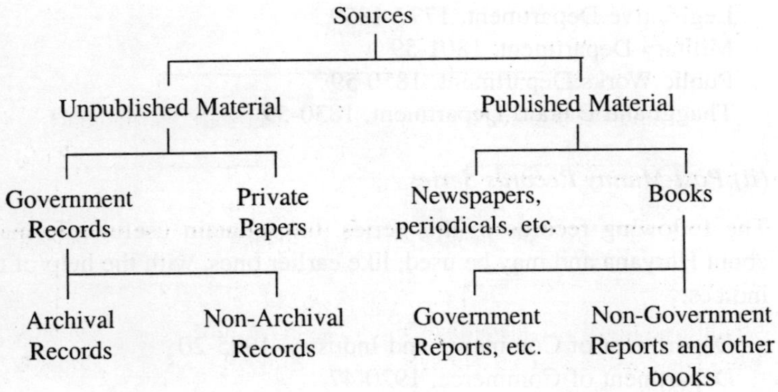

UNPUBLISHED MATERIAL

As indicated above, the unpublished material is of two types: (A) Government Records; and (B) Private Papers.

A. Government Records

1. NATIONAL ARCHIVES OF INDIA, NEW DELHI

This material is available in the archives/government record rooms of which the National Archives of India, New Delhi is the most important. This great repository preserves records of the central government that occupy, by a rough estimate, about 75,000 running feet of shelves. The main archival series of records date from 1748, although copies of earlier collections have been obtained from various sources (notably the Indian Office Records, a section of the Commonwealth Relations Office, London and from France, the Netherlands and Denmark). Of these records the following ones contain some useful information pertaining to the history of modern Haryana:

(i) Pre-Mutiny Records Series

The following pre-mutiny records starting from 1803 are found in this series. Material relating to Haryana can be culled from these records with the help of their indices:

Finance Department, 1810-59
Foreign Department, 1757-1859
Home Department, 1704-1859
Legislative Department, 1777-1859
Military Department, 1801-59
Public Works Department, 1850-59
Thaggi and Dakaiti Department, 1830-59

(ii) Post-Mutiny Records Series

The following records in this series, too, contain useful information about Haryana and may be used, like earlier ones, with the help of their indices:

Department of Commerce and Industry, 1905-20
Department of Commerce, 1920-47
Ministry of Commerce, 1947 onwards
Department of Education, Health, etc., 1923 onwards
Foreign Department, 1860 onwards
Home Department, 1860 onwards
Department of Industries, 1921 onwards
Legislative Department, 1861-1947
Military Department (including successor bodies), 1860 onwards
Public Works Department, 1860 onwards
Reforms Office, 1919 onwards

(iii) Residencies and Agencies Records: The Punjab States

The Punjab States Agency was formed in 1921, when the states which had formerly been in political relations with the Punjab Government, were placed in direct relation with the Government of India. To begin with, the two Haryana states, Jind and Loharu came under the Agency. Subsequently, Pataudi and Kalsia came in (1936). The following agency records of the Agency are preserved in the Archives in different series.

(iv) Punjab Government Records

Commissioner Ambala Division, 1867-1930, 71 bdls
Confidential files, Native States, 1897-1931, 1 bdl
Financial Commissioner, Punjab, Excise Cases, 1888-1918, 1 bdl
General and Judicial Departments, Proceedings, 1849-60, 3 bdls
Native States, Proceedings, 1934-5, onwards
Pataudi State, Special Bundle, 1881-1900, 1 bdl
Revenue and Agriculture, 1849-1932, 9 bdls
Residency Files, 1946-7, 51 bdls

(v) Regional Commissioner, PEPSU Records

Various Registers, 1947-54, 94 bdls

(vi) Newspapers

Complied by the Home Department, these printed reports contain some useful material concerning Punjab, 1864-1911: 120-6, 26 vols.

2. HARYANA STATE ARCHIVES

Haryana State Archives, Panchkula,[3] which came into being in 1975 in pursuance of the Section 65 of the Punjab Government Reorganization Act, 1966 (31st of 1966) has the following highly useful records/material for our purpose:

(i) Delhi Division Records

These records are divided into three groups: (a) Delhi Division Records (Press Listed); (b) Delhi Division Records (Non-Press Listed); and (c) Delhi Division Records (Principal Matters).

(a) Delhi Division Records (Press Listed)

These include the divisional commissioner's main correspondence with his deputy commissioners and with the Punjab Government in the Political Department (1857-64); General Department (1857-80); Revenue Department (1957-30); Judicial Department (1851-71); Education Department (1961-8); and Military Department.

(b) Delhi Division Records (Non-Press Listed)

These include correspondence of different nature with Punjab Government or with subordinate offices. The papers are not properly arranged.

(c) Delhi Division Records (Principal Matters)

These records in 97 bundles pertain to different departments, like Finance, P.W.D., Agriculture, Irrigation, Judiciary, etc. These are of late nineteenth century.

(ii) Ambala Division Records

These records are also divided into three groups: (a) Ambala Division Records (Press Listed); (b) Ambala Division Records (Non-Press Listed); and (c) Ambala Division Records (Principal Matters).

(a) Ambala Division Records (Press Listed)

These records consist of the divisional commissioner's correspondence with his deputy commissioners, and with the Punjab Government in the General and Political Department (1857-80); Revenue Department (1956-80); Judicial Department (1857-64); Military Department (1857-73); and Public Works Department (1864-80).

(b) Ambala Division Records (Non-Press Listed)

These records covering the period 1822-84 pertain to all departments of the divisional commissioner's office.

(c) Ambala Division Records (Principal Matters)

These records consist of 120 bundles covering collections of correspondence and other papers of different departments relating to certain important subjects, such as granting rewards for services rendered during the Revolt of 1857, pensions, estates, allotting land for railways, education, famines, etc.

(iii) Hisar Division Records

These records are also divided into three categories: (a) Hisar Division Records (Press Listed); (b) Hisar Division Records (Non-Press Listed); and (c) Hisar Division Records (Principal Matters).

(a) Hisar Division Records (Press Listed)

The record consists of divisional commissioner's main correspondence with his deputy commissioners and with the Punjab Government in the Political and General Department (1857-64); Revenue Department (1857-80); Judicial Department (1851-78); and Education Department (1851-68).

(b) Hisar Division Records (Non-Press Listed)

These records are un-arranged documents pertaining to different departments.

(c) Hisar Division Records (Principal Matters)

These records in 124 bundles relate to financial, agricultural, judicial matters, etc.

(iv) District Records

The Archives has acquired the following useful records pertaining to Haryana history:

(a) Records of D.C. Offices

AMBALA
General Records, 1920-61
Confidential Records, 1898-1956
Secret Records

GURGAON
General Records, 1857-80
Confidential Records, 1912-69

HISAR
General Records, 1901-57
Confidential Records, 1897-1964

KARNAL
General Records, 1850-1954
Confidential Records, 1878-1967

ROHTAK
General Records, 1910-58
Confidential Records, 1910-63

SONEPAT
General Records, 1842-1900
Revenue Records, 1842-1900

(b) Records of Superintendents of Police Offices

AMBALA
Confidential Records, 1918-62

GURGAON
General Records, 1857-1953
Confidential Records, 1913-64

(c) Zila Parishad Office Records

(d) Persian and Urdu Records

These records are in bound volumes and cover the following three main groups: [5]

(a) Miscellaneous Papers, 74 vols. They contain copies of orders, instructions and demi-official letters issued by the resident at Delhi, political assistants in the cis-Sutlej territories to other British officers, Panjab chiefs and Indian princes in North India.

(b) *Haquat-i-Hai-Deh Subha Delhi* (Facts about villages in the province of Delhi), 6 vols. These manuscripts relate to 5,000 villages, most of which are now in the Haryana state (whereas some are in Delhi). They contain useful information, especially for the purpose of economic history.

(c) *Boundary Disputes, 1920-40.* These records in 10 vols. contain evidence of withnesses produced for the settlement of claims to certain villages by the British government and Patiala state.

3. OTHER ARCHIVES

(a) The West Bengal State Archives, Calcutta[6] has the following useful records pertaining to Haryana, for this region was part of the Bengal Presidency from 1803 to 1834:

Bengal Revenue Consultations, 1805-33

Revenue Letters from Bengal to the Court of Directors and vice-versa.
Home Miscellaneous Series
Bengal Political Consultations, 1805-35
Bengal Judicial Civil and Criminal Consultations
Public Consultations and Bengal Political Consultations, 1806-35.

(b) For the period from 1835 to 1857 when Haryana (officially Delhi Division) formed one of the eight divisions of the North-Western Provinces with its headquarters at Delhi, the Central Records Office, Allahabad[7] preserves some useful material in the following departments:

Proceedings of the Board of Revenue, North-Western Provinces, 1835-55.

Abstracts of The Proceedings of the Sadar Board of Revenue, North-Western Provinces, June 1854-December 1857.

(c) From 1858 to 1947, Haryana was a part of Punjab and, therefore, all the records of this period are found in the Punjab Records Office, Lahore, Pakistan.[8] These records are very useful and are available in the following departments:

Home Department, 1858-1947
Political Department, etc., 1858-1947
Public Relations Department, etc., 1858-1947
Education Department, 1858-1947
Miscellaneous, 1858-1947

(d) The Commonwealth Relations Office, London (the India Office Library) is also a rich repository of records pertaining to the Haryana region.[9]

4. DISTRICT AND TEHSIL RECORDS ROOMS

(i) A lot of highly useful material lies—yes, in bad state, in dark dingy stores—at the district records rooms at every district headquarters. This material is a useful source of information relating to political, social and economic aspects of life.[10]

(ii) Some useful material is also preserved at tehsil headquarters and village *patwarkhanas*. Especially, the following records are very important at *patwarkhanas: Shjra Kistwar*, *Khatauni*, *Istemal Register*, *Khasra Girdawari*, *Misl Haqiqat*, *Intiqal*, *Jamabandi*, *Lal Kitab*. Of all these records (of parwaris) *Lal Kitab* is immensely useful for capturing a full picture of a village's social and economic life.[11]

Printed Records

A large number of records containing information on Haryana are also found in printed form. Of these, the important ones are: Parliamentary Papers; Selection from Government Records (printed in separate volumes) and official reports. This material is given in the bibliography at the end.

B. Private Papers

Private papers are immensely helpful for reconstruction of our history. Unfortunately, however, Haryana state is badly placed insofar as this source is concerned. There are many reasons for this. First, the region is dominated by agriculturists who usually do no preserve their papers. Secondly, until the other day, it was a very backward region with very low percentage of literate persons living over here. In the third place, some politically awakened persons who were in the habit of preserving papers had to destroy these owing to the hostile attitude of the colonial masters towards them. (Fallen into the hands of the latter, these papers would have put their owners into great difficulties.) Despite all these reasons, however, we are fortunate that the following private papers have come to us:

Zaildar Ghasi Ram Papers

The house of Zaildar Ghasi Ram of Auhalana has a large number of useful papers. The papers date from 1885 to 1947 and throw light on political and other aspects of life in the Auhalana zail in particular and Haryana in general.[12]

Bhagat Phool Singh Papers

Bhagat Phool Singh was a famous Arya activist and social reformer of pre-1947 days from Khanpur. His papers throw useful light on social, cultural and educational matters. There are several papers in his collection relating to Hyderabad Satyagraha (1938-9) also.[13]

Murlidhar Papers

Murlidhar of Ambala was one of the 73 leaders who formed Congress at Bombay in 1885. He was also a social activist. A large number of his papers throw light on political and social affairs in Haryana from 1882 to 1922 (when he died).[14]

Aryanand Sharma Papers

Pt. Aryanand Sharma was a prominent freedom fighter and a social activist from Ambala. His papers (in Urdu), throw welcome light on the freedom movement in the district from 1885 through 1947.[15]

Praja Mandal Papers

These papers throw useful light on the Praja Mandal activities in Dojana, Pataudi, Luharu, Jind, Kalsia and other States.[16]

Harihar Lal Bhargava Papers

Harihar Lal Bhargava was a prominent freedom fighter from Gurgaon. His papers give some information on the non-cooperation movement (1921-2) in the district.[17]

Radha Krishan Verma Papers

Radha Krishan Verma was a prominent freedom fighter from Bhiwani. His papers throw light on political affairs in his locale from 1936 to 1955.[18]

Mohan Swami Vaidya Papers

Mohan Swami was a prominent freedom fighter from Rohtak. His papers deal with political development from 1939 through 1977.[19]

Lala Sham Lal Papers

Lala Sham Lal was a very important freedom fighter from Hisar. His papers give useful information pertaining to freedom struggle in his district.[20]

Neki Ram Sharma Papers

Neki Ram Sharma was an eminent freedom fighter of Haryana. As such his papers throw light on political activities pertaining to the entire state.[21]

Published Material

As noted above, published material relating to history of Haryana is of two types: (1) newspapers, periodicals, etc., and (2) books.

(1) Newspapers, etc.

As far as newspapers are concerned, the Haryana region is very backward. There were only three newspapers worth the name in the nineteenth century issued from here, namely (i) *Haryana*,[22] (ii) *Rifa-i-Aam*,[23] and (iii) *Khair-Andesh*.[24] And even these did not last long. In the beginning of the present century, two more newspapers were born: (i) *Jat Gazette*[25] (1916); and *Haryana Tilak*[26] (1923). Both were weeklies in Urdu. These continue till today. In 1930s another newspaper, *Gramya Sevak*[27] was started from Hisar. It continued till 1942. It was a Hindi weekly devoted to nationalist cause.[28]

Besides, there were some newspapers from Punjab, like *The Tribune, Civil and Military Gazettee*[29] in English; *Pratap*, *Milap*, *Paisa*, *Aihsan* and *Zamindar*[30] in Urdu which gave coverage to developments in Haryana. As such, these newspapers are a useful source of information relating to history of Haryana.

After 1966, some research journals/periodicals were also published from here. Of which *Haryana Research Journal*[31] (Rewari), *Journal of Haryana Studies* (Kurukshetra)[32] and *Saptsindhu* (Chandigarh) gave useful research material on different aspects of life in the state.

(2) Books

Books relating to Haryana are, as indicated above, divided into two categories: (a) official reports, etc., and (b) general books.

(a) OFFICIAL REPORTS, ETC.

These are largely published by the Punjab Government (as Haryana was a part of Punjab then). Of these the oldest are *Administration Reports, Punjab*.[33] They were brought out every year from 1849 to 1935. They contain very useful administrative, social and economic information arranged usually under the following heads, physical and political geography; administration of the land; production and distribution; revenue and finance, etc. After 1935 these reports began to be issued by different departments separately.

Equally important, if not more, are the census reports. These multi-volume official publications are a mine of information dealing with almost every aspect of life in the region. Although regular census operations began with effect from 1881, a few census were taken before 1881 also in 1834, 1855, 1868. After 1881, decennial census were taken in 1891, 1901, 1911, 1921, 1931, 1941, 1951, 1961, 1971, 1981, 1991 and their reports are available in every standard library in the state and elsewhere.[34]

Like the census reports the revenue settlement/assessment reports are also useful sources of information. The British authorities began to take special interest in the matters relating to land revenue ever since they occupied this region (1803-5). To begin with, they took to summary settlements for one year. These were followed after a while by triennial settlements and by still longer ones, especially in the 1820s ranging up to twenty years in some cases. The regular settlements were, however, set on foot only after 1836-7. The summary settlement and assessment reports of the years before 1836-7 are for the most part unprinted. A few important ones of these are, however, available in print in 'the Selections from Records' series of the Government of the India and those of North-Western Provinces and Punjab. The assessment reports and settlement reports are available in print in separate volumes after 1837.[35] They contain immensely useful economic, social and other information.

During the period under study several commissions and committees were set up by the Central Government to enquire into problems concerning the state. Of these the following are mine houses of information: *Indian Famine Commission Report* (1889), *Indian Famine Commission Report* (1901), *Indian Industrial Commission Report*[36] (1916-18), *Punjab Evidence* (1919), *Report of the Royal Commission for Agriculture* (1928), *Punjab Famine Report*, 7 vols., (1899-1900)[37], etc. There are some reports of provincial level enquiries also.

After 1870s the Punjab Government published several works on social customs covering different districts of Haryana.[38] There were similar works on castes also, like *Punjab Castes*[39] by Sir Denzil Ibbetson, *A Glossary of Castes and Tribes of Punjab and NWFP* by H.A. Rose.[40]

The Parliamentary Papers,[41] Proceedings of the Punjab Legislative Council[42] (1920-36) and Punjab Legislative Assembly[43] (1937-66) provide useful data about political, economic, educational, social and cultural conditions in Haryana. And so do district histories, like *Tarikh-i-zila Rohtak*,[44] *Tarikh-i-Zila Gurgaon*,[45] etc., written under official patronage and published in 1860s in Urdu. The *District Gazetteers* also contain useful material.[46]

The *Gazetteers* were, to begin with, issued in single volumes. But after 1902, these were issued in two volumes entitled A & B (A contained descriptive part, and B statistics).[47] The *Gazetteers* were revised quite often—vol. B usually after every census, and vol. A whenever the need arose.[48]

(b) General Books

Besides these works, several books on different aspects of life in India and Punjab written before independence[49] and general histories of the state written after 1966[50] throw a great deal of light on the history and culture of Haryana. (These books are listed in the bibliography.)

The above sources contain rich material on the history of Haryana in modern times. This material is mostly found in English. Some material is also found in Urdu and Hindi. Unfortunately, the material is scattered at different places and it is very difficult to reach it. The Haryana State Archives should acquire its copies from different sources so that scholars could make proper use of it easily.

NOTES

1. For the uninitiated the word 'archives' may be new or confusing. Archives is essentially a repository of government records. However, non-government records, like private papers of individuals and non-government documents of historical importance can also be preserved there.
2. See, for details, *Handbook to the Records of the Government of India in the Imperial Records Department, 1748-1859*, Calcutta, 1925; D.A. Low et al., *Government Archives in South Asia*, Cambridge, 1969.
3. The account is based on my personal survey of records/material.
4. See *An Introduction to the Haryana State Archives*, published by the Archives.
5. The Account is based on my personal survey of records.
6. The records pertaining to Haryana (i.e. Delhi Territory) may be consulted with the help of the indices of different departments.
7. For details see S.P. Sen (ed.), *Sources of History of India*, vol. I, pp. 149-50.
8. See Guide to the Archives for details about its holdings.
9. See Guide to the records office for details about its holdings.
10. See Bibliography at the end.
11. These records are mostly in Urdu and not well preserved. It is very difficult to use them.

12. In K.C. Yadav Collection.
13. Ibid.
14. Ibid.
15. Ibid.
16. Ibid. Haryana State Archives and Jawaharlal Nehru Memorial Museum and Library, Delhi also have material on the Praja Mandals.
17. In the Haryana State Archives.
18. Ibid.
19. Ibid.
20. Ibid.
21. Ibid.
22. For details see K.C. Yadav, *Haryana: Itihas Evam Sanskriti* (hereafter *Haryana*), vol. II, pp. 1-12.
23. Ibid.
24. Ibid. It was started by Murlidhar from Ambala in 1889. It lived for a short duration only.
25. Ibid.
26. Ibid.
27. It was started by the veteran freedom fighter Hardev Sahai.
28. Nationalist newspaper started in 1881 by Dayal Singh Majithia (Lahore).
29. Loyalist newspapers from Lahore.
30. Urdu newspapers published from Lahore.
31. Published from Rewari, 1966.
32. Published by Kurukshetra University (since 1969).
33. From 1849 to 1866-7, the report was entitled *General Report on the Administration of the Punjab Territories* and from 1867-8 to 1920-1 *Report on the Administration of the Punjab and its Dependencies*, from 1921-2 onwards the title remained *Punjab Administration Report.*
34. The census were conducted on the following dates: 1 Jan. 1855; 10 Jan. 1868; 17 Feb. 1881; 26 Feb. 1891; 1 March 1901; 10 March 1911, 18 March 1921; 26 Feb. 1931; 26 Feb. 1941; 26 February 1951; 26 Feb. 1961, Feb. 1971, Feb. 1981, and Feb. 1991.
35. For details about census reports pertaining to Haryana see K.C. Yadav, S.R. Phogat, *History and Culture of Haryana: A Classified and Annotated Bibliography*, pp. 18-21.
36. For a comprehensive list of settlement and assessment reports see ibid., pp. 182-90.
37. For these reports see ibid.
38. See ibid.
39. See Bibliography at the end.
40. Ibid.
41. Ibid.
42. Ibid.
43. Ibid.

44. Ibid.
45. Ibid.
46. Ibid.
47. Ibid.
48. For details about *Gazetteers* see K.C. Yadav, S.R. Phogat, op. cit., pp. 21-3.
49. See Bibliography at the end.
50. Ibid.

3

Advent of the British and People's Resistance

The Old Order Changeth

Having presided over the destiny of the Indian empire of the Mughals for about fifty-one years, Aurangzeb closed his eyes in death on 3 March 1707. As ill luck would have it, he was succeeded by unworthies; and what Demosthenese, the famous Greek political philosopher and orator said to his countrymen at the time of the fall of the Athenian empire in the Fourth century BC could well have been said by them, too, with regard to their handling the affairs of the Mughal empire—'The gods alone preserve our Empire, for we on our part are doing all we can to destroy it.'

As a result of the follies and foibles of these weak successors of Aurangzeb, province after province slipped out of their hands at a stupendous speed; and by the end of the eighteenth century of the once mightiest empire in the world there remained a tiny kingdom comprising a small belt of territory around the imperial capital. And unfortunately even this small kingdom was not to remain under the Mughals for long. For in 1803, when Shah Alam, a blind old shadow was sitting on the great throne of the great Akbar and Aurangzeb, 'a power from across the seven seas'—the British—appeared on the scene. Their main aim in so doing was obviously to bring Shah Alam under their protection, for he, notwithstanding his total deprivation of 'real power', dominion and authority, was still acknowledged by almost every state and every class of people in India as the sovereign power. And as such, 'he could form a dangerous instrument in the hands of any one possessing sufficient power, energy and judgement to employ it in prosecuting views of aggrandizement and ambition'.[1]

But possession of Shah Alam was by no means an easy job, for he was under the strong protection of Daulat Rao Sindhia, a very powerful Maratha chief at that moment. He could not be secured without reducing the Maratha chief. In consequence, there came the Second Anglo-Maratha War (1803). The British Governor-General, Wellesly,[2] deputed General Lake,[3] the most experienced of his military commanders in India, to break the power of Daulat Rao and to capture Shah Alam, while his own brother Arthur Wellesly, the future Duke of Wellington, fought in the Deccan to humble the Maratha power over there.

According to a well planned strategy, General Lake left his head-quarters, Kanpur, on 7 August 1803. He captured Aligarh four weeks later, causing Perron, the unfaithful French commander of Sindhia's forces in the north to desert his master in his hour of need. Next, he stormed Delhi. The French officers incharge of the metropolis wanted to surrender without fighting, but their brave soldiers did not let them do so; rather they compelled them to march out for fighting the English instead of surrendering like cowards or effecting their own escape.[4] In consequence, the two armies fought a pitched battle at Pratapganj, a small village about 6 miles south of Delhi (11 September). The people of Haryana extended all possible help to the Marathas; the Jats under Hira Singh[5] of Ballabhgarh, Ahirs under Rao Tej Singh[6] and the Sikhs (about 5,000) under their local chiefs[7] were a great support. The Maratha army gave good account of itself, but the treachery and cowardice of officers who were unfortunately all foreigners (French) caused their defeat.

A New Order

The victorious British marched into Delhi, the historic capital of India, on 14 September. It was, indeed a great day for them. The French officers, one and all, who carried out the administration of the city surrendered to them at once.[8] And so did Shah Alam, the blind old shadow on the historic Mughal throne. The British were now the masters of Delhi, of the Mughal Empire and all that which belonged to them.

General Lake treated Shah Alam with 'respect and attention'.[9] Besides, to satisfy his ego, the old emperor 'was allowed to exercise his authority in the capital and its environs, but of course, under the superintendence and control of British Resident. After this, the old general fought two brilliant actions and broke the power of Sindhia and obliged him to purchase peace at their terms by signing the Treaty of Sirjianjan Gaon on 30 December 1803. It was according to this treaty that Sindhia re-linquished his hold over Haryana and several other territories.[10]

The People's Reaction

It is generally believed that except for a few persons whose material interests were directly affected, the general masses nowhere opposed the British rule (in their respective lands) in India. Rather they 'welcomed it as heralding the dawn of peace, prosperity and security'.[11] This belief, at least in case of Haryana, does not stand historical scrutiny. The people in this region, hundreds of them, from every walk of life came forward to oppose the British when they came to occupy their land in 1803 with obstinate valour which has ever characterized them.

Why was it so? What made these people fight the way they did? Admittedly, it was not the feeling of nationalism, for the same was conspicuous by its absence in the India of that time. Their being inspired with the writings of Russaou, Voltaire or Locke or anything of that sort was surely out of question. Then? The reason was perhaps the same which in 1842 Captain Preston, a 91-year-old veteran of the American War of Independence gave in answer to an enquiry as to why he participated in the War: 'Young man, what we meant in going for those red coats was this: We always had governed ourselves, and we always meant to. They did not mean we should.'[12] Surely the people of Haryana, like Americans, had always governed themselves and they always meant to. But the newcomers—the Feringhees—did not have faith in such a thing: wherever they went they smothered the self-governing institutions in that land. Here, too, the Haryanavis were sure, they would do the same; and hence they took up arms against them, as they did earlier in the case of other such invaders.

It is creditable indeed that those people, having seen with their own eyes the mighty Daulat Rao Sindhia (whom they supported in the previous war) being so badly crushed by the British (1803), could still dare to oppose a so-called invincible power. On the other hand, the challenge from a simple village-folk when the mighty rajas and nawabs lay prostrate before them was too insulting to bear with for the British. Consequently, after the Maratha affair became somewhat settled, they (the British authorities at Delhi) despatched columns in all directions to humble them. As a result, the two sides were locked in a deadly struggle.

Trouble in the North

In the upper region, what now makes the districts of Ambala, Yamunanagar, Kurukshetra, Kaithal, Jind and Karnal, Gurdit Singh and Bhanga Singh, the chiefs of Ladwa and Thanesar respectively had formed a confederacy, of all the Sikh chiefs—except for Bhag Singh of Jind and Lal Singh of Kaithal who had surrendered to General Lake soon after the battle of Delhi (11 September) in the late Anglo-Maratha War—to oppose the British laying their hands on them. Happily, at this critical juncture, their people stood behind them.[13] In order to curb these hostile activities of the Sikh chiefs, whose effects were seen in both sides of the river Yamuna, the British sent a force under an experienced officer Col. Burn. The old Colonel, who had anticipated little opposition from the loose confederacy of the Sikhs, got many a battle for a pretty long time—stretching beyond a year. The Sikh soldiers, inspired by their brave leaders, 'fought like devils'; and hundreds of them, including Sher Singh, the chief of Buria, laid down their lives, neither shirking nor flinching from their path. But despite all this, they lost to the enemy who was by all means superior to them in arms, ammunitions and military tactics. The defeat was bitter and it led many a chief to do away with the confederacy. As a matter of fact, by the end of March 1805, the confederacy was almost broken, most of the chiefs having accepted the terms of 'general amnesty' proclaimed by the British to them.[14]

However, Gurdit Singh, the brave and redoubtable prince of Ladwa still held out. The British, in view of his having organized the confederacy and being 'a great rebel', had also excluded him from the amnesty. However, that mattered little to the chief determined to fight till the last. But determination alone cannot bring about success. Greatly weakened by the desertion of almost all his friends, Gurdit could not put up a tough fight. Having outmanoeuvred him at Karnal, Col. Burn ultimately broke his power (April 1805). But, surprisingly, the defeated chief was treated quite leniently by the British—only a part of his paternal jagir, that is pargana of Karnal, was confiscated. He was allowed to retain the pargana of Ladwa.[15]

Thus by April 1805, the power of the Sikhs was broken and all their opposition, at least for the time being, was quelled. Yet the British were in no mood to hold the tract under their control—directly or indirectly; they let it remain into the hands of its original holders under treaties from the Marathas.[16] Many British writers have criticized the Delhi authorities for giving up such a valuable piece of territory 'for ever to the leaders of adventurers' instead of keeping it under their control. Perhaps the critics have evaluated the whole issue without putting it into correct historical perspective. The fact of the matter is that it was not a part of the Company's policy to hold such far-off lands beyond the Yamuna. Nor was it possible for them to keep the fierce, warlike population living there under perfect control, without wasting a lot of money, energy, etc., which they could hardly afford to spare at that time. Naturally, in such circumstances, the game would not have been worth the candle burnt to play it.[17]

Defiance in the South

The lower region, corresponding to the present districts of Gurgaon, Faridabad, Rewari and Mahendragarh was placed 'under the direct control of the Kampany Sarkar' and some 'native chiefs', mostly the British creations. Surprisingly, the resident, his assistants and other lower officials, as also the above-mentioned 'native chiefs' who tried to set up new government in the region were manfully challenged by the local people who refused to acknowledge them as their masters. They did not pay land revenue or any other tax. No official, high or low, 'could afford to visit their villages without a company of infantry moving with him for his protection'; and even then he was threatened with destruction and 'taunted with the menace of having muskets taken as play things for the villagers' children'.[18]

Not only that, the brave and warlike Meos, Ahirs, Jats and Ranghars did not hesitate to come out in open to destroy them. They followed guerilla tactics and kept the British forces in utter harassment all the time. They had become so daring that even Delhi, the headquarters of the government, 'was parcelled out into shares to them of which each co-partnership monopolized the plunder of its allotted portion'.[19]

The suppression of these war-like people was not an easy job. To subdue a single unfortified village, says Matcalfe, 'a force of five battalions with cavalry and artillery was deemed necessary.' The brave villagers, 'when besieged, instead of awaiting the assault, sallied forth against this force.' Though inferior to their enemy in arms, ammunitions and military knowledge, they fought with courage and valour. However in those circumstances, their fight could only be a fight to be lost—yet it was not before a decade's hard efforts on the part of the British forces that they were fully subdued.[20]

Trouble in the West

In the Western region (Sirsa and Fatehabad tehsils of the present district of Sirsa), the Bhattis, a tribe of Muslim Rajputs who were in preponderance there, challenged not only the authority of the chiefs appointed by the British in their territory but also organized regular predatory incursions inside the territories of the neighbouring chiefs and even that of the

British. Their leaders were Khan Bahadur Khan and Zabita Khan, the chiefs of Fatehabad and Sirsa (including Rania) respectively.[21] In order to put a check on these warlike people, the British deputed a strong garrison force at Hansi under the command of Mirza Illahi Beg, and gave him the title of *nazim* (governor). But the Bhattis proved too strong to be subdued by the *nazim*: they routed his forces and killed him. Obliged to take stronger action, the British sent a force under one of their experienced commanders, Col. Browning. But as ill luck would have it, the Bhattis gave a crushing defeat to the enemy. The British lost a large number of their men, Col. Browning being one of them.[22]

Thus beaten, the British authorities at Delhi were obliged to postpone the suppression of the Bhattis for some time. As a result, the situation became grave. In consequence, a sizeable column under Col. Ball was sent in 1809 to subdue them. The Bhattis gave tough opposition to the column and eventually overpowered it.[23] But determined as the British authorities were this time to subdue these daring people once for all, they sent Col. Adams at the head of a bigger force in November, 1809.[24] The new British commander launched his first attack straight away on Fatehabad (3 December). The attack was very forceful, but brave Bhattis did not lose heart and gave tough fight. But quite unexpectedly, they had to yield because of the treacherous and cowardly behaviour of their leader, Nawab Khan Bahadur Khan, who fled away from the battlefield.[25]

Emboldened by the victory, Adams launched a quick attack on Rania and Sirsa (19 and 21 December respectively). The Bhattis opposed him manfully here, too, but the story of Fatehabad got repeated here too. The nawab of Sirsa, Zabita Khan also fled away like Khan Bahadur Khan.[26]

Surprisingly, the British treated the defeated Bhatti chiefs sympathetically: Zabita Khan was allowed to retain parts of the *jagir* of Sirsa and Rania and Khan Bahadur was granted a pension of Rs. 1,000 per mensum in place of his *jagir* of Fatehabad.[27] Perhaps, expediency demanded this. In any case, a heroic struggle had come to an end.

The Troubled Centre

The central region (comprising the modern district of Rohtak and the eastern parts of the Hisar and Bhiwani) was a strong habitat of the ferocious Jats and Ranghars. To begin with, they challenged the authority of Nawab Bambu Khan (brother of the notorious Rohilla chief Ghulam Qadir), the first British grantee of their territory. They did not pay him any revenue and harassed him so much that he left the uncomfortable possession soon after he received it (1805).[28] Unhappy with the development, the British appointed their 'trusted servant' Ahmed Bakhsh Khan as Bambu's successor. Being 'a man of guts and unusual intelligence', it was hoped that the new ruler would overcome the popular opposition. But what happened actually was quite contrary to these expectations: the new ruler failed miserably in his job and relinqui-shed the charge of the state forthwith.[29] Next came Abdus Samad Khan, whose 'personal bravery, local knowledge, and influence justified a confident expectation of success in the establishment of his authority'. But hopes were belied in his case too: the brave people defied him as manfully as before. In the struggle that ensued, the nawab was a big loser—he lost his eldest son and son-in-law in the battles of Bhiwani and Bohar respectively. Demoralized by these losses, the nawab resigned the grant in 1807.[30]

Now British approached Raja Bagh Singh of Jind and Bhai Lal Singh of Kaithal to hold this region, since their possessions lay quite close to it. But to their great disappointment, both the chiefs declined to accept the offer.[31] When Nijabat Ali Khan, the nawab of Jhajjar, saw that nobody was coming forward to occupy this tract, he offered his services.[32] But to him the British would not give it for the reason that a man in possession of such a big tract in proximity of Delhi could prove harmful to them at the time of a crisis.[33]

Now that the Sikh chiefs refused to accept this tract and to Nijabat Ali the British would not give it (for the reason mentioned above), the only alternative with them was to take it up under their direct management. But this, too, was not an easy job. The people everywhere were up in arms and accepted nobody's overlordship. Minto, the governor-general told the British Resident at Delhi to act at the point of military strength to crush these people. Consequently, a big force consisting of four battalions of Native Infantry, a strong regiment of cavalry, Skinner's Horse, a few companies of the Irregular Horse, with a train of artillery was sent in March 1809, under the charge of Gardiner, assistant to the resident at Delhi.[34] In the beginning, a little difficulty attended their proceedings in and around Beri, Dighal, Kanauhar and Niganna.[35] Eventually they overpowered the rebels with some effort. But at Balliali, a big village in Hisar, they met stiff opposition at the hands of about 2,000 people on 14 May. The villagers fought gallantly, but they were ultimately defeated by the enemy who was superior in number as well as in arms and ammunition.[36] Next, they attacked Bhiwani, a stronghold of the rebels (27 August). The people gave a good account of themselves. For two long days they continued their action and kept the enemy at bay. But on the third day (29 August), they could not maintain their position and retreated to the town.[37] Since the British force were equipped with heavy artillery, they breached the walls of the town in no time and made an assault in two columns. The right column was checked by the inhabitants who fought with courage. The left column also met stiff opposition. But ultimately the two columns succeeded and the place was carried. There were heavy losses on both sides. One officer, eighteen privates were killed and 120 wounded on the British side, whereas on the Indian side about one thousand persons lost their lives. The victors slaughtered their foes mercilessly.[38]

By the end of 1809, as the above discussion shows, the hard efforts of about seven long years on the part of the British had been fruitful: they had quelled all opposition to their rule throughout the length and breadth of the territory.

The *cis-Sutlej* Region

After quelling opposition in the region, the British turned their attention towards the so-called *cis-Sutlej* chiefs to whom they had left in the as-they-were position after vanquishing them in 1805. But now in 1809, they were obliged to change their policy *vis-a-vis* these chiefs since they feared a serious danger to their existence as a political power in the east by their enemies—the French, the Turkish and the Persian emperors, who, they supposed, were seriously mediating the subjugation of India in coalition, if necessary, with Maharaja Ranjit Singh, the ruler of Punjab, their next door neighbour.[39] In such an eventuality, the northern Haryana in the hands of petty chiefs, mostly belonging to the same religion as of Ranjit Singh, outside the British influences, could present a great danger to the British. In Consequence, they changed their original policy of keeping the Yamuna as the farthest limit of their kingdom in the north-west. They decided to cross the Yamuna now. But their problem was: how to tackle the independent chiefs beyond the Yamuna? Fortunately, before the British could do any serious work in this regard, Ranjit Singh solved the problem for them. Harassment and the fear of total extinction at his hands[40] sooner or later, converged these chiefs to come to the British for help.[41] Adept in the art of fishing successfully in troubled waters, the British seized the opportunity with both hands and afforded protection to the *cis-Sutlej* chiefs on the following conditions:

(i) They (chiefs in the *cis-Sutlej* region) shall in future be secured from the authority and influence of Maharaja Ranjit Singh.
(ii) All the country of the chiefs thus taken under protection shall be

exempted from all pecuniary tribute to the British.

(iii) The chiefs shall remain in the full exercise of the same rights and authority in their own possessions which they enjoyed before they were received under the British protection.

(iv) Should a British force, on purpose of general warfare, be required to march through the country of the said chiefs, it is necessary and incumbent that every chief shall, within his own possessions, assist and furnish to the full of his power, such force with supplies of grain and other necessaries which may be demanded.

(v) Should an enemy approach from any quarter, for the purpose of conquering this country, friendship and mutual interests require that the chiefs join the British army with all their force, exerting themselves in expelling the enemy, act under discipline and proper obedience.

(vi) All European articles brought for the use of the army shall be allowed to pass without molestation.

(vii) All horses purchased for the use of cavalry regiments shall be allowed to pass without molestation or the demand of duty.[42]

Thus, by the fall of 1809, practically speaking, the whole of Haryana was 'under the control of the Kampany Bahadoor'. They were now—not in 1803 when Daulat Rao Sindhia made it over to them vide the treaty of Sriji-anajan Gaon—the real masters of the territory.

NOTES

1. Governor-General-in-Council to the Court of Directors, 13 July 1804.
2. Governor-General from 1798 to 1805.
3. He was born on 27 July 1744, son of Charles Lake; entered the Ist Foot Guards in 1758; saw many actions; became General; C-in-C in India, and member of the Council, 1801-5; made a Viscount on his return to England; died 20 February 1808.
4. For cowardice and treachery of the Sindhia's French officers, see J.N. Sarkar, *Fall of the Mughal Empire*, vol. IV, pp. 251-60, 280-310.
5. Ibid.
6. K.C. Yadav, *Ahirwala Ka Itihas* (hereafter *Ahirwal*), pp. 54-8.
7. J.D. Cunningham, *History of the Sikhs*, p. 114.
8. The French officers surrendered on 14 September.
9. Shah Alam had shown his earnest desire to place himself under the protection of the British Army quite long before their advent into the city. The Governor-General-in-Council to the Secret Committee to the Court of Directors, 12 April 1803.

10. For the full text of the treaty see Aitchison, *Treaties, Engagements and Sunnuds*, vol. IV, pp. 384-9. The relevant parts of the treaty were as follows:

ARTICLE 2

The Maharajah cedes to the Honourable Company and their allies in perpetual sovereignty all his forts, territories, rights and interests in the countries which are to the northward of those of the Rajahs of Jeypore and Jodhpore and of the Rana of Gohud of which territories and c., a detailed list is given in the accompanying schedule.

SCHEDULE 2

	(Rupees)
Jagheers . . . belonging to Ajit Singh and Heera Singh Jat	
Pergunnah of Furedabad	1,26,500
Pergunnah of Furedabad, Foujdarry Delhi	6,000
Lands under the Khalsa Mootsuddees to the west of the River Jumna Pergunnah of Boodhorpoor	6,000
The Zemindaree of Runjeet Singh in Doab	
To the west of the River Jumna	13,23,370
Kutoba Bysakh	
To the West of the Jumna	73,284
Baboojee Sindia to the west of the Jumna	
Paniput	99,478
Mungothla	50,000
Govurdhun	10,000
Seth Singh Seik	
Karnal to the west of the River Jumna	14,000
Yeshwant Rao Sindia and Raghojee Kudum, 2 Mahals to the west of the Jumna	
Nornoul and Kanthee	1,64,000

11. See for instance, R.C. Majumdar, *History of Freedom Movement in India,* vol. I, p. 47
12. The conversation being very interesting, I put it here in full:

Did you take up arms against intolerable oppressions?
'Oppressions'? replied the old man, 'I did not feel them'.
What? Were you not oppressed by the Stamp Act?
I never saw one of the stamps, I certainly never paid a penny for one of them.
Well, what about the tea tax?
I never drank a drop of the stuff; the boys threw it all overboard.
Then I suppose you had been reading Harington or Sydney and Locke about the eternal price of Liberty.
Never heard of 'em. We read only the Bible, Catchism, Psalms and Hymns, the Almanac.

Well, then what was the matter? And what did you mean in going to the fight?

Young man, what we meant in going to the red coat was this: We always had governed ourselves and we always meant to. They did not mean we should. Quoted in Morison, *The Oxford History of the American People*, p. 112.

13. K.C. Yadav, *Ahirwal*, pp. 29-32; *Glimpses of Haryana*, ed. Buddha Prakash, pp. 33-49; Griffin and Massey, *Punjab Chiefs and Families of Note*, vol. I, pp. 20-1; J.D. Cunningham, op. cit, pp. 114-16.
14. Col. Burn met his first opposition near Panipat at the hands of a Maratha General, Ika Rao. Undaunted by the rout of his master at Delhi and Laswari recently, he gave quite a tough battle to his enemy, surrendering only when his head was not on his shoulders.
15. See J.D. Cunningham, op. cit., p. 115. Sir Richard Temple has criticized the conclusion of peace with the rajas on these terms as an act of 'bad grace'. *Memoirs of my Indian Career*, vol. I, p. 39. See also *District Gazetteer, Karnal*, pp. 25-6; Griffin and Massey, op. cit., vol. I, p. 12.
16. *District Gazetteer, Karnal*, pp. 25-6; *Settlement Report of Karnal*, paras 94-6, pp. 22-5.
17. See for instance, Griffin and Massey, op. cit., vol. I, p. 55.
18. John Kaye, *Selections from the Papers of Charles, Lord Metcalfe,* vol. I, p. 55.
19. Ibid.
20. Ibid.
21. NAI, Foreign Political Consultation, no. 56, 10 April 1809; *Hisar District Gazetteer*, pp. 32-3.
22. Ibid.
23. James Mill, *History of British India*, vol. VII, p. 139.
24. Ibid., pp. 138-9.
25. NAI, Foreign Political Consultation, no. 94, 28 December 1810; no. 20, 7 January 1811.
26. Ibid., nos. 57-60, 9 July 1811.
27. Ibid., no. 40, 26 Jan. 1811; J.S. Mill, op. cit., vol. VII, p. 139.
28. George Hamilton, *Hindostan*, vol. I, pp. 455-8.
29. Ibid.
30. Ibid; *Rohtak District Gazetteer*, pp. 25-6.
31. NAI, Foreign Political Consultation, no. 42, 14 December 1807.
32. Ibid.
33. Ibid., no. 104, 6 Feb. 1809.
34. Ibid, J.S. Mill, op. cit., vol. VII, pp. 138-9.
35. Ibid.
36. NAI, Foreign, Political Consultation, no. 56, 10 April 1809.
37. Ibid., no. 1, November 1809.

38. J.S. Mill, op. cit., vol. VII, pp. 138-9.
39. J.D. Cunningham, op. cit., p. 123, Griffin and Massey, op. cit, vol. I, p. 54, G. Auber, *Rise and Progress of the British Power in India*, vol. II, p. 461.
40. J.D. Cunningham, op. cit., pp. 123-9.
41. Ibid.
42. Ibid., pp. 353-4.

4

New Administration: Popular Discontent, 1809-1856

A New Structure, a New System

As indicated in the preceding chapter, the Haryana territory had been brought under effective control of the 'Kampany Bahadoor' by 1809. To begin with, the new masters converted the territory into an administrative unit quite akin, in almost every respect, to a *subah* of old times. The Resident in whom great powers were vested was its governor: he was a magistrate, judge, collector and a police officer, all combined in one. However, for smooth and easy functioning, he was helped by a number of junior officials, designated as Assistants (their number varying from two to four from time to time).[1]

The British were fortunate in the Residents who came to rule here during the period under study. Archibald Seton, a man reputed for his ripe experience in revenue, judicial and public work,[2] did his job very well at the initial stage. In May 1811, he was succeeded by another brilliant man, C.T. Metcalfe.[3] Though still in his twenties, Metcalfe was full of wisdom and patience. He gave to the territory a novel system of administration—the Delhi system, 'a combination of native practice and regulation spirit'.[4] This was not a permanent arrangement, however, for as soon as its author left the region, the Delhi system underwent changes (1819). First of all, the civil and political functions of the Resident were separated and given to two persons—the Resident and the Commissioner.[5] Secondly, the territory from Delhi to Rewari and Hansi-Hisar being too unwieldly to be administered as a single administrative unit, was divided into three divisions: (i) Northern Division, including Panipat, Sonepat, Rohtak, Hansi, Hisar; (ii) Central Division, including the city of Delhi and its environs; and (iii) Southern Divison, including Palwal, Hodal, Mewat, Gurgaon and Rewari.[6] In 1820, yet another, though not very significant, change took place. In view of the practical difficulties arising out of the plural headship of the Resident and Commissioner, the designation of the latter was changed to Deputy Superintendent and he was placed under the control of the Resident.[7]

These arrangements, however, did not last long. In May 1822, the Board of Revenue for the Western Provinces took over the administration of the territory. The Board was composed of three members. The Board's decisions were taken after mutual discussion by simple majority—of course, subject to confirmation of the Bengal Government. It was expected that being somewhat broad-based, the board would run the administration more efficiently and in a better way than the Resident. No such thing meets the eye in their proceedings, however.[8]

Meanwhile, the year 1833 brought another set of changes in administration. By the Charter Act of that year, the North-Western Provinces was formed after cutting it from the Bengal Presidency with its headquarters at Agra.[9] In the new set-up, the Haryana territory was made one of the six divisions of the province.[10] Its official designation was 'Delhi Division' and it comprised the districts of Panipat, Hisar, Delhi, Rohtak and Gurgaon.[11] The administration of the upper parts of Haryana, i.e. the present districts of Karnal and Ambala, was conducted through an official designated as superintendent of the political affairs and agent to

TABLE 1: ADMINISTRATIVE ARRANGEMENT, VILLAGES, TOWNS, AREA AND POPULATION, HARYANA, 1855

Districts	No. of towns & villages	Area (sq. miles)	Population	No. of persons per sq. mile
Panipat	538	1,270	3,89,085	306
Hisar	653	3,294	3,30,852	100
Delhi	568	790	4,35,744	552
Rohtak	300	1,340	3,77,013	281
Gurgaon	1,274	1,939	6,62,486	342
Princely States				
Bahadurgarh	28	48	14,400	300
Ballabhgarh	121	190	57,000	300
Dujana	31	71	6,390	90
Farrukhnagar	18	22	4,400	200
Jhajjar	250	1,230	1,20,700	180
Loharu	54	200	18,000	90
Pataudi	40	74	6,660	90
Total	3,875	10,468	24,22,730	212

the Government in the territory of the Protected Sikh and Hill Chiefs, at Ambala,[12] until 1849 when they were placed under the charge of the Punjab Government. The former, i.e. the Delhi Division, however, remained a part of the North-Western Provinces throughout the 'Kampany' period. Besides this, there were some princely states, Bahadurgarh, Jhajjar, Dojana, Pataudi, Loharu, Ballabhgarh, Farrukhnagar, Jind and Kalsia, which were ruled by local princes under the superintendence of the Resident. The district and princely state-wise population, etc., of the region has been given in Table 1.

New Revenue Administration

The chief concern of the 'Kampany Bahadoor' in this period was to manage the land affairs in the region, for agriculture was the chief means of economy of the people of Haryana and land revenue the chief source of income of the Government. The Government proceeded with a declaration that

> from the earliest time to the present period, the public assessment upon land has never been fixed and according to established usage and custom, the rulers have exercised a discretionary and despotic authority. The tenants and cultivators of the soil have been exposed to rapacity and oppression. The Government had, therefore, decided in order to include the cultivators to feel secure, and extend their efforts, to make a three years settlement with them to be followed by a second for the same period and then by one of four years.[13]

This was, however, only a pious belief which was not transformed into a working reality by the authorities. In accordance with the Regulation IX of 1805, the early revenue officials, ridings on horses and elephants like the rajas and nawabs, accompanied by a band of troopers, toured the region in 1807 and made a settlement for one year. After some time, triennial settlements were made. As time elapsed and conditions became settled, longer settlements were effected with the bigger villages. By 1820 there were settlements ranging from three to twenty years. But it did not make much difference in those days whether the settlement was for short duration or longer period, for all the settlements were very heavy—only less than 50 per cent of the gross produce was left with the peasant.[14]

Law and Order

For the enforcement of law and order a strong body of police was recruited and detachments posted to different parts. The practice of the

Regulation Provinces, where the police were supposed to inquire into crimes, whether they were reported or not, was not in vogue in Haryana. The police had to be asked to come in. In any case, the police helped in reducing crimes and establishing law and order in the region.[15]

Administration of Justice

For the administration of justice the whole territory was divided into two parts: that of the city of Delhi and the countryside. In the city there were three courts for civil cases. The lowest court for petty suits of the value of Rs. 100 was conducted by three Indian commissioners, a *qazi*, *mufti* and a *pandit*. The second court was for ordinary suits. Here the Assistants decided the cases. The third or the highest court was of the Resident which chiefly heard appeals from the lower courts. The criminal adjudication was conducted by the Resident and his Assistants. The panchayats administered justice in the villages.[16]

In the princely states, the chiefs were given powers to run internal administration of their states. But they were under the political superintendence of the resident and enjoyed powers and privileges on condition of fidelity and military service to the British Government.[17]

The Popular Reaction

How did the people react to these administrative arrangements? For sure, they did not like them—for obvious reasons, the chief which was denial of self-rule. The people here always managed their own affairs in the villages[18] which were variously called by early British administrators as 'little republics',[19] 'tributary republics'and so forth.[20] They elected their executives as councils or panchayats which, in the words of Thomas Fortescue 'settled everything of common interest for the village': the cultivation of common lands, the rents to be paid for realization of grazing and hearth fees, the exemption of certain persons from rent payment, the building and repair of village rent houses, supervision of the system of special watchmen (*thikar*), the cleaning of the village tanks; and such like things. The accounts of the village funds would be submitted yearly for the sanction of the whole body of proprietors, but this was not done regularly. Certain other matters by general custom also needed their special assent, such as the breaking up of jungle land, the cutting and selling of the trees of the common land, the grant of a revenue free holding by the villagers, and the like.[21] The dispensing of justice, deciding cases, civil as well as criminal, of the villagers was also the job of the council. In deciding cases it usually chose an arbitrary board of generally five persons, well-known for their impartiality, objectivity, just views, intelligence and position. They were '*panch parmeshwara*' (god-like-judges) whose decisions were binding on the disputants. Justice was given right at once without paying even a single penny to anybody.[22]

As against this, the British courts gave justice mostly arbitrarily: written words were not there to guide the dispensors of justice in the courts and if at all some documents were there, these were not paid any heed. A few representative illustrations to this effect may be enough to prove the point. Charles Metcalfe, for instance, gave punishment to offenders without weighing their guilt or fault. To one Roshan Khan, a policeman, he is reported to have given life imprisonment, accompanied by hand labour for having been suspected to have stolen 7 lbs. of thread.[23] Another man, Ramadaya was imprisoned for seven years in 1815 on a similar charge of theft, for his making attempts to escape from the jail thrice, Ramadaya's sentence was increased in proportion to 56 years.[24] Yet another man Makhan Singh was sentenced to seven years rigorous imprisonment for forging the signatures of Metcalfe.[25] Surprisingly enough, Metcalfe could deal with the prisoners in any way he liked. For instance, he sent some diehard criminals to their villages for an indefinite period just to enable them to cultivate their lands and thereby prevent loss of revenue to government.[26] Yet in another case he passed judgement on the absentee offenders without giving them any chance of defending themselves. In fact, no trial was held and the judgement was passed privately. Metcalfe was, however, reprimanded for this lapse.[27] Another official, Henry Middleton, the superintendent of the Delhi Territory is said to have given to his assistants powers of granting solitary confinement for life.[28] Lastly, the worst thing was that there was no provision for appeals over assistants and there was no 'writ of certiorari'. Even death penalties were awarded without printed regulation.[29]

Naturally, the people's reaction to this judicial system was one of dread and hatred. No better words than those of the informants of Col. Sleeman, contracted by him during his tours in 1853 through the N.W. Provinces can explain the real position:

> Your Court of Justice, they said, are the things we dread most, sir; and we are glad to escape from them as soon as we can. . . . The truth, sir, is seldom told in these courts. There they think of nothing but the number of witnesses as if all were alike; here (in India), sir we look to the quality. When a man suffers wrong, the wrong doer is summoned before the elders (composing Panchayats) and the

offender dreads their vengeance. In your *adalats*, sir, men do not tell the truth so often as they do among their own tribes or village communities; they prejure themselves in all manners, without shame or dread, and there are so many men about these courts who understand the rules and regulations, and are so much interested in making truth appear to be falsehood and falsehood truth, that no man feels sure that right will prevail in them in any case. The guilty think they have just as good a chance of escape as the innocent.[30]

Since the local institutions were built up according to the requirements of the people, they felt securer and happier under them. The new administration destroyed these institutions. Resultantly, the people felt insecure and unhappy.[31] Not to speak of the sufferers even many British administrators lamented the loss of these institutions. Richard Temple, for instance, observed:

I have always thought that throughout India a very great deal of harm has been done by the interference of our authorities, both executive and judicial, with indigenous village corporations. I look upon the discouragement of the small indigenous municipalities as the great blot and weakness in our rule and think it is by no measures compensated.[32]

Denial of self-rule and bad justice were followed by economic exploitation of the worst type. The colonial government made many tall claims to better the lot of the people. But what they did was just the opposite. Substantion: Haryana was, as noted above, predominantly an agricultural territory. The 'Kampany Bahadoor' in settling and collecting revenues was nothing short of a robber. The Government's dues in most of the cases were more than 50 per cent of the gross produce. These dues were fixed arbitrarily. The farmers were neither consulted nor their consent obtained in anyway while fixing them. We have it on the testimony of their own brethren, the later settlement officers, that when the settlements were made, 'the headmen (of the villages) were imprisoned till they agreed to the terms offered and having accepted them, till they furnished security for payment'.[33] Despite all this, however, the poor peasants could not pay the land revenue as Table 2 shows.

Consequently, they became defaulters and had to visit jails four to five times in a matter of few years. In the later years, however, when the high-handedness of the settlement officers became well-known and their work began to be adversely criticized even in their own circles, some changes were effected. As a result, the settlements began to be conducted somewhat thoughtfully. But being a colonial outfit, the government could not afford to be anything but harsh.[34]

The mode of collection of land revenue was as extortionate as the

TABLE 2: OUTSTANDING DUES, 1811-18[35]

Year	Total land assessment (Rs.	As.	Ps.)	Outstanding balances (Rs.	As.	Ps.)
1811-12	9,87,030	11	6	10,073	6	11
1812-13	10,39,560	0	0	60,304	15	6
1813-14	12, 56,502	12	0	18,967	2	1
1814-15	12,15,470	13	6	34,215	8	3
1815-16	13,88,978	0	0	95,913	3	0
1816-17	17,01,663	0	0	1,24,318	0	0
1817-18	17,23,691	0	0	2,68,797	0	0

assessments were oppressive. The collections were made in February and September, long before the harvest. It was but natural that people should have offered some protests to their making collection at such a wrong time when practically speaking they had nothing with them in cash or kind. The government, strangely enough, did not realize their mistake and made their collections almost everywhere at the point of bayonet. Extent of severity in this regard could be well assessed from the fact that in a small tract in Karnal, 136 horsemen were retained for the collection of land revenue, while 22 sufficed for police duties of the same tract.[36]

The ultimate outcome of such a revenue policy could be anybody's guess. It completely shattered the peasant's economy, as we would see later, and made people unhappy. Similarly, the upper stratum of the society was not cared for? In the beginning, the government did not adopt any unsympathetic attitude towards them. This was obviously due to their having no interest in the occupation of the territory beyond the Yamuna. But after 1809 there was a clear-cut shift in their policy. They became interested in the possession of the extensive territories on the other side of the Yamuna and wanted to rule the masses living there without the intervention of any powerful section of their own countrymen.[37] As a first step towards the new goal, the government declared all the estates in the region—numbering over four score-with the exception of Ballabhgarh, Farrukhnagar, Pataudi, Jhajjar, Bahadurgarh (or Dadri), Dujana and Loharu in the lower region and Jind, Kaithal, Ladwa, Thanesar, Shamgarh, Kunjpura and Ambala in the upper region as grants for one life only. Interestingly, even these so-called permanent estates were, as a matter of fact, not really permanent as far as their existence was concerned for good, for these could be confiscated any time if their rulers failed to leave behind male successors. As a consequence of this measure, most of the important estates in the upper region met their doom: Ambala in 1823; Kaithal in 1843; Ladwa in 1845; Thanesar in 1850, to name a few only.[38]

By their measures of confiscation and resumption of various estates, the government created a class of 'bitter enemies' (John Kaye). To know the exact feelings of this class towards the Government, the following statement of Rao Tula Ram of Rewari, wherein he expresses his reaction on hearing the news of the fall of the British at Delhi on 11 may 1857, may be cited. Writing to Emperor Bahadur Shah, the Rao observed:

The *pargana* of Rewari together with other *parganas*, yielding the annual rent of about rupees twenty lakh was awarded in *jagir* to my forefathers by the *sanads* issued by the Emperors of India (Mughals) which remained in possession of my forefathers till the domination of the British Government. The above mentioned *jagir*, too, had been in their possession when the British took possession of the said *jagir* from them; and the property worth rupees one lakh was given as a lease in perpetuity in its place. Consequent upon this injustice my forefathers passed their lives in adverse financial circumstances. They were praying to God, the Almighty, day in and day out for the time when the Imperial Government (of the Mughals) be able to gain the lost power again so that they may again be in possession of their lost *jagir.* Thanks to God, the Almighty, that after the prayers of day and night the much desired day has arrived, that is the said territory has again come under the Empire of Your majesty. I am extremely pleased to see these days full of happiness.[39] Besides the dispossessed dynasts, their followers (who were shorn of official ranks and emoluments on the destruction of their estates) also cherished strong anti-government feelings in their hearts.[39]

In sum, the 'Kampany' rule was ruinous for one and all—from the humble to the highest in the land.

Popular Discontent

Political scientists almost unanimously hold that no self-respecting people can be satisfied with a foreign rule no matter how wise or good it might claim to be. If ever proof was needed for this aphorism, the 'Kampany' rule over Haryana during the period under study provides it. By their self-centred imperialistic policy and actions, the British *huqqam* (rulers) produced here in abundance what Francis Bacon (1561-1626) in his famous essay 'Of Seditions and Troubles' calls the 'Causes and motives of seditions'. They rose up, as discussed in the next chapter, to finish off all vestiges of such a raj whenever and wherever an opportunity came their way.

NOTES

1. K.C. Yadav, *Haryana: Studies in History and Culture* (hereafter *Haryana: Studies*), p. 40; P.G.T. Spear, *Twlight of Mughals*, p. 84.
2. He had served as an agent to the governor-general at Rohilkhand for quite some time before joining at Delhi.
3. For his life and work at Delhi see D.N. Panigarahi, *Charles Metcalfe in India*; P.G.T. Spear, op. cit., pp. 84-98.
4. Ibid.
5. NAI, Foreign Political Proceedings, no. 52, 2 April 1918. Ochterlony was appointed resident and Fortescue as commissioner. The latter, however, could not live here for long; he left in 1820 owing to bad health.
6. Ibid. The name of the territory was changed to 'Delhi Division'.
7. D.N. Panigrahi, op. cit., pp. 39-41.
8. The members of the Board were: Ross, Elliot and Fraser. Ross, however, left Delhi in Dec. 1821 and Batson was appointed in his place. For the working of the Board, see ibid., pp. 41-3.
9. K.C. Yadav, *Haryana*: *Studies*, p. 83.
10. Ibid., the six divisions were, Delhi, Meerut, Rohilkhand, Agra, Allahabad and Benaras.
11. For the details of area, etc., of the Haryana districts see Martin Montgomery, *The History of Indian Empire*, vol. I, p. 514.
12. The Agency to govern them was created for the first time in April 1810. The agent, who held the charge of the Agency, worked in subordination to the Delhi resident. His headquarters were located at Ludhiana. In 1815, however, the Agency's designation was changed to the present designation and the headquarters were shifted to Karnal and remained there till March 1822 when finally these were moved to Ambala. For details see Farooqi, *British Relations with the cis-Sutlej States*, 1809-23, *Punjab Govt. Records*, Monograph no. 19.
13. See Martin Montgomery, op. cit., vol. I, pp. 514-20.
14. For details see Buddha Prakash (ed.), *Glimpses of Haryana*, p. 81.
15. Ibid.
16. See, K.C. Yadav, *Haryana*, vol. II, p. 57, p. 82.
17. Ibid.
18. H. Tinker, *Local Self Government in India, Pakistan and Ceylon*, p. 5, *Settlement Report, Rohtak*, p. 40.
19. C.T. Metcalfe's *Minute of the Board of Revenue*, 17 November 1830.
20. For details see *JHS*, vol. IV (1972), pp. 24-32.
21. Quoted in ibid.
22. Ibid.
23. Ibid.

24. Ibid.
25. Ibid.
26. Ibid.
27. Ibid.
28. Ibid.
29. Ibid.
30. Ibid.
31. Ibid.
32. Ibid.
33. Ibid.
34. *Settlement Report, Karnal*, 1878, p. 48.
35. *JHS*, vol. IV (1972), pp. 24-32.
36. John Kaye, *History of Sepoy War, 1857-58*, vol. I, pp. 153-4.
37. David Ross, *The Land of Five Rivers and Sind*, p. 231.
38. See *Settlement Report, Karnal*, pp. 21-35.
39. NAI, Mutiny Papers, bundle, no. 34, document no. 12.

5

Uprisings and Outbursts, 1809-1856

The reasons mentioned in the preceeding chapter to which many more, such as racial hatred, arrogant behaviour of the rulers towards the ruled, denial of the share in government, etc., may be added, created an atmosphere of suffocation for the people during the period under study. It can be anybody's guess that the brave people of Haryana, who were not accustomed to tolerate such impositions, should have felt like doing away with such a raj. But because of the strong hold of the rulers they could not do much to rise as a body against them. Of course, whenever and wherever the hold seemed easier to break they did not hesitate to do it, as noted below.

Chhachhrauli Disturbances

Chhachhrauli, a small principality of the Karorsinghia sardars, with an area of about 63 sq. miles and a population of less than 9,000 in the present tehsil of Jagadhari in Yamuna Nagar district became the first trouble-spot for the British after the death of its chief, Bungail Singh (1809). As the deceased chief had no male heir, Jodh Singh, the chief of Kalsia, who, by virtue of being the head of Karorsinghia misl, claimed his right to get the state of his brother *mislman*, came and occupied it.[1]

A staunch friend and faithful ally of Maharaja Ranjit Singh of Punjab, Jodh Singh was an enemy of the British. He had, in fact, showed open hostility to them on more than one occasions.[2] As such, he could not be an acceptable successor to a thoroughly loyal chief to the British. Accordingly, David Ochterlony, the British Resident at Delhi, declared him an usurper and demanded his withdrawal from the state after leaving all its management into the hands of Rani Ram Kaur, the widow of Bungail Singh. To this Jodh Singh said no. As a result, Ochterlony had to take 'the most drastic step' to throw him out by force. But before doing so, the old man gave him another 'chance to withdraw within five days, failing which you would face serious consequences'. The ultimatum bore fruits and the Karorsinghia chief, aware of his inferiority to the British in deciding the issue on the battlefield, withdrew from the state forthwith.[3]

But Jodh's withdrawal was by no means for good. He came back after a couple of years (1818) and reoccupied the state. Enraged beyond description, the British authorities viewed the reoccupation with serious concern. They despatched a strong force at the head of an experienced commander, Brigadier-General Arnold (October 1818) to undo the new arrangement. It is interesting to note that this time the people of the state chose to take sides with Jodh Singh. This was perhaps due to the fact that Rani Ram Kaur, who ruled this state after Jodh Singh's exit in 1818 on the promptings of the British, failed to give a good government to them. Naturally, therefore, they welcomed the change; and when Arnold came to undo it, they fought against him. But the chief and his people proved no match to the superior British force and lost the day. Jodh Singh was thrown out and the territory was annexed to the British raj.[4]

Trouble in Rania

Soon after Chhachhrauli cooled off, Rania (Sirsa) got hot. Although Nawab Zabita Khan of the state had passed under the British authority in 1810, yet he did not behave like a 'faithful feudatory'. We are told by Fagan, the editor of the *District Gazetteer of Hisar*, that caring little for the British authority, he encouraged his people (Bhattis) to carry on regular plundering expeditions in to the British territories adjoining his state. When all the measures of the Delhi government failed to effect any improvement in the situation, a force was sent (1818). The Bhattis fought well for some time but their power was broken once for all. The state was confiscated and 'brought under the direct control of the Kampany Bahadoor'.[5]

The Peasant Revolt of 1824

In 1824 there was a serious trouble from an unexpected quarter. It has been discussed earlier that the agrarian system of the Company was quite defective: their revenue assessments were high; the modes of collection were severe and at times barbaric; and hardly anything was done in the name of relief work at the time of famines or droughts which, unfortunately, occurred quite frequently. In these circumstances, it was natural for the peasants to have harboured great resentment against the British. But, as the situation then was, they could not express it openly.[6] However, in 1824, the situation improved a bit in their favour: the Kampany Bahadur was locked in a war with Burma and the peasants had heard of their suffering reverses and losses there. This was, they thought, the right occasion to strike and finish the exploiting regime once for all. Accordingly, they rose up in open revolt.

The lead was taken by the brave Jat peasantry of Rohtak. They were soon followed by other communities inhabiting the district and their numbers and strength swelled a great deal—so much so that the British authorities with limited resources at their disposal proved incompetent to check them. The bold peasants finished off all the vestiges of the Feringhee rule from their land.[7]

The success achieved by the Rohtak peasants inspired their fellow-beings elsewhere too; and hundreds of them came forward to do the same in the districts of Gurgaon and Hisar. They attacked government buildings and offices, plundered treasuries and cut off all communications in their respective places. The people of Bhiwani attacked and plundred even a military transport passing through their territory.[8]

The British authorities at Delhi were alarmed to have known of the developments in the region so contiguous to Delhi. To prevent it from taking serious turn, they had to apply full force and check the rebellion forthwith. And this they did by sending a strong military contingent of the Gurkhas (October 1824). The peasants fought well. Suraj Mal, the leader of the peasants, showed conspicuous gallantry. However, a crowd could hardly stand for a long time against a disciplined contingent of army well equipped by all means: they lost the ground and suffered heavy casualties.[9]

Pratap Singh's Revolt

There was a rising in Jind in 1812. It so happened that the local ruler, Raja Bhag Singh, suffered a severe paralytic attack in March 1813. Unfit to run the administration of the state, the ailing chief wished to appoint Prince Pratap Singh, the ablest and wisest of all his sons as his regent to do his work. But the British government, to whom the anti-British bearing of the prince was known, stood in his way and got appointed Rani Sobrahi in place of the prince.[10] This was unbearable for Pratap Singh and he raised the standard of revolt on 23 June 1814. Being a popular figure in the state, the local forces also revolted and joined him forthwith. The prince occupied the fort (Jind) and established his government after putting the Rani, the puppet of the British, to sword.[11] The British viewed the whole affair pretty seriously and asked the Resident at Delhi to send a force against Pratap Singh. The prince, finding the Jind fort unfit from military viewpoint to give a fight to the invading force, retired to a relatively stronger position at Balawali, a fort in 'the wild country' about Bhatinda. The local population extended all sorts of help to him.

The British forces chased the prince hotly. But on reaching near Balawali they found that it was not possible for them to achieve their aim with their present strength. Hence they got some reinforcements from Ludhiana. Meantime, the prince also measured his strength *vis-a-vis* the new force; and left the fort without any fight. He crossed the Sutlej at Makhowal and entered Punjab where he was joined by Phula Singh Akali.[12] This being the territory of Maharaja Ranjit Singh, the British government asked the Sikh ruler to oust the rebel prince from there. Ranjit Singh, who did not think it proper to annoy the British for so trivial a matter, sent his troops right at once from Phillaur for this purpose. But to his surprise, his troops refused to fight against the prince. In fact, they openly praised the prince fighting against the Feringhee for a right cause.[13]

Having improved his position a good deal by getting help from the local papulace and Phula Singh, the Akali leader, Pratap Singh crossed the Sutlej after some time and entered into his old territory again. This was a bad news for the British who at once sent instructions to the Sikh chiefs of Patiala, Nabha and Kaithal to send their troops to check his advance. The chiefs obliged the British commander promptly but the problem faced earlier by the troops of Ranjit Singh was experienced by the troops of these chiefs too. Their soldiery refused to fight against the prince accompanied by Phula Singh. Compelled by the circumstances, the British authorities despatched their own troops again.[14]

Pratap Singh again took position in the Balawali fort (28 January 1815). The British forces attacked him with full force. An obstinate struggle ensued which went on for quite some time. But ultimately the British succeeded in subduing the prince who was taken prisoner.[15] But during the course of his march towards Delhi, the prince managed to escape and reached Lahore. Unfortunately, this proved to be a fall out of the frying pan into the fire. Ranjit Singh instead of giving him shelter, handed him over to the British who placed him in confinement at Delhi. There he lived as a prisoner, leading a wretched life till his death in 1816.[16]

After the above happenings, the administration of Jind was entrusted to Prince Fateh Singh. Though Raja Bhag Singh did not like the arrangement, yet he did not oppose it. In fact he had neither the will nor the means to do it. Broken in every sense of the term, Bhag Singh died in 1819 when Fateh Singh became a full-fledged ruler of the state. Fateh Singh's rule proved short-lived, however, for he, too, died three years later (1822). Sangat Singh, his only son (11 year old), succeeded him.

Challenge from Sangat Singh

Sangat Singh, the boy Maharaja, also disliked the British. As he grew up, the dislike turned into intense hatred. Besides this, the young Maharaja was also friendly with Maharaja Ranjit Singh. He visited him quite often. These direct and regular visits to the Lahore durbar were unpalatable to the British and they passed strictures against him for this 'default'. The Maharaja, it seems, was quite determined to tread upon this very path, for even the 'reprimands' could not stop him from visiting Lahore.

In order to make the presence of the British agent at his court meaningless, the Maharaja shifted his residence from Jind to a place about 60 miles from there and conducted the administration of his state from there. His anti-British feelings had developed to such an extent that he never treated the British officials, who happened to visit his state, with due respect. Like master, like servant: his employees also maltreated the Feringhees whenever and wherever they came across them. One Lt. Talbot, for instance, was robbed of all his belongings in broad day light in Jind itself and no state official cared to help him.[17]

The British government noted the hostile behaviour of Sangat Singh with grave concern. But, before they could think of doing something to stop him from carrying on with such affairs, he died a sudden death on 2 November 1834. Annoyed as the British government were with the deceased Maharaja, they forfeited a number of his estates (150 villages in Ludhiana, Mudki, etc., were taken under direct control while some estates in the trans-Sutlej region (Halwara, Talwandi, etc.) were given to Ranjit Singh).[18]

The deceased Maharaja left no heir behind him. Sarup Singh, his cousin, succeeded him. Although very friendly and loyal to the British heretofore, the confiscation of the above-mentioned estates sowed the seeds of disaffection in his heart. But weakling as he was, he could not do anything but grumble here and there; and remained loyal.[19]

Balawali Rising

Unlike their Maharaja, the people of Balawali, who had great veneration for Prince Pratap Singh and had fought for him against the British in a number of actions, reacted manfully to the taking over of their *ilaqa* under their direct management. They organized themselves to fight it out. Gulab Singh Gill,[20] formerly a risaldar in Jind army, and Dal Singh, brother-in-law of Prince Pratap Singh were their leaders. They also got a good deal of inspiration from Mai Sul Rani, the widow of Prince Pratap Singh.

A British force was despatched against the 'rebels' in early 1835. The 'rebels', too, gathered in large numbers. Besides, the people of the neighbouring villages, like Bhai Ghakian, etc., and the Akalis of Gurusar, a place of pilgrimage, also joined hands with the them.[21] The British attacked them with full force (March 1835). The 'rebels' fought well, but being inferior to their enemy in military knowledge, strategy, tactics, arms and ammunitions, they lost the day. Their casualties in the action were quite heavy—Gulab Singh being one of the killed. Dal Singh and Mai Sul Rani were apprehended and put behind the bars along with hundreds of their supporters.[22] And thus ended a popular revolt after a great deal of bloodshed.

Murder of Fraser

About this very time, a very serious occurrence took place in the southern part of the state. It related to the murder of William Fraser,[23] the resident at Delhi (1835). This officer, who had served in Haryana in the capacity of an assistant for long, was a typical representative of the old Sahibs. He was haughty, cruel and licentious. His visit to a village always meant oppression, at times for collection of revenues and at times for 'setting something in order'. No fair faced woman, if caught his glance, could have remained safe from him. (The higher stratum of the society was his main target in this respect.) It is alleged, for instance, that he had subjected Shamsuddin, nawab of Loharu's cousin sister to his seductive designs. The nawab resented it. There was yet another reason: the resident also took sides in the family feud of the nawab of the local chiefs.[24] Nawab Shamsuddin had some dispute over the division of property with his brothers—Aminuddin and Jiauddin. The court decided it in favour of the former.[25] But Fraser, who was annoyed with the nawab over his cousin sister's case, incited the losing party to reopen the case.[26] Not only that, Fraser abusing his position as resident, played Amin's and

Jia's cards himself openly and got them victory. Accordingly, the state was divided: Aminuddin and Jiauddin got Loharu whereas Shamsuddin retained Ferozepur-Jhirka.

This was too much to bear with for Shamsuddin. He deputed one Karim Khan,[27] his *daroga-i-shikar* and a Mewati marksman, Anya to kill Fraser. The two men went to Delhi at once (September 1834). But difficult as their job was, they could not materialize it for many a month. Nevertheless, on 22 March 1835, they got an opportunity when Fraser was going from a dinner party to his residence. They shot him dead.[28]

Since Nawab Shamsuddin was a known enemy of Fraser, the Delhi authorities lost no time in working out his complicity in the murder. Anya, to his bad luck, turned approver and confirmed the whole thing. The case was, therefore, decided against the Nawab and Karim Khan; and both of them were awarded the extreme penalty of law, i.e. death by hanging.

The decision gave a rude shock to the general public, especially the Muslims, in Delhi. As indicated above, Fraser was quite notorious for his ruthless oppression of the people and his licentious character. The murder of such a man was naturally nothing short of deliverance for the people, and both the 'offenders'—Karim Khan and Nawab Shamsuddin—were treated as great souls dying for a noble cause.[29] On the day of hanging of Karim Khan (28 August 1835), it is said, the people prayed for him in almost every mosque in Delhi. Respect due to a martyr was accorded to him: flowers were placed and lamps (*chirags*) lit on his grave. He was called *gul-i-shahid.*

Nawab Shamsuddin was hanged on 8 October 1835. The gallows were erected between Kashmiri Gate and Mori Gate. The people of Delhi were terribly upset on that day. The government anticipated disturbances. To avert any untoward happening in the city, they made heavy security arrangements. Despite all sorts of discouragement, however, over 8,000 people assembled and accompanied the nawab on his last journey. Clad in green, the nawab climbed the gallows courageously. It is said that after death the nawab's head moved slightly pointing towards the Quba. This was a fair indication of his being an innocent and a martyr.[30]

There was an interesting side-effect of the execution of the nawab. The people felt very strongly on this point and wished to express their opinion through press. But the existing press would not oblige them. This led to the birth of the Urdu press: the *Delhi Akhbar* came out in 1836, followed later on by *Sayyad-ul Akhbar* (1837), *Siraj-ul-Akhbar* (1841), *Karim-ul-Akhbar* (1845), *Qiran-us-Sadan* (1845), and *Sadiq-ul-Akhbar* (1853).[31]

Kaithal Uprising

There was a big trouble at Kaithal in 1843, when Bhai Udai Singh, the chief of the state died. Since he left no male heir after him, the state (valued at Rs. 4 lakh per annum) was taken into possession by the British. This was a 'highly distasteful' act to the Phulkian chiefs—the rajas of Patiala, Nabha and Jind—who, as relatives of the late chief, were naturally desirous of succeeding to the state and thus 'retaining the possessions in the family'. They placed their case before Greathed, the government's special agent at Kaithal (sent to take possession of the state). Their proposal was rejected and they became quiet.[32]

However, the widow of the deceased raja and the people of Kaithal, unlike the Phulkian chiefs, were not prepared to accept the 'act of spoliation' lying low. They rose up and ousted the usurpers of their raj from their place. This was an unexpected thing for the British authorities who at once despatched a column to reduce the rebels. The people showed fight for some time, but inferior as they were militarily, they could not stand for long. The town of Kaithal and the fort were re-occupied. The rani was arrested along with his hundreds of followers. A reign of terror was let loose in the state for some while.[33]

Ajit Singh's Revolt

Two years later, the bugle of revolt was blared at Ladwa, a small town and headquarters of the state of the same name, not far from Kaithal. The local ruler, Raja Ajit Singh was well-known for his contempt and hatred for the British. The Delhi authorities, naturally, felt quite bad about it and wanted to see him off the *gaddi*. But to their great chagrin, they could not get any solid excuse to implement their scheme. Yet, it had to be done—even if it meant inventing some imaginary lapses on the part of the raja.

By 1845, the British cup of tolerance was more than full and they declared the raja to be 'a traitor, disloyal to their rule'. Besides, his system of administration was reported as corrupt and inefficient by one and all.[34] How baseless this charge against the raja was can be seen from the following observations of George Compbell, the deputy commissioner of Kaithal and Ladwa in the forties:

> The Raja of Ladwa was by no means a model ruler—indeed our officers had considered him a very bad one—yet, when I went into his revenue accounts and system, I was surprised to find how regular everything was and how much that we had supposed to be highhandedness was really very precisely regulated by custom and precedent and the subject of very exact account.[35]

Yet he was pronounced a bad, corrupt ruler and a rebel and put under surveillance at Saharanpur (1845).[36] But the cage could not hold the lion for long. On the occasion of the outbreak of the first Anglo-Sikh War, the Ladwa chief, as if by some magical touch, effected his escape. Having mustered a contingent of several thousands of his people, he joined the Sikh army under Ranjor Singh, which had crossed the Jullundur Doab, to the neighbourhood of Ludhiana and fought many an action. Early in January 1846, while on his way to collect his family from his fief of Badowal (near Ludhiana), he invaded Ludhiana and burnt down the contonment which 'the paucity of infantry and the want of cavalry on the spot enabled him to do with impunity'. On 21 January, in conjunction with the Sikh army under Ranjor Singh, he humbled a British force under Henry Smith at Badowal. After this, he fought at several other places on the other side of the Sutlej during the course of the war.[37] After the war, his state was confiscated and he died as a fugitive, as we shall see later.

Sikh Chiefs' opposition

Ajit Singh's other fellow-chiefs in the cis-Sutlej tract behaved more or less in the same manner during the first Anglo-Sikh War, 1845-6. Many of them joined the Sikh forces openly, whereas others remained only passively obstructive to the 'new masters'.[38] This was too much to be tolerated by the British and they inflicted severe punishment on these 'disloyal chiefs' after the war.[39] The Raja of Ropar lost his 106 villages in Ropar and Kharar parganas.[40] The Sodhis of Anadpur had to part with 72 villages in the same pargana.[41] As regards smaller chiefs, 'less severe measures were considered sufficient. Their powers were reduced so that in future they could not indulge in 'open disaffection or neglect'.[42] Their status was also changed—they were transformed into jagirdars.[43]

The suppression of the aforesaid outbursts in no way cooled the hearts of the people; nor did the repression that followed in their wake could kill their spirit. They were still ready to rise up again against the *zalim sarkar* (cruel government) should they get any suitable opportunity. Fortunately, they got the opportunity in May 1857, and they seized it with both hands. No matter where their castes, creeds or professions were, they rose up in thousands throughout Haryana to smite the slavery down, as is seen in the next chapter.

NOTES

1. Martin Montgomery, op. cit., vol. I, p. 522; J.D. Cunningham, *History of the Sikhs,* p. 127.
2. J.D. Cunningham, op. cit., pp. 124-5, 127.
3. NAI, Foreign Political Consultation, 14 July 1810, no. 18; 21 July 1810, no. 43; 23 November 1810, no. 42.
4. G. Hamilton, *Hindostan*, vol. I, p. 464; J.D. Cunningham, op. cit., p. 127.
5. *Hisar District Gazetteer*, 1910, p. 34.
6. Ibid.
7. J.S. Mill, *History of British India*, vol. IX, p. 116.
8. Ibid.
9. Ibid.
10. Lepel Griffin, *Rajas of the Punjab*, vol. II, pp. 342-52.
11. Ibid.
12. Ibid.
13. Ibid.
14. Ibid.
15. Ibid.
16. Ibid.
17. Ibid.
18. Ibid.
19. Ibid.
20. He was a resident of Balawali.
21. Lapel Griffin, op. cit., vol. II, pp. 381-2.
22. Ibid.
23. William Fraser (1784-1835) was son of Edward S. Fraser; came to Bengal in 1799; became secretary to Ochterlony in 1805; served at various other places in different capacities till 1826, when he became member of the Board of Revenue, N.W.P.; became Resident at Delhi in 1830.
24. Fraser, it is said, was 'self witted to such a great extent that no power could be entrusted to him without some risk of its being abused. For details see C.P.N. Singh, *Mughal Samrajya-ki-Jiwan Sandhya*, p. 97; K. Nigam, *Delhi in 1857*, p. 18; D.N. Panigrahi, *Charles Metcalf in India*, pp. 53-4; Mrs. Chopra (ed.), *Delhi, History and Places of Interest*, p. 56.
25. The feud started in 1827 on the demise of Ahmed Baksh Khan. Shamsuddin, being the eldest of all his brothers, advanced his claims to the whole estate, whereas his two younger brothers, Aminuddin and Jiauddin, pressed for its division. After a year's litigation, the estate's division was ordered by the supreme government. Accordingly, Ferozepur-Jhirka went to the share of Shamsuddin and Loharu to the younger brothers. The government changed their decision, afterwards for the two brothers failed to manage the affairs of their estate (Loharu). Shamsuddin was given Loharu, too, on the condition of a cash payment of stipends to the two brothers (1853).

26. This was a misuse of his powers on the part of Fraser. Shamsuddin was right in his approach throughout. Even C.T. Metcalfe admitted this fact: 'If there be any right point', he said, 'of the judgement of Government, it is, I conceive, with the party opposed to that which Fraser patronizes, Shamsuddin being heir to his father in his territorial possessions.' Metcalfe to Bentinck, 1 November 1833, vide P.G.T. Spear, *Twilight of the Mughals*, p. 184.
27. Ghalib, the celebrated Urdu poet, informs us that according to one report Karim Khan had decided to kill Fraser on his own, whereas according to another one he had taken the decision at the instance of the nawab (*Nuhar-Safa*, 47). To us the later version seems to be more correct, for it is corroborated by facts received from other sources (which we have seen in the text above).
28. For details see P.G.T. Spear, op. cit., pp. 185-6.
29. It was generally believed by the people at that time that Ghalib, who was on bad terms with Shamsuddin, had done *mukhabari* (informant's job) to the British against the nawab. Ghalib, however, refuted this charge against him and held one Ibn-un-Fatehullah Beg, a friend of the nawab, responsible for communicating all information in this regard to the British. See *Kuliat-Nasar*, p. 162; *Zikr-i-Ghalib*, p. 72.
30. For these details see *Tarikh-i-Safahat Urdu*, pp. 97-101; Chopra, op. cit., pp. 56-7.
31. Chopra, op. cit., p. 57.
32. Lapel Griffin and Massey, *The Punjab Chiefs and the Families of Note*, vol. II, pp. 27-8.
33. Ibid.
34. Panigrahi, op. cit., p. 47.
35. Griffin and Massey, op. cit., vol. II, pp. 27-8.
36. George Campbell, *Memoirs*, vol. I, p. 58.
37. Griffin and Massey, op. cit., vol. II, p. 39.
38. Ibid., p. 57; Cunningham, op. cit., pp. 270-1
39. Lapel Griffin and Massey, op. cit., vol. II, p. 57.
40. Campbell, op. cit., vol. 1, p. 39.
41. Griffin and Massey, op. cit., vol. II, pp. 57-8.
42. About the smaller chiefs, Griffin says: 'The majority had not shown their loyalty in 1845 in any more conspicuous way than in not joining the enemy.'
43. Ibid., pp. 57-8.

6

The Mighty Challenge, 1857

The British rule of half a century from 1803 to 1857 had produced a great deal of discontent and disaffection among the people of Haryana. They made certain attempts, as seen in Chapter 4, to do away with the exploitative colonial raj. These efforts were, however, too feeble and too unconcerted to be effective. The British could fail them easily. But in May 1857, a different situation presented itself. The entire northern India rose up against the *zalim* raj as one man and struck a powerful blow. The people of Haryana were, as was expected, in the forefront of the great uprising.

Outbreak of the Revolt

At the close of the year 1856, the government of India introduced in the Indian army an improved type of firearm, the enfield rifle, in place of the 'brown bess' on grounds of expediency. The cartridges for the new rifle were greased with an ingredient containing 'cow's fat and hog's lard' to make them slip readily into the barrel. A large number of such cartridges were manufactured at Fort William in Calcutta and supplied to the three depots at Dum-Dum, Ambala and Sialkot for instruction in the use of the new weapon.[1]

No sooner was the new weapon introduced than a complication arose. In the early days of January 1857, a Bengali clerk at Calcutta had been assigned the task of translating into vernaculars details regarding the make and use of the cartridges in the enfield rifle. While going through the original text in English he learned, to his great surprise and horror, that the grease used in the lubrication of the cartridges contained animal fat of cows, pigs and goats. The clerk spread the news which was later on confirmed by a khalasi attached to the magazine at Dum-Dum where cartridges for the enfield rifles were manufactured. The news literally spread like wildfire among the sepoys of the Bengal Army.[2]

On 22 January 1857 the military authorities at Dum-Dum came to know of this 'strange hysteria that had seized the native sepoys'. Denials, explanations and reasoned arguments were put forward by persons in authority. But the belief proved hard to remove, so much so that very efforts made to root it out only fixed it more ineradicably in the popular mind. The sepoys firmly believed that the government was determined to convert them to Christianity. And the first deliberate attempt in that direction, they said, was to destroy the caste, both of the Mohammedans and Hindus, by making them use the fat of hog and cow.[3] There is enough evidence to show that the sepoys' fear of the violation of their religions by the greased cartridges was not completely unfounded. The cartridge did contain cows' fat and hogs' lard at first. The fact was conceded by various English writers, and even by the government in the House of Commons.[4]

Naturally, the sepoys were in consternation. The question that agitated every mind and that trembled on every tongue was: 'Shall we tolerate the violation of our religion?' The answer was in the negative. To devise some counter-measures, panchayats were formed in every corps. They vehemently criticized the government, openly expressed their resentment and unanimously decided to expel from all communion, those sepoys who at any of the depots, used the cartridges at all. Besides, 'sedition was vigorously spread from one regiment to another by letters, medicants and such religious agencies as Dharma Sabha of Calcutta until at last a general spirit of mutiny pervaded the whole of the Bengal Army and northern India'.[5]

In north-western India the first military station to feel the contagion of the mutiny was Ambala. Besides being a large cantonment, this city was also one of the three musketry depots to which detachments from different regiments in the Punjab and the North-Western Provinces had been detailed for training in the use of the notorious enfield rifle. Sham Singh, a sepoy of the 5th Native Infantry stationed here, told Forsyth, the deputy commissioner of Ambala towards the end of April 1857:

> The great body of the sepoys were in highly indignant and excited state under the apprehension that they were all to be compelled to use the offensive cartridge; and that they had resolved that whenever such an order be issued every bangalow in the station should be in flames.[6]

He further exposed a conspiracy giving the details thus:

> Two native infantry corps were to seize the magazines; the Light Cavalry to seize the guns; the heelropes of the horses of the M.M.'s 9th Lancers were to be cut and the horses let loose; and a general rise and massacre to ensue.[7]

A police official (the bazar kotwal) also confirmed the existence of such a conspiracy, though in a different way by deposing that a pandit had told him that according to Hindu astrological calculations, it was certain that blood would be shed within a week either in Delhi, Meerut or Ambala.[8] The British authorities got ready to meet the serious situation.

The Rising at Ambala

The first bugle of the great uprising of 1857 was blared at Ambala on 10 May 1857, about nine hours before the outbreak at Meerut took place. Ambala sepoys rose up, as noted above, according to their plan of rising, the sepoys of the 60th Native Infantry left their lines line as one man, seized arms from the regimental kote, and arrested their European officers. But to their great surprise, the next moment they found themselves surrounded by a superior number of European forces. Under such circumstances, the sepoys could not proceed ahead with their plan. Nor could the British troops fall upon them for, in the words of an eyewitness, 'They (sepoys) had their officers as prisoners and threatened to shoot them if we came down'. So both the forces stood still for a while and then a bargain was struck which, in the words of the same eyewitness, was something like this: 'If we (Englishmen) did not (attack them), they (sepoys) would return quietly'. The Englishmen had no other alternative but to agree to their proposal.

The 60th Native Infantry was not even fully quiet when the 5th Native Infantry turned out at 12 o'clock (noon). The British troops being too alert to be swept over by a surprise, immediately rushed up to the troubled spot and surrounded the 5th Native Infantry by their cavalry and artillery, superior in number and fire-power to them. So the rising of the 5th Native Infantry was also checked.[9]

About the same time trouble bursted forth at the third spot too—the treasury. Here a detachment of the 5th Native Infantry was on duty and when they heard that their brethren had risen, they also rose up. But again promptitude on the part of the British saved the situation.[10]

The British were too alert to be caught napping at Ambala. As a result, the 'rebels' failed to transform their intentions into a working reality. But their counterparts at Meerut fared better. They finished off all vestiges of the British rule from their place on 10 May and succeeded in doing the same at Delhi the next day. They placed Bahadur Shah II on the throne of Akbar and Aurangzeb and announced the heralding of a new era.[11]

District Gurgaon in Revolt

On hearing the news of the happenings at Ambala, Meerut and Delhi, the brave and bellicose people of Haryana rose en masse and opposed the British authorities tooth and nail. At Gurgaon, the local populace along with some sowars of the 3rd Cavalry of the Meerut fame (who had reached that place on 13 May) turned out W. Ford, the collector-magistrate and established their rule. This led the people to believe that the British rule had ceased to exist. Consequently, the flames of rebellion flared up in the most virulent form in the whole of the district.

In Mewat, the sturdy and warlike Mewatis came out in large numbers and formed a *dhar* (a crowd turned into a somewhat organized gathering) to finish the British rule. Sadruddin, a tall, handsome Meo peasant from Pinnghawa stood at their head.[12] Sadruddin's first attack was on the loyalist elements living in towns. His men met with little opposition at Tauru, Sohna, Ferozepur, Punhana, and Pinnghawa, but they had quite a tough time dealing with the loyal Khanzadas[13] at Nuh. The struggle went on for quite some time, but ultimately the rebels were successful on account of their superiority in numbers. Thereafter 'the Rawat Jats of the region near Hodal and the Rajputs of Hathin, who were supposed to be on the side of the (British) government were attacked with the help of the Surot Jats of Hodal and Pathans of Seoli'.[14] The fight continued for several months with the loyalists suffering heavy losses.[15] On receipt of the SOS signal from the Rawats, the British authorities before Delhi despatched a movable column for Hodal to help them, but despite Government help, the Rawats were completely routed.[16]

In the middle of June, Major W. Eden, the political agent at Jaipur, happened to pass through Mewat at the head of a contingent comprising about 6,999 men and 7 guns on his way to Delhi. But finding Mewat in a 'most deplorable state of anarchy', he thought it advisable to settle it before going to Delhi.[17] But he soon found that the job he had assigned himself was not an easy one. He was offered stiff opposition by Mewatis between Tauru and Sohna. Had he not been in possession of artillery, his forces would have suffered heavy losses.[18]

Major Eden halted at Sohna for three days. Ford and thirty European officers came down from Mohana and joined him here. After that, Eden moved towards Palwal and remained between that place and Hodal for some time.[19] Interestingly, at this stage there was a rebellion among his own troops and a powerful group of the Rajputs led by Thakur Shiv Nath Singh, an ex-minister of Jaipur, even made a murderous attack on Eden on 20 July.[20] Under these circumstances, Eden had to return to Jaipur at once, leaving Mewat in the hands of the sons of the soil.[21]

In Ahirwal,[22] the people waged a gallant struggle under the leadership of Tula Ram and his cousin Gopal Dev, both descendants from the Raos of Rewari whom Farukhsiyar had granted a *jagir* worth Rs. 20,00,000 per annum. The Raos had helped the Marathas in 1803 in their fight against the British and as a result when the latter came out successful in the struggle, they confiscated their *jagir* and gave them instead an *istamarari* grant of about 87 villages worth Rs. 1,00,000 per annum. This was a great blow to the Raos which shattered their position.[23] This made the sufferer unhappy with the British raj: naturally, the fall of the British fortunes on 11 May 1857 was a most welcome piece of news to them.[24]

On 17 May 1857, the Raos went to the tehsil headquarters at Rewari with four to five hundred followers and deposed the tehsildar and thanedar. They appropriated the cash (Rs. 8,36,427) from the tehsil treasury, took all the government buildings in their possession and proclaimed under the sanction of Emperor Bahadur Shah their rule over the parganas of Rewari, Bhora and Shahjahanpur consisting of 360, 52 and 9 villages respectively. For their headquarters they chose Rampura, a small fortified village, one mile south-west of Rewari. Tula Ram, the elder Rao became raja and Gopal Dev his commander-in-chief.[25]

Tula Ram organized various departments, and collected revenue and taxes.[26] He took donations and loans amounting to Rs. 1,50,000 from the *mahajans* of Rewari[27] and raised a big force[28] (about five thousand men) and set up a large workshop in the fort of Rampura where a substantial number of guns, gun carriages, and other small arms and ammunition were manufactured.[29] The Rao enforced law and order and defended his state from outside attacks.[30]

These activities pleased Bahadur Shah and he confirmed the Rao in his *jagirs* of Rewari, Bhora and Shahjahanpur.[31] The Rao, in return rendered all possible help to Emperor Bahadur Shah and the rebels waging war against the British in Delhi. For instance, he sent Rs. 45,000[32] through General Bakht Khan, at such a critical time when non-payment of the salaries to the sepoys had caused great insecurity and anxiety,[33] though his small sum did not improve the situation.[34] The Rao also supplied the Delhi forces with large quantities of other commodities. Jiwan Lal says that in August there was a scarcity of opium in the army, and consequently many soldiers died. On 24 August 1857 Bahadur Shah sent a request to Tula Ram to send some opium to Delhi. This may have been supplied because the appeal was not repeated: nor was Tula Ram scolded in any way for non-compliance of the royal orders. Again in

September a request was made to the Rao for the supply of sulphur for manufacturing powder when there was none to be found in the city.[35] At the time of scarcity of food grains, the Rao sent forty-three carts of grain for the rebel forces.[36] About this very time sacks were needed. The Rao promptly supplied 2,000 of them.[37] This shows that the Rao kept open the supply line of the besieged garrison in Delhi.

In the south-east, the sturdy Jats, Rajputs, Ranghars, rose in revolt effectively. At Palwal, Mirza Gafur Ali and Harsukh Rai, both small tradesmen[38] held the torch of revolt. At Faridabad, the leadership was assumed by Dhan Singh Rajput.[39] Raja Nahar Singh,[40] and Nawab Ahmed Ali led[41] at Ballabhgarh and Farrukhnagar respectively.[42] The contemporary records indicate that the people of this district had freed themselves of the British control completely by the end of the second week of May 1857.[43]

Rohtak in Flames

Almost similar thing happened in district Rohtak. On hearing the news of the fall of Delhi, all the Jat clans rose up and finished off all vestiges of the British rule from their localities. Unfortunately, however, they could not throw any local leader worth the name from amongst themselves to control the new situation. This resulted in chaos and confusion and different Jat clans started their age-old infights again.[44]

The Ranghars, living in the midst of the sturdy Jat population, behaved a bit differently, however. Their struggle was very intense for two reasons: First, a large number of Ranghar soldiers whose regiments had mutinied came and joined them. Secondly, they found good leaders in Bisarat Ali and Babur Khan. The former was from Kharkhauda. He had joined the army and by dint of his hard work and ability had become a risaldar there. He was brave and clever. Babur Khan was a resourceful local peasant chaudhari who was held in high esteem by the people for his good virtues and behaviour.[45]

The Ranghars under these two leaders freed the whole of their locale from the British control. Despite their best efforts, however, they could not take Rohtak, the seat of the district administration which was ably defended by Loch, the deputy commissioner. But fortunately for them, this situation did not last long. On 24 May, there came a movable column under Tafzal Hussain. Deputy Commissioner Loch tried to oppose the column with the help of Tehsildar Bakhtawar Singh, and Thanesar Bhure Khan and the local troops, but he was overpowered by them. Having suffered defeat, Loch ran away, leaving the district headquarters in the hands of the rebels.[46] They burnt all the public buildings and records.[47]

After three days the Rohtak rebels were joined by a force (Haryana Light Infantry) from Hansi, Hisar and Sirsa which strengthened their position a great deal. It is unfortunate, however, that Tafzal Hussain did not take any steps to restore administration in the district. He only collected Rs. 1,10,000 from the district treasury and then returned to Delhi via Mehan, Sampla and Mandauthi, plundering the houses of Europeans and the loyalist element at all these places. Nor did the local leaders like Bisarat Ali and Babur Khan did anything worthwhile at Rohtak after Tafzal had left the place.

The news of maladministration reached Bahadur Shah at Delhi who at once issued a *firman* to the people of Rohtak, warning them:

> That one man is not to stretch out the hand of violence against another, and that all are to continue in full subjection to the authority and power of the powerful landholders who are known to be the well-wishers of the State; civil establishment and a sufficient military force will very soon be sent to make all necessary arrangements. Anxious concern for welfare and comfort of his subjects is cherished by His Majesty, but all such as shall be guilty of acts of turbulence or disobedience against lawful authority will be most harshly punished.[48]

It seems the royal instructions were complied with and some sort of order was preserved in the district with the help of the local chaudharis.[49]

These developments perturbed the British authorities. Rohtak in close proximity of Delhi and through which the G.T. Road to Delhi passed was an important place. Therefore, a column comprising the 60th Native Infantry (of the Ambala fame) was despatched from Panipat on 28 May,[50] with Deputy Commissioner Loch to bring the district under their control.[51] Since the regiment was already disaffected and had risen in revolt against the British on 10 May (at Ambala), Loch undertook this responsibility with a great deal of hesitation. He grumbled: 'Despatching a mutinous corps to settle a disturbed district appears to me to be a new principle of administration'.[52] But it could not be helped: the despatcher of the regiment had his own difficulties, and he had done so under compulsion. He did not want to keep the regiment at Ambala. He could not send it to Delhi. So he chose Rohtak,[53] thinking that perhaps it would be least harmful there. But it was not to be. No doubt Loch, marching with this regiment, reoccupied the district headquarters easily, but it proved to be short-lived. The rebels made secret negotiations with the 60th Native Infantry. As a result, the regiment rose up in open mutiny on 10 June: 'not a single man remained true to his colours'. The European officers, too alert to be caught napping, saved their lives by fleeing in time. Leaving Rohtak to the care of the rebels, the sepoys made their way to Delhi, reaching there in full numbers.[54]

The British authorities before Delhi took a serious view of the loss of the district again. Since the G.T. Road passed through the district, its rebel population could greatly impede the passage of men and material (from Punjab to Delhi).[55] It was, therefore, considered very essential from the military point of view that the district be recovered without any loss of time. Accordingly, Major General Wilson, commanding the Delhi Field Force sent Lieutenant Hodson with a force comprising six officers, 103 men of the Guides, 233 of Hodson's Irregular Horse and 25 of the Jind Horse (361 in all) in the early hours of 15 August 1857.[56]

Hodson proceeded with speed. But he was checked at Kharkhauda, a village about 20 miles from Rohtak (at about 12 o'clock on 25 August).[57] The villagers, and specially the leave men[58] of the irregular corps who had taken position in one of the strong buildings belonging to a lambardar of the village right in the centre of the town, opposed him bravely under the inspiring leadership of Risaldar Bisarat Ali.[59] Even Hodson admitted: 'They fought like devils.'[60] But because of their large numbers and superior fire power, the British soon overpowered them. Risaldar Bisarat Ali fell fighting along with twenty-five of his men. The British also suffered a number of casualties on their side.[61]

Hardly had Hodson finished this encounter when intelligence reached him that Rohtak had become a rallying point of a considerable large number of rebels under a new peasant leader, Sabar Khan.[62] He at once left Kharkhauda and after a short halt and respite at Bohar reached Rohtak at about 4 o'clock the following afternoon.[63] Here, he formed his men just outside the town and rode forward with two officers and a few sowars to reconnoitre.[64] But his movements were soon checked by fire from rebels collected in large numbers inside a fortified building in the vicinity of the old civil station.[65] With lightening speed Hodson brought up his men and detaching two troops to take up defensive position, he made a dash at the main gate.[66] The rebels repulsed his attack successfully, and prevented him from entering the building from any other side.[67] Disappointed and dejected, Hodson withdrew his men to the old Kacheri compound near the junction of the roads coming in from Delhi, Bohar and the town of Rohtak and bivouacked there for the night.[68]

In the early hours of 17 July, Hodson was attacked by Sabar Khan with about 300 Ranghar horsemen belonging to different irregular cavalry regiments and a mass of footmen certainly not less than 900 or

1,000 in numbers.[69] They took shelter in the bushy hides in close proximity of the town and 'incessantly poured in a galling fire'.[70] In this position, the British cavalry could cause little harm to them: their only hope lay in drawing them out.[71] To accomplish this, Hodson sent out 'one troop to the right second to the left and placed the rest in the centre, pushing the Guides to the front'.[72] Thus disposed, they defied the efforts of the rebels to outflank them, presenting a front wherever they appeared. Hodson then ordered them to retire slowly. The plan succeeded admirably. On seeing the cavalry retiring the rebels came out, yelling and shouting and followed up Hodson's party. When he had drawn them about three quarters of a mile out in the open, Hodson ordered his men to turn about and charge. His men immediately fell on the 'astonished enemy in every direction, and took a heavy toll'.[73] The rebels retreated but Hodson did not pursue them.[74] That was the end of the indecisive battle of Rohtak where both the parties broke away without either of them registering a victory.[75] Hodson tells his story thus:

> Unfortunately, I had no ammunition left, and therefore could not without imprudence remain so close to the north of the town and encamped near the first friendly village that we came to.[76]

Leaving some important places, such as Kharkhauda, Sampla, Meham under the care of the raja of Jind,[77] and some local chaudharis, Hodson left the district and went to Delhi.[78]

Hisar Revolts

Hisar was hotter than Rohtak.[79] Muhammed Azim, the assistant patrol of Bhattu, a young, energetic descendant of the royal family of Delhi, proclaimed the end of the British rule and established his authority over most of the region.[80] At Hansi, Hukam Chand, a middle aged Jain businessman and his young nephew Faqir Chand and a Muslim friend Meena Beg played an important role and enforced law and order there.[81] Nur Muhammed Khan, the nawab of the ex-state of Rania, began to rule his erstwhile state. All these local leaders accepted the central authority of Emperor Bahadur Shah.[82]

The winds of change blowing in the district were also felt by the troops stationed at Hansi, Hisar and Sirsa. On 15 May, the men of the 4th Irregular Cavalry[83] revolted at Hansi and made their way to Delhi.[84] Fourteen days later the entire wing of the Haryana Light Infantry and the detachment of the Dadri Cavalry stationed there mutinied. Major Stafford, the commanding officer and other officers who had been informed of the uprising earlier (by a junior commissioned officer and a loyal civilian employee named Murari) managed to escape, while others, about eleven men, women and children, were massacred. Their bungalows were set on fire, and the town of Hansi was plundered.[85]

On 27 May, a wing of the Haryana Light Infantry under Subedar Shahnur Khan and men of the Dadri Cavalry under Rajab Beg rose up at Hisar.[86] It started at about 1.00 p.m. when a few persons clad in green attacked the Hisar Fort where Wedderburn, the deputy commissioner was living with his family. The men at the gate did not object to their entry into the Fort, and as though the whole thing was pre-planned led them in. Shahnur Khan, the commander, whose tent was pitched just near the sentry-post, did not check them. Two Englishmen, Hallet and Taylor came on hearing the noice, but they were shot down before they could do anything. The shots served as a signal for a popular uprising—troops were joined by the civil population in the twinkle of an eye. They broke open the district jail, released about two scores of prisoners from there, plundered and destroyed the houses and bungalows of the Europeans and seized the district treasury containing Rs. 1,70,000. Wedderburn, the deputy commissioner and twelve other Europeans were killed. Thereafter the sepoys went to Hansi to join their comrades.[87]

The news of the catastrophes at Hansi and Hisar was conveyed to the European residents at Sirsa before it reached the rebel troops.[88] The former became greatly demoralized and fled without losing any time. Capt. Roberts, the superintendent of Bhatinda and his family moved to Ferozepur via Dabawali and Bhatinda. Other Europeans, about 17 in all, went to Sahuwala with Donald, the assistant superintendent, and took shelter in the Patiala state. Hillard, officer commanding of the contingent and Fell, assistant patrol went into the barracks of the sepoys and tried to keep them 'true to their salt'. But sepoys did not listen to them at all and asked them to leave at once. The rebel sepoys occupied the tehsil treasury. They seized Rs. 8,000 from there and went to Hansi where all the rebel troops of the district had assembled. After staying there for some time, they made their way to Delhi via Rohtak.[89]

Thus by the first week of June, the entire district of Hisar was free of the British rule.

Panipat and Thanesar

The news of the outbreak of the revolt at Meerut and Delhi was also a glad tiding for the people for Panipat[90] and Thanesar. Barring those living in big towns where the government had made great arrangements with the help of the local chiefs[91] the disaffected people rose up everywhere.[92] Commenting on the state of district Panipat, Capt. Mac Andrew informed the Government of India on 1 June 1857: 'I find the country considerably disorganised; the revenue and police officers are in the state of flight, many of the zamindars and big villagers are quite refractory.'[93] Capt. MacAndrew's counterpart in Thanesar was confronted with a similar situation in his district.[94]

The British authorities made a prompt appeal to the chiefs of Patiala, Nabha, Jind, Kunjpura and Karnal to help them retain their hold at least over the G.T. Road passing through the two districts.[95] These chiefs, to their good fortune, obeyed the orders at once. The Maharaja of Patiala came to Thanesar with 1,500 men and 4 guns on 15 May. On the 17 May the raja of Jind sent 400 men. Kunjpura and Karnal gave 350 and 150 of their men respectively for Panipat. The troops controlled the G.T. Road and the main towns situated on it.[96]

The rebel army in Delhi took a serious view of the developments in the two districts and a movable column was sent out to undo the work of the British authorities in the third week of May. Although no writer of the uprising mentions it, a contemporary Indian named Tajuddin, a well-informed man from Punjab, has stated that this column fought a pitched battle with the British forces around Panipat (near Karnal) and killed a large number of their men, including their Commander-in-Chief, General Anson[97] and obliged them to beat a hasty retreat. I have elsewhere questioned the truth of the contention of the historians that General Anson had died of cholera at Karnal.[98] He was killed. In utter haste, under the heavy pressure of the Indian column, the retreating British forces buried the old general (at Karnal) without military honours.[99]

Soon afterwards, however, the position of the British column improved with the arrival of fresh reinforcements from Punjab. Karnal again fell into their hands, but not the rest of the two districts. The people in the distant of the British parganas of Ladwa, Pehowa, Kaithal, Pundri, Assandh rose up en masse. They drove out the revenue and police officials, made the loyalists surrender, and destroyed all traces of the British rule in their localities.[100]

District Ambala

There was upsurge in district Ambala[101] too. As noted above, like the Indian soldiery stationed at Ambala, the civil populace was also ill-disposed towards the British.[102] John Lawrence, the chief commissioner of Punjab, requested the Commander-in-Chief, General Anson, to disarm the Ambala troops at once.[103] The commander-in-chief reached Ambala on 15 March to carry out the work. But when he took the matter in hand, the local military authorities pointed out that they had pledged themselves not to disarm the sepoys.[104] Under these circumstances, General Anson did not think it wise to carry out the suggestion of the chief commissioner and devised another plan to render the troops harmless. He divided them into small detachments and despatched them to far-off places[105] retaining only the 5th Native Infantry at Ambala.

The plan of the old general proved a failure. After the Delhi Field Force had left Ambala, one-fourth of the 5th Native Infantry men deserted at night.[106] The remaining sepoys—two companies stationed at Rupar under Captain Gardiner made an alliance with Sardar Mohar Singh,[107] a rebel sardar of that place. And gave a lot of trouble to the local administration. Gardiner, who tried to intervene, was openly insulted. Gardiner reported the matter to the Ambala authorities, who at once called the troops back. Most of the sepoys absconded on the way to Ambala. The remaining ones were tried by a court-martial and discharged from service without pay.[108] Their Indian officers were sentenced to death.[109]

Like their brethren in uniform, the civil populace in the district, also stood against the British. In the words of Forsyth, the deputy commissioner: 'The district population had decidedly not enlisted themselves warmly on the part of the government.'[110] He was surprised to find that even the jagirdars and landlords who derived great benefits from the English rule showed sympathy to the rebels. His astonishment knew no bounds when he found that not a man came forward from the whole of the district who could give him any clue regarding the Jullundur mutineers when they passed through the district in the month of June. If somebody gave information for the fear of the loss of his jagir, the facts tended to be inaccurate. Even the feudal chieftains, like

> the Mir of Garhi Kotah showed great lukewarmness, for which the Deputy Commissioner fined him one thousand rupees in the month of June. This Mir entertained and helped the Jullundur mutineers. Consequently, his fort was dismantled by the order of the Chief Court and heavy fine was imposed upon him. Similarly the Pathans of Khizarbad and the headmen of villages of Ferozepur, Narsingh Garh, Thuska and Govindpur were heavily mulcated for rebellious behaviour.[111]

The wealthy bankers of Jagadhari 'displayed a sprit of disloyalty and closefistedness unworthy of a class who owe all their prosperity to the fostering care and protection of the British government'.[112]

Despite their hatred for the British, the civil population of Ambala could not rise in open revolt against the British except at Rupar where Mohar Singh, an ex-kardar of the former ruler of Rupar made a vain attempt to end the British rule from that place.[113] The reason for general civilian inactivity was that heavy precautionary measures had been adopted by the British authorities. A large number of military and police personnel belonging to the raja of Patiala, Nabha and Jind had been stationed throughout the district.

Thus except for some parts of district Ambala, a few towns of Thanesar district and Jind state, the whole of Haryana was free from British control by the end of May 1857. In the words of Cave-Brown: 'Huriannah, the land of fertility, was in a blaze'.[114]

Some Pertinent Questions

A pertinent question may arise here: Though the revolt was wide-spread, how many people actually participated in it? It is difficult to answer the question with any arithmetical accuracy, for no counting of heads raised against the foreign power during the uprising was attempted by any side, British or Indian. A rough estimate is not impossible, however. Like any other rising or a revolution, the present rebellion was initiated by a small militant minority committed to acting on behalf and in the best interest of the great majority.[115] And this must explain the interesting phenomenon that almost all the classes, excepting a part of the nobility, supported the rebellion. Surprisingly, even such sections of the Haryana population that derived maximum benefits from the British rule were not prepared to back them (British) during their hour of need. In the district of Rohtak, for instance, about 59 *mafidars* who were granted rent free tenures and other privileges by the British government expressed their sympathies for the rebels.[116] Similarly, the jagirdars of Thanesar 'did not help' when asked to assist the British authorities by supplying information regarding the rebels, movements. They did not give anything. 'And if somebody supplied any information,' says the deputy commissioner of Thanesar, 'of the fear of loss of his jagir, it was all to deceive them.'[117] The attitude of the mahajans of Jagadhari gave a rude shock to the deputy commissioner of Ambala. To quote his own words: 'On this occasion the wealthy bankers of Jagadhri displayed a spirit of disloyalty unworthy of a class who owe all their property to fostering care and protection of the British government.'[118]

Popular Uprising

In the light of what has been said, can we accept Dr. Sen's observation that 'outside Oudh and Shahabad there is no evidence of that general sympathy which would invest the mutiny with the distinction of a national war'?[119] Haryana, as also some other regions, by all means qualify to be included in the list of Dr. Sen.

One more question: Who were the leaders who led the popular upsurge? The answer is summarized in Table 1.

TABLE 1: LEADERS OF THE UPRISING

District	Place	Leader (profession)
Delhi	Delhi proper	Bahadur Shah (feudal chief)
	Sonepat	No leader
Gurgaon	Gurgaon	No leader
	Mewat	Sadruddin (peasant)
	Ahirwal	Tula Ram (feudal chief)
	Palwal	Gafur Ali (small tradesman)
		Harsukh Rai (do)
	Faridabad	Dhanu Singh (peasant)
	Ballabhgarh	Nahar Singh (feudal chief)
	Farrukhnagar	Ahmed Ali (feudal chief)
		Ghulam Mohd (serviceman)
	Pataudi	Akbar Ali (feudal chief)
Panipat	Panipat	Imam Ali Qalandar (priest)
	Karnal	No leader
	Jalmana	No leader
Thanesar	Thanesar	No leader
	Ladwa	No leader
Rohtak	Kharkhauda	Bisarat Ali (peasant and ex-risaldar)
	Sampla	Babur Khan (peasant)
	Dojana	Hasan Ali (feudal chief)
	Dadri	Bahadur Jang (feudal chief)
	Jhajjar	Abdur Rehman (feudal chief)
		Abdus Samad (General)
Hisar	Bhattu	Moh. Azim (serviceman)
	Hansi	Hukam Chand (serviceman)
	Rania	Nur Moh. Khan (feudal chief)
	Loharu	Aminuddin (feudal chief)
Ambala	Ambala	No leader
	Rupar	Mohar Singh (serviceman)
	Jagadhari	No leader

Table 1 gives names of twenty-one leaders. Of these ten were feudal chiefs (seven ruling and three dispossessed), four were 'state' or British government officials, one was a religious leader and the rest of them (seven) were petty tradesmen and peasants. A perusal of the contemporary evidence indicates that out of the ten feudal leaders, four played very significant roles,[120] three behaved dubiously[121] and only two,[122] who were dispossessed chiefs, were active and effective. Out of the four officials, three did their jobs well, whereas one[123] of them indulged in double dealing. The one maulavi and the seven petty tradesmen and peasant leaders played their parts effectively and kept the flame of freedom burning until their last breath.

An interesting feature of the leadership story is that the feudal chiefs did not opt to lead the people on their own initiative, but they were forced by the people to do so. I think this explains that wherever the feudal element gave lead, the intensity of the struggle was less, but wherever the masses were led by their own men, the struggle was hot and grim.[124]

A word about communal problem. Contemporary evidence shows that in Haryana healthy communal relationship was brought about in 1857 by the positive efforts of the rebels. The contemporary records speak of these efforts at length. Take, for instance, the actions of Raja Nahar Singh of Ballabhgarh. He gave a detailed account of the measures taken by him for fostering communal unity in his state to Emperor Bahadur Shah thus:

> Although I in my heart profess the Hindu religion, still I follow the dictates of the Muhammadan leaders and am obedient to the follower of that creed. I have gone so far as to erect a lofty marble mosque within the fort of Ballabhgarh. I have also made a spacious idgah close to my fort.[125]

Besides this, the Jat raja had appointed many Muslim officials to responsible posts in his administration. The Muslim chiefs of Jhajjar, Dadri and Pataudi had also behaved in the same vein with their Hindu subjects and offered them high posts in their respective states. The Muslim chief of Dadri helped Tula Ram, the Rao of Rewari, in suppressing his own co-religionist Ahmed Ali, the nawab of Farrukhnagar who, instead of waging war against the British was fighting his neighbours in furtherance of his personal interests.[126] Not only in towns or at the headquarters of the local states, but even in villages the atmosphere was quite congenial. Contemporary accounts paint a lively picture of the joint endeavours of the Haryana villagers against the British and their allies. For instance, the Meos (Muslims) attacked and killed the loyal Khanzadas, their own brethren at Nuh (district Gurgaon).[127]

Next, the Rawat Jats of Hodal village and the Rajputs of Hathin, who were supposed to be on the side of the (British) government, were attacked by a large gathering of the Surat Jats of Hodal, Pathans of Seoli and the Meos.[128] On another occasion, the Meos joined with Ahirs under the leadership of Rao Tula Ram and attacked the Rajput of the Bhora pargana who were disturbing the Rao at the instigation of the ruler (Muslim) of Farrukhnagar.[129] In Panipat we find an example of the Muslim Ranghars coming to the rescue of their Jat (Hindu) brethren of the village of Ballah[130] when the latter were attacked by a British force under Captain Huges on 14 July.[131] In Hisar, Hindus and Muslims assembled and fought under Prince Muhammad Azim.[132] In the second week of November, all the rebels of Haryana and their leaders, Prince Muhammad Azim of Bhattu, General Abdus Samad Khan of Jhajjar, Rao Tula Ram of Rewari and Ahmad Ali (Risaldar), commandant of the Jodhpur Legion, assembled at Narnaul under a common banner, irrespective of caste, creed or religion, and opposed the British on 16 November 1857.[133] Moreover, there is not even a single instance where a Muslim's hand might have extended to desecrate a temple or a Hindu's towards destroying a mosque. They lived or fought and perished like brothers for a common cause, against a common enemy.[134]

NOTES

1. For details see K.C. Yadav, *The Revolt of 1857 in Haryana* (hereafter *Revolt*), pp. 38-50.
2. Ibid.
3. Ibid.
4. Ibid.
5. Ibid.
6. Ibid.
7. Ibid.
8. Ibid.
9. Ibid.
10. Ibid.
11. How little we know about the Ambala rising can be seen from the following except from a latter of the late Dr. R.C. Majumdar, a well-known historian and author of a standard book on the Revolt, which he very kindly wrote to me on 21 April 1969: 'That there was an open Revolt of the sepoys there (Ambala) on the morning of the 10th May (1857) before the outbreak at Meerut is, I confess, a news to me and probably to many others. I congratulate you on bringing this point to public notice.'
12. Jawala Sahai, 'Sketches of Munity (Gurgaon District)', p. 7.

13. They are an allied caste of the Meos, and claim to have sprung from the Rajputs of the Yadava clan. For details see Sharaf-ud-din, *Tarikh-i-Mewat,* pp. 79-134.
14. The compiler of the *Gurgaon District Gazetteer* (pp. 24-5) has tried his best to twist the facts to show the rebels' risings were acts of looting and plundering. But he fails to hide the truth completely.
15. Ibid.
16. *Gurgaon District Gazetteer*, records this episode thus (pp. 24-5): 'Suddenly a strong hostile force of mutineers appeared, British troops had to retreat and many Rawats were surprised and killed'.
17. Jwala Sahai, *The Loyal Rajputana*, pp. 258-9.
18. Jawala Sahai described it thus: '(Major Eden's) artillery opened fire to different quarters, burnt villages and destroyed a number of the Meos'. Ibid.
19. *Gurgaon, District Gazetteer*, pp. 24-5.
20. N.R. Khadgawat, *Role of Rajasthan in the Struggle of 1857*, p. 174; NAI, Foreign Secret Consultations, nos. 440-52, 18 December 1857.
21. Ibid.
22. Ahirwal literally means the 'Abode of Ahirs', an agricultural caste which is found in great majority in this region. Its headquarters, for socio-cultural purpose, is Rewari. For details see Chapter I.
23. For details see K.C. Yadav, *Rao Tula Ram*, pp. 1-14; 'History of the Rewari State (1555-1857)', *Journal of Rajasthan Institute of Historical Research,* April-June (1975), pp. 23-6.
24. NAI, Mutiny Papers, Bundle no. 34, Document no. 12.
25. *Gurgaon, District Gazetteer*, p. 21; NAI, Mutiny Papers, Bundle no. 34, document no. 34—Petition of Rao Tula Ram to Emperor Bahadur Shah (Persian) without date; PSA, File R-192, pp. 281-3.
26. PSA, File R. 192, pp. 281-3.
27. Ibid.
28. Man Singh, *Abhirkuldipika*, p. 169; *Trial of Bahadur Shah* (hereafter *Trial*) edited by K.C. Yadav, p. 256.
29. Hodson, *Twelve Years of a Soldier's Life in India*, pp. 331-2; *The Bombay Overland Times* in its issue of November, 1857 spoke very highly of the brass guns which were manufactured in the gun foundry of Tula Ram at Rampura.
30. PSA, File R. 180, pp. 47-53.
31. NAI, Mutiny Papers, Bundle no. 34, Document no. 3, n.d.
32. *Trial*, p. 256.
33. India Office, Home Miscellaneous, p. 725, quoted by P.G.T. Spear, *Twilight of the Mughals*, p. 209.
34. Ibid.
35. Ibid.
36. *The Punjab Government Records*, vol. II, part I, p. 7.
37. PSA, File R. 192, pp. 281-2.

38. For short life sketches of these leaders see K.C. Yȧdav. *Revolt*, Appendix 1.
39. Ibid.
40. Ibid.
41. Ibid.
42. Ibid.
43. Ibid.
44. *Rohtak District Gazetteer*, pp. 32-42.
45. Cave-Brown, op. cit., vol. II, pp. 142, 144.
46. *Settlement Report*, *Rohtak*, p. 37.
47. Quoted in *Rohtak District Gazetteer* (1910), p. 34. Also see NAI, Foreign Secret Consultations, nos. 100-3, 25 September 1857.
48. *Settlement Report*, *Roḥtak*, p. 37.
49. *Trial*, p. 19.
50. NAI, Foreign Secret Consultations, nos. 100-3, 25 September 1857.
51. Ibid.
52. Ibid.
53. Ibid.
54. Ibid.
55. It was feared that the people would also lay their hands upon the 'Siege Train' from Ferozepur to Delhi. See Cave-Brown, op. cit., vol. II, p. 144.
56. Ibid., vol. II, p. 144.
57. Hodson, *Twelve Years*, p. 265.
58. Forest, op. cit., vol. I, p. 352.
59. The risaldar had earlier been decorated with the Order of Merit. See Cave-Brown, op. cit., vol. II, p. 145.
60. Hodson, op. cit., p. 265.
61. Cave-Brown, op. cit., vol. II, p. 145.
62. Forest, op. cit., vol. I, p. 352.
63. Cave-Brown, op. cit., vol. II, p. 145.
64. Ibid.
65. Forest, op. cit., vol. II, pp. 352-4.
66. Ibid.
67. Cave-Brown, op. cit., vol. II, p. 145.
68. Hodson, op. cit., pp. 267-8.
69. Cave-Brown, op. cit., vol. II, pp. 146-7.
69. Ibid.
70. Ibid. Eighty persons were killed and 150 wounded.
71. Ibid.
72. Ibid.
73. Ibid.
74. Cave-Brown wrongly says that Hodson's men followed them up to the very walls of the town. This has been denied by Hodson.
75. Forest, op. cit., vol. I, pp. 352-7.
76. Hodson, op. cit., pp. 267-8.

77. Forest, op. cit., vol. I, pp. 352-7.
78. PSA, File R. 131, contains along list of such local chaudharis of Rohtak, Meham, Gohana and Sampla tehsils, who extended all sorts of help to Lt. Hodson with money and material. After Hodson's retreat they held their local places for the British after the uprising was crushed. These loyal persons did not belong to any particular caste or community. They were Jats, Ranghars, Mahajans, Bhats, and Brahmans.
79. Martin-Montogomery, op. cit., vol. II, p. 514, *Hisar District Gazetteer*, p. 33.
80. N.A. Chick, *Annals of the Indian Rebellion*, p. 713. Also see NAI, Foreign Secret Consultations, nos. 100-93, 25 September 1857; *Hisar District Gazetteer*, p. 35; Kanhayya Lal, *Tarikh-i-Baghwat-i-Hind,* pp. 196-9; Jwala Sahai, *The Loyal Rajputana*, pp. 290-1.
81. Parliamentary Papers, House of Commons, nos. 215-23, July 1857, p. 290.
82. Ibid., F. Cooher, *Crisis in the Punjab* (by a Punjabee Employee), pp. 1-11.
83. NAI, Foreign Secret Consultations, nos. 204-7, 9 July 1857; *Hisar District Gazetteer*, p. 35; Cave Brown, op. cit., vol. II, pp. 274-5; N.A. Chick, pp. 710-12.
84. The entire force comprised two companies of the Haryana Light Infantry; 96 sowars of the 4th Irregular Cavalry; and some 8 sowars of the Dadri Cavalry.
85. NAI, Foreign Secret Consultations, nos. 100-3, 25 September 1857; *Hisar District Gazetteer*, p. 33; N.A. Chick, op. cit., p. 760.
86. For details see 'Narrative of events at Hisar by an eye witness' (Munshi Bakhtawar Singh) vide Kanhayya Lal, *Tarikh-i-Baghawat-i-Hind*, pp. 196-9; Report of Capt. Stafford, vide N.A. Chick, op. cit., pp. 706-7; NAI, Foreign Secret Consultations, nos. 100-3, 25 September 1857.
87. Ibid.
88. N.A. Chick, op. cit., pp. 706-7.
89. Ibid., pp. 710-12, *Hisar District Gazetteer*, pp. 34-6; Jwala Sahai, op. cit., p. 47.
90. Kaye and Malleson, op. cit., vol. VI, p. 139.
91. For details see *HRJ*, vol. I, no. 2 (1966).
92. Ibid.
93. Ibid.
94. Ibid.
95. Kaye and Malleson, op. cit., vol. VI, p. 139; NAI, Foreign Secret Consultations, nos. 162-3, 26 June 1857: Mc-Andrew informed the government on 7 June: 'I find the country considerably disorganised, the revenue and police officers are in the state of flight, many of the Zamindars and big villagers are quite refractory.'
96. *The Punjab Government Records*, vol. VIII, part I, pp. 27-8.
97. See Tajuddin's statement dated 29 May 1857, vide *The Punjab Government Records*, vol. VII, part II, pp. 201-6. Reference to an expedition to Panipat is also found in the NAI Mutiny Papers, Bundle no. 69, Document no. 71, n.d.

98. *Proceedings of the Bhartiya Itihasa Parishad*, Delhi, 1967.
99. Martin-Montgomery, op. cit., vol. II, p. 179; Richard Collier, *The Sound of Fury,* p. 81.
100. K.C. Yadav, *Haryana Mein Swantrata Andolan*, p. 98.
101. Martin-Montgomery, op. cit, vol. I, p. 517.
102. NAI, Foreign Secret Consultations, nos. 15-31, 26 June 1857.
103. *The Punjab Government Records*, vol. VIII, part II, p. 329.
104. Ibid.
105. See the account of Rohtak above.
106. *The Punjab Government Records*, vol. VIII, part II, p. 329.
107. Ibid. vol. VIII, I p. 39; Cave-Brown, op. cit., vol. I, p. 212.
108. *The Punjab Government Records*, vol. VIII, part II, p. 11.
109. Ibid. Cave Brown, op. cit., vol. I, p. 213.
110. *The Punjab Government Records*, vol. VIII, part I, p. 41.
111. Ibid., pp. 41-2.
112. Ibid. p. 42.
113. See K.C. Yadav, *Revolt*, Chapter VIII for a detailed account of this rising.
114. Cave-Brown, op. cit., vol. I, p. 226.
115. This was so in the French Revolution, the American War of Independence, and even in the more recent Russian Revolution.
116. PSA, File R. 131.
117. *The Punjab Government Records*, vol. VIII, part I, pp. 41-2.
118. Ibid.
119. Ibid.
120. These were of Dujana Dadri, Loharu and Pataudi.
121. Bahadur Shah, Nahar Singh and Ahmed Ali.
122. Tula Ram and Nur Mohd. Khan.
123. Hukam Chand Jain (Qanungo) of Hansi.
124. Ibid.
125. NAI, Foreign Political Consultations, nos. 51-5, 4 March 1859.
126. NAI, Mutiny Papers, Bundle no. 34, Document no. 2.
127. *Gurgaon District Gazetteer*, pp. 5-6.
128. Ibid.
129. NAI, Foreign Political Consultations, nos. 581-6, 6 August 1858.
130. For details see *JHS*, vol. II (1970), pp. 35-9.
131. Ibid.
132. Ibid.
133. Ibid.
134. Ibid.

7

Return of the Raj

The 'rebels' managed the administrative affairs of 'free Haryana' to the best of their ability. But they had their weaknesses which contributed to their fall. In the first place, their leaders from the princely class betrayed them. Secondly, they had no military leader of merit who could fight the British forces effectively. They suffered from perpetual shortage of money and war equipment. And above all, they were part of a central organization which was not compact and powerful and once this central organization collapsed its regional/ local outfits were also bound to fail as the following paragraphs show.

District Hisar

In the first week of June, General van-Courtland,[1] the deputy commissioner of Ferozepur, attacked the Hisar district on instructions from John Lawrence, the chief commissioner of Punjab. His forces consisted of about one thousand men and two guns. Captain Robertson acted as a political officer under him.[2] He started the operation with the pargana of Sirsa where he encountered opposition from Nur Samad Khan, the ex-nawab of Rania.[3] A pitched battle was fought at Odhan on 17 June. The nawab's men 'fought like dare devils'. As many as 530 of them fell fighting. But eventually, owing to superiority in firearms, the victory went to van-Courtland. The nawab effected his escape. He was, however, chased and caught while passing through Ludhiana district. He was condemned to death by hanging.[4]

One June 18, the village of Khatravan, where Capt. Hillard and his brother-in-law were killed was attacked. The assault came so sudden that the villagers could neither come out to fight nor flee away to save their lives. They were ruthlessly butchered. Their houses were burnt to ashes.[5] Next day the British attacked Khairka. Unlike the residents of Khatravan, the villagers here were on guard and offered a tough battle to the enemy.

But ultimately the British superiority in number and firearms again decided the fate of the battle. As many as 300 villagers died fighting.[6]

Overjoyed with the victory, van-Courtland went to Sirsa on 20 June. About 800 men with two guns of the raja of Bikaner joined him there.[7] The general sent the Bikaner contingent under Capt. Pearse to Hisar via Bhadra, and he himself stayed back to reduce the pargana of Sirsa. This took the general a little more than a fortnight.[8] Meanwhile, Pearse reached Hisar (26 June) and re-established British authority there. On 8 July the general also left Sirsa for Hisar. On the way, he met with opposition at the hands of the inmates of the villages through which he passed. However, he conquered them easily. He reached Hisar on 17 July. The local population, especially the Bhattis, Ranghars, Pachhadas and others in and around Hisar were mercilessly slaughtered. The house of Prince Muhammad Azim was plundered and destroyed and his begum captured.[9]

Leaving a strong garrison force under Capt. Mildway at Hisar, van-Courtland proceeded to Hansi. There the rebels had collected in large numbers. But the arrival of the British forces had the desired effect and they fled away without offering any fight. But gain of Hansi proved to be a loss of Hisar. For as soon as the general stepped out of Hisar, Prince Muhammad Azim attacked the city with a force consisting of 1,500 cavalry, 500 infantry and three guns. His arrival in the region was hailed by the people, and several hundred of them collected round him in a short time. Despite this, however, Mildway fought a pitched battle in which about 300 of Azim's men lost their lives. The rebels did not give way to despair and continued their fight. Ultimately they won and occupied Hisar. This arrangement proved to be short-lived, however. For soon after the occupation, van-Courtland reached the place and drove Azim out.[10]

After their exit from Hisar, the rebels went towards Tosham on 25 September. They attacked the tehsil headquarters, killed the government officials (Tehsildar Nandpal, Thanedar Pyare Lal and Qanungo Khazan Singh) plundered the treasury and looted the loyalist bankers.[11] Next, they directed their attention towards Hansi with a view to attacking and plundering the tehsil headquarters there. But van-Courtland foiled their plan by checking them at Hajimpur, a village near Hansi. The rebels fought right heroically. But they tasted defeat. Almost the same thing happened at another village, Ruhnat.[12]

The reverses demoralized the rebels. But fortunately for them, they were reinforced at this critical hour by the rebel sepoys belonging to the 10 Light Cavalry from Ferozepur and a contigent of cavalry from

Jhajjar.[13] Capt. Pearse, however, chased them boldly. The two forces met at village Mangla. The rebels fought bravely but again the superiority in numbers and firearms decided the fate of the battle. About 400 rebels lost their lives.

It was indeed a big loss. But they did not lose guts and reorganized their forces to fight the last battle at Jamalpur on 30 September. The fate favoured the British this time too.[14] There was nothing left for Prince Azim in Hisar now. So he, along with his trusted men, moved into the Gurgaon district and joined Rao Tula Ram of Rewari. The two leaders fought against the British at Narnaul on 16 November. Nothing was heard of the prince after the fall of Narnaul.[15]

The rebellious element thus crushed, General van-Courtland established order throughout the district. The work of persecution also went side by side. The proprietary rights of Mangala, Jamalpur, Hajipur, Ruhnat, Odhan, Khatravan, Khairka and Jodhka were forfeited while heavy fines were levied on scores of other villages.[16] He hanged nearly 133 persons and confiscated their properties. Fearing such a fate hundreds of persons ran away to distant places.[17] The clever ones changed their colours and turned into loyalists overnight. But unfortunately for them, many of them were hanged for duplicity.[18]

District Thanesar

In the district of Thanesar the restoration work was comparatively easy. Lt. Pearson and Capt. McNiel (deputy commissioner) settled the parganas of Kaithal and Ladwa respectively without any difficulty. Thereafter the combined forces of both these officers attacked the Asandh-Jalmana sector where they met with stiff opposition from the rebel stationed at the villages of Asandh, Jalmana, Bhatru and Chatru. Eventually the villagers were defeated. Their houses were plundered and burnt to ashes. The district was restored to the old masters.[19]

District Panipat

The British found no big problem in settling the district of Panipat either. Barring the town of Panipat and a village named Ballah. At the former place the Imam of the shrine of Bu Ali Shah Qalandar gave a tough fight to the British. But ultimately he was defeated, caught and hanged.[20] At Ballah, Ram Lal, a Jat peasant, held the torch of revolt. Capt. Hughes of the Ist Punjab Cavalry came near him in the second week of July. When

Ram Lal heard of his approach he collected a large number of rebels at the village. The gates of the villages were barricaded with heavy timber and 900 matchlockmen and a large number of people stood guarding the village.

When Hughes reached the village, the rebels opened fire and brought down one of his men and two or three horses. Hughes made a retreat which relaxed the rebels. But that was not a retreat in the real sense of the word. That was his trick. He reattacked the village in the night from the other side which was less strongly defended. His sowars got down from their horses and joining the footmen rushed into the village with great speed. But the very next moment the brave peasants took a quick turn and pounced upon them. There was no alternative for Capt. Hughes but to flee away. And he did that. In the action three of his men were killed and many more wounded.[21]

Capt. Hughes, however, did not give way to despair even after testing second defeat. He moved towards the jungle and encamped at a short distance from the village. The news of Hughes' defeat spread in the neighbourhood. Meantime, about 3,000 Ranghars came to Ballah and joined hands with the Jats. Then the two together launched an attack on Hughes in the morning (14 July). The assault was very powerful, and Hughes had no choice but to flee again. But lucky as he was, right then reinforcements comprising two guns and a number of cavalrymen of the nawab of Karnal, and 50 sowars of the Patiala raja arrived for him.[22] This strengthened Hughes and he struck back. It was a powerful punch. Moving up 'by a flank manoeuvre', he overpowered the rebels. In the bloody fight the latter lost about 100 lives.[23]

Hughes' next target was the village (Ballah). He asked his artillery to fire hell. As a result, the defensive walls and the strongly barricaded gates of the village were damaged. The villagers, who had been left behind to guard it, came out in the open and fought a grim battle in which again the British came out victorious, losing 'two native officers and three troopers'.[24] This was the last centre of revolt in Panipat. By the end of July, the whole of the district passed again under the control of the British.

Fall of Delhi

Meanwhile Delhi fell (20 September). The defeat of the rebels at Delhi, the nerve-centre of the whole movement, had a paralysing effect on all the other centres of revolt. The position of the British improved hundredfold. In high spirits, they sent out columns in different directions to subdue the people up in arms against them. General van-Courtland,[25] the deputy commissioner of Ferozepur, was sent to subdue the Rohtak district. His column consisted of a considerable body of native levies.[26] The news of the fall of Delhi had a demoralizing effect on the people. And this explains why the general found his job easy: the large villages submitted without a blow; many mutinous soldiers surrendered; the old order was restored (26 September).[27]

Ahirwal Attacked

Brigadier-General Showers led out another column of 1,500 men with a light field battery, 18 two-pounder guns and small mortars on 2 October 1857

> to punish the Gujars in and around Tughlaqabad, Gurgaon and Rewari; to attack and destroy Ranghar insurgent horsemen in the vicinity of the latter place; to attack and destroy Rao Tula Ram and his followers and to raze his fort (at Rewari); to annex the King's jagir of Kotqasim; and in conjunction with the civil officers, to settle the Gurgaon district.[28]

The column realized its first two aims without any difficulty. The Gujars and Ranghars 'around Thughlakabad, Gurgaon and Rewari slipped away on its advent'.[29] It had, however, a light skirmish with some sowars of Rao Tula Ram on 5 October at Pataudi, a small town near Rewari. In the words of Hodson, who accompanied the column: 'They fired at our advance and bolted at speed'[30] to inform heir master about the strength of the column. The Rao studied the situation seriously and foresaw that a fight with he British forces in the mud fort of Rampura (Rewari), in the changed circumstances after the fall of Delhi, would result in complete destruction of his army without any serious loss to the British. So he left his fort before Showers' arrival.[31] Showers occupied the fort (6 October) without any opposition. But Showers was not happy. He had got the nest but not the bird.[32]

Disappointed Showers sent a message to Tula Ram to the effect that 'if he would come in and give himself up, as well as him guns and arms, he should be treated on his merits'.[33] But the Rao turned down the inducement.[34] Showers stayed at Rewari for a week and 'settled' the villages around it. Then, on 12 October, he left for Jatusana[35] where some horsemen of the nawab of Jhajjar surrendered without resistance.[36] Next, going via Kosli, Ladain, Matanhail, he reached Chhuchhakwas (near Jhajjar), the hunting resort of the nawab (of Jhajjar) on 16 October.[37] The

Showers contacted the nawab who took no time in surrendering. He was made a prisoner at once.[38] Next day (17 October), Showers attacked Jhajjar.[39] The forces of the nawab, most of whom had already left the town during the night, fled away.[40] Showers 'captured' the nawab's fort where he got 21 guns, 30,000 arms, horses and elephants without any opposition.[41] The prisoner-nawab was sent to Delhi (under C.T. Metcalfe)[42] on 17 October. The administration of the state was entrusted to Col. Lawrence.[43]

After making these arrangements, Showers divided his column into two parts. The first part comprising Hodson's Horse and the 6th Dragon's Guards under Col. Gustance and Capt. Hodson was despatched to Kanond, the treasury fort of the nawab of Jhajjar via Nahar and Kannia, on 19 October.[44] He himself marched with the remaining troops to Dadri where he arrested the nawab of that place without encountering any opposition. Like his Jhajjar counterpart, the Dadri chief was also sent to Delhi.[45]

Col. Gustance's men moved speedily (about 3 miles an hour) towards their destination (Kanond). They halted for a while at Nahar, 30 miles from Jhajjar, where they were joined by some reinforcement.[46] In the night, however, the British force was attacked by a party of rebels from Jhajjar and Delhi. The latter fought bravely but being inferior in men and material they were defeated. They lost 40 of their men, 50 horses and a few nine-pounder guns.[47]

Thereafter, the British forces resumed their march and reached Kanond at about 7 a.m. where they captured 'one of the strongest, best planned and best kept forts in India' without firing a shot.[48] There 14 heavy guns, one 8-inch mortar, two 6-pounder guns and a large quantity of small arms and ammunition fell in their hands. Besides that, the nawab's treasure amounting to Rs. 5 lakh was also seized.[49] Leaving Capt. Tozer in command of the garrison[50] (comprising a wing of the 23rd Punjab Infantry and some men of Tohana Horse), Showers left for Delhi via Sohna (22 October).[51]

Mewat Region

It is quite interesting that the fall of Delhi and the presence of Brigadier-General Showers' column in the region had no effect on the people of Mewat. There the fire of revolt was still burning in every village. Obviously, this made Showers very uneasy and he decided to reduce this region before going back to Delhi. Showers, however, did not know that it was not an easy job. The difficulties that he confronted within

Mewat are best described in Showers' own words thus:

> From the time I entered the Gurgaon district, I was in enemies' country, that in all my encampments and during every march I was exposed to the attacks by the enemies' horsemen. I had to anticipate attacks from every village that I passed, where I had to be continually on alert against an enemy. I may well be understood that the protection of captured property was of secondary consideration.[52]

Battling with the villagers on the way, Showers somehow reached his way to Farrukhnagar. Unlike the Mewatis, Ahmed Ali Khan, the nawab of this place surrendered without any resistance. The nawab was arrested and sent to Delhi.[53]

After this Showers left for Ballabhgarh. On the way, a few miles short of Sohna, he met with tough opposition. The villagers attacked and killed about 60 of his men in a hand-to-hand fight. An eye-witness gives an interesting account of the exploits of brave Mewati in this strife:

> A Mewati, a huge fellow, armed with shield and sword was put up half way down the *khud* (pit) at our feet. Twenty shots were fired; but no, the bold fellow held steadily on springing from rock to rock, descending to the bottom of the dell, and then mounting the opposite rock.[54]

The brave man, who put up this heroic show for quite a long time, was ultimately killed by the Guides.

The Column remained around Sohna and Tauru for a few days and then, leaving the tract in the charge of a Gorkha detachment of the late 22 Native Infantry under Captain Drummond, it proceeded to Ballabhgarh (31 October). There Showers sent a word to the raja to present himself and surrender his fort. The raja complied with the orders with promptitude. The raja was apprehended and sent to Delhi.[55] The British troops plundered his fort and palace. The raja's womenfolk were deprived of their ornaments. Some of them were even stripped naked.[56] What a wonderful show of British civilization!

Showers returned to Delhi in the first week of November with immense booty (valued at £ 70,000), 70 guns and a large quantity of ammunition, besides the prisoner-chiefs of the region.[57] But despite all these apparently impressive gains, Showers' campaign could hardly be called a success. He had failed to realize his main aim, that is, capturing Tula Ram, or General Abdus Samad Khan of Jhajjar, or Muhammad Azim of Bhattu, who had acted as 'centres' of revolt in the various districts of Haryana.[58] In a way, the attack of Showers came as a blessing in disguise to these persons[59]—they left their respective places on Showers' approach and moved into Rajasthan (Shekhawati) where they met a rebel force from Rajasthan, the Jodhpur Legion[60] and formed a junction with it.[61] After this, they marched to Rewari and reoccupied it.[62] But strategically speaking, Rewari was not a good place to camp; so they abandoned it in the first week of November and occupied Narnaul. This was relatively a stronger place. According to Col. Malleson:

It lay under a hill about four hundred feet high, which formed part of a ridge extending some miles to the south-east. It was covered in front by low walls, forming admirably defensive cover. A large and well-filled tank with steep banks, standing much above the surrounding plain, distant only about two hundred yards from the village (town?) and commanding the road to it, afforded another strong position which infantry might advantageously have occupied. The ground to the left was broken and uneven, but the plain in front was level and broad, admirably adapted to the movements of cavalry, in which arm the rebels were very strong.[63]

The Battle of Narnaul

The British authorities at Delhi (General Penny) were disturbed by these developments. Hence they sent a strong column composed of the Ist Fusiliers, the 7th Punjab Infantry, a troop of Horse Artillery (of the 3rd Brigade), a heavy battery of 9-inch howitzers and 18-pounders, a portion of the Corps of Guides and the Multani Horse[64] under Colonel Gerrard, 'an officer of conspicuous merit'[65] to destroy the rebels. The column left Delhi on 10 November 1857 and reached Rewari three days later. They at once occupied the fort of Rampura. Here they were joined by two squadrons of the carabineers.[66] After a day's rest at Rewari (Rampura), Gerrard proceeded to Narnaul via Kanond (Mahendragarh).[67] He reached the latter place in the evening where he was joined by the Haryana Field Force[68] (comprising the 23rd Punjab Infantry, Patiala Infantry and Haryana Infantry).[69] At about 1 a.m. on 16 November, Gerrard marched to Narnaul. The distance was about 14 miles[70] but the sandy nature of the ground made the march rather difficult. The guns could only be dragged along with difficulty and the infantry had to halt again and again to give them time to catch up.[71] In consequence, the column reached Nasibpur, a small village, 2 miles north-west of Narnaul at 12 o'clock and halted for a short while.[72] But they had hardly relaxed for a while when 'they saw a little cloud of dust rising over a sloping ground at their front'. It was a rebel force advancing to pounce upon them after having abandoned their strong fort in the centre of that town.[73] It was really a blunder on the part of the Indians, from military point of view, to have chosen to take the offensive instead of awaiting an attack by the British, 'for so strong was indeed their position that had they had the patience to await attack, Gerrard would have found that all his work had been cut out for him'.[74] Any way, the British forces at once stood up to meet the challenge—the Carabineers and the Guides on the right, linked to the force at the centre (by a wing of the 7th Panjab Infantry and six light guns) comprising the Ist Fusiliers, the heavy 18-pounders, a company of the Guides Infantry and the 23rd Punjab infantry. The Irregular Cavalry and Multani Horse formed the left flank, connected with the centre by the Sikh Infantry with four light guns.[75]

The action began a little before 12 o'clock.[76] The first Indian charge was irresistible and the British force was scattered before them like chaff before the wind. The Patiala Infantry and the Multani Horse on the British left were completely disheartened.[77] The whole of the right flank fled. But at this juncture the Guides and the Carabineers came to their rescue and saved the situation.[78] A graphic picture of their engagement with the Indian cavalry has been given by Malleson and Holmes. 'The enemies (Indians) met the shock of the Guides and the Carabineers right gallantly', remarked Holmes.[79] Malleson said:

> It was a gallant conflict. Never did the enemy (Indians) fight better. There was neither shirking nor flinching. Never was there a charge more gallant, and certainly, never were the British cavalry met so fairly or in so full a swing by the rebel force.[80]

This violent action did not last long, however. The British fire, especially of the artillery was too much to stand for the rebels. The Guides and the Carabineers, under the cover of the artillery fire made a heavy attack; and though the rebels 'fought with the courage of despair, though they exposed their lives with resolution which forbade the thought of yielding, they were fairly borne down'.[81] Next, the 1st Bengal Fusiliers, swooping upon the weak Indian artillery, captured some of their guns.[82] This encouraged the British cavalry on the right and they pressed through the Indian ranks and successfully overpowered them on the right and in the centre.[83]

But soon the situation took an unexpected turn when Col. Gerrard, the British commander, was mortally wounded by a musket ball.[84] The result that the British troops were demoralized. Taking full advantage of the circumstance, the Indians swooped down upon them. The demoralized British forces could not stand the charge and the Multani Horse fled away in bewilderment.[85] The Indian cavalry recaptured its lost guns and inflicted heavy losses on the enemy. The right and the left wings of the British forces were thrown into confusion.[86]

Appreciating the gravity of the situation, Major Caulfield, the officiating British commander, ordered his artillery to start heavy bombardment on the Indian troops and his cavalry and infantrymen to charge straight on with full force into their front ranks. The Indians fought back furiously and stood their ground. The British artillery fire nevertheless broke their backbone and split their force into two parts—the troops in the front got engaged in the close quarters battle and those in the middle and at the rear fled to go out of the range of the British guns. Meanwhile, Kishan Singh and Ram Lal, the two best Indian commanders, received musket shots and died. This disheartened the Indian forces under their command and they retreated.[87]

The British resumed advance in the same old order until they came to the dry bed of a rainy stream following between Nashibpur and Narnaul. The British guns were unable to cross the rivulet owing to sand, so they diverged to the right and took up a position near the Horse Artillery guns, whilst the 23rd Punjab Infantry and Patiala Infantry with other units of the cavalry crossed the stream and advanced towards the Indian camp.[88] The heavy artillery and infantry fire confused the Indians, and they ran pell-mell in all directions. In most of the cases they retreated to the town and hid in the buildings. Their pursuit was however quick and inexorable, and they were very soon driven out of the town.[89]

The rebels lost the day and when the sun went down, there remained none in Narnaul except heaps of corpses here and there.[90] Though Tula Ram and General Samad Khan escaped,[91] Rao Kishan Singh,[92] Ram Lal,[93] Samad Khan's son[94] were killed. The British took nine Indian guns and a large quantity of other standard arms.[95] The total loss on the British side was 70 killed and 45 wounded.[96] Their commander Col. Gerrard, and Capt. Wallace were the star casualties.[97]

Tula Ram's Exploits

After the fall of Narnaul Tula Ram kept the flame of freedom burning. He entered Rajasthan. His trusted lieutenant, Man Singh gives a vivid description of his Rajasthan tour in his book *Abhirkuladipika*. However, he keeps silent over the discussions that took place between his master and the Rajput princes. The reason for this silence is not far to seek. The recording of details of discussions would have meant loss of life and property to his master and his friends. However, a Russian scholar, Professor Aleixi Raikov, has recently supplied the desideratum. He has unearthed some very important documents in the Russian Archives at Leningrad, which bespeak that Tula Ram met Raja Takhat Singh of

Jodhpur on 26 August 1859 and after great persuasion 'converted' him to his views: to work for India's freedom with Russian help. The Maharaja wrote a letter to the czar saying that 'having commissioned the Rao Raja (Tula Ram) with the task of explaining our case to your Government, I have your Majesty's attention to everything you will learn from him either verbally or in written form on my behalf'. After this, the Rao visited Bikaner on 30 August 1859, and convinced the raja of the place to follow the chief of Jodhpur. Accordingly, Sardar Singh wrote an identical letter to the czar. And so did Sawai Ram Singh of Jaipur on 3 September 1859.[98] Accompanied by his relatives, Harshai and Tara Singh, besides some attendants, Tula Ram moved down to Kotah and Bundi. He met the Hada princes of both the states. They, however showed their unwillingness to tender any help to them.[99] After this, Tula Ram went to Kalpi (Madhya Pradesh), the stronghold of the rebels and stayed there for some time. Eventually in the last days of 1859, he moved to Bombay and went out of Hindustan to enlist the support of other countries, like Afghanistan, Iran, and finally Russia to fight the British imperialism. He did not succeed in his mission, however, and died at Kabul on 23 September 1863.[100]

The story of Tula Ram is that of heroism, valour, patriotism and self-sacrifice. With four to five thousand Ahirs, Jats, Rajputs and Ranghars, he struggled hard against the superior British forces in 1857. Tula Ram is the solitary example of pursuing the same goal until the last breath. He was the first Indian to plan the overthrow of British imperialism with foreign help, when the great revolt petered out.

The Last Flicker

A word about the situation in Haryana. Ahirwal was quiet by November 1857. But not Mewat, which was still afire with revolt. In the third week of November 1857, Captain Drummond, incharge Sohna sector received intelligence through the 'native officials' of Sohna, Hathin, and Palwal that 'several thousand Meos and a few hundred cavalry men were congregated about Kot and Rupraka and had been attacking the "loyal Rajput villages" for several days'. Besides this, they were also intent on plundering the Government treasury at Palwal.[101] Captain Drummond, with a force comprising a detachment of Hodson's Horse, another of Tohana Horse, some 120 men of the Kumaon battalion, at once proceeded to Rupraka. On the way, he was reinforced by a company of the Ist Punjab Infantry (Coke's) from Ballabhgarh.[102] He burnt all the Meo villages on the Sohna-Rupraka route and destroyed their crops. Panchanka, Geopur, Malpuri, Chilli, Utawar, Kot, Mugla Mitaka, Kullulka, Guraksar, Malluka, and Jhanda, were among these unfortunate villages.[103] When the column reached Rupraka, 3,500 Meos and others drawn up in front of the village met them bravely. They lost 400 lives. But they could not carry the day, for the British forces possessed superior fire power.[104] The action at Rupraka, says Captain Drummond, was very important because

not only have the Meos been defeated, their villages and property burnt and destroyed, but the friendly Jat villages who have hitherto been kept in a state of siege by constant aggression on the part of their enemies, are relieved.[105]

In the Raisina region, Clifford, the assistant collector of Gurgaon played havoc in order to satisfy his thirst for vengeance. He was told that his sister was

stripped naked at the Palace (Delhi), tied in that condition to the wheels of gun-carriages, dragged up in the 'Chandni Chowk', or Silver Street of Delhi, and then, in the presence of King's sons cut to pieces.[106]

He 'had it on his mind that his sister, before being murdered, was outraged by the rebels'. Naturally his heart burned with the desire for revenge. He went from village to village and destroyed the countryside with fire and sword. In his own words: 'He had put to death all he had come across not excepting women and children.'[107] But he could not carry on his ruthless campaign for long, for he was killed by the Meos of Raisina and Muhammadpur.

Sadruddin, as noted above, had collected a large number of Mewatis under his banner. He held the pargana of Pinanghwa. The Gurgaon authorities directed their attention towards him in the third week of November when they sent Capt. Ramsay with a force from Palwal 'to crush him'.[108] But Sadruddin was not there—he was then at a small village called Mahun.[109] The British forces made for that village the next day and reached there at 7 a.m. The rebels took up a defensive position. Exchange of shots continued till mid-day. Then the British troops bombarded the village with guns. This silenced the rebels' fire and three Gorkha regiments advanced upon the village from three directions. There was some fight but the rebels were beaten. The victors cut down many Meos, including Sadruddin's son.[110] But Sadruddin escaped. Making an assessment of the fight after the battle, Macpherson, the joint-magistrate of Gurgaon and the chief actor in the action, observed:

Altogether I look upon it that is, the action a most successful affair, say about

70 rebels killed. The whole number of the rebels assembled was so small that, their resistance was to me a subject of the greatest surprise.[111]

Having crushed the last of the uprisings in Mewat, the column retreated, but not before making a severe example of the villages and people suspected to have taken part in the rebellion. Especially, the villages of Shahpur, Bali Khera, Kherla, Chitora, Nahirika, Sujan Nangla, Baharpur, Kaheri tested the bitterest pills—they were completely destroyed; many people were killed.[112]

Effects of the Uprising

After the uprising was crushed, the Haryana territory was detached from the North-West Provinces and merged with Punjab[113] in February 1858. The Punjab system of administration was immediately introduced all over the region, which was divided into two divisions: (1) Delhi Division, comprising the districts of Delhi, Gurgaon and Panipat with divisional headquarters at Delhi; and (2) Hisar Division, comprising the districts of Hisar, Sirsa and Rohtak along with a portion of the confiscated Jhajjar state, with divisional headquarters at Hisar. Each division was placed under a commissioner who had various administrative and political duties to perform. He was also a sessions judge for criminal trials and sole appellate and controlling authority in every branch of administration. Under him were the deputy commissioners. They were in-charge of the districts and performed multifarious duties with the help of subordinate Indian officers.[114]

As regards the 'native states', the policy of the government was very harsh, many local princes were hanged without proper trial. The chiefs of Ballabhgarh and Jhajjar pleaded and gave unimpeachable evidence that they were loyal to the British, but to no avail. They were killed without any reason or rhyme. The nawab of Farrukhnagar also pleaded 'not guilty' but his case was weak. The nawabs of Dadri, Dujana, Pataudi and Loharu were not so unlucky however. They were left off. The confiscated states of Ballabhgarh and Farrukhnagar were merged with the Gurgaon district and those of Jhajjar and Dadri were parcelled out among the loyal chiefs of Punjab—Narendra Singh of Patiala got the pargana of Narnaul worth Rs. 2,00,000 a year.[115] Sarup Singh of Jind was given the state of Dadri worth, Rs. 1,03,000 per year, and some villages in the Kanond (Mahendragarh) pargana worth Rs. 21,000;[116] and Bharpur Singh of Nabha received the parganas of Bawal and Kanti (Jhajjar state) worth

Rs. 1,06,007 per year. The states of Pataudi, Dujana and Loharu were, however, permitted to remain as these were.[117]

The Punjab Government held the Haryana territory in contempt for a long time. Those at the helm of affairs did not forget the role of the Haryanavis in the uprising and denied them benefits of their rule.[118] They were not given educational facilities. Until 1927 there was not even a single college in this region and there were hardly any good high schools worth the name. The people here were exclusively farmers, but they received nothing by way of agricultural assistance. The doors of government services were almost closed upon them. Means of communication were neglected. In short, the people were reduced to a deplorable condition.[119]

NOTES

1. He was an officer of European extraction who had served under Ranjit Singh, and who subsequent to the campaign of 1845-6 had accepted civil office under the British government. John Kaye, *A History of Sepoy War*, vol. II, p. 107.
2. *Hisar District Gazetteer*, 1910, p. 35.
3. The state of Rania had been confiscated by the British government long before the outbreak of the uprising. The nawab was provided with some pension. In 1857 Nawab Nur Samad Khan was head of the family. He and his family got the following pensions: The nawab: Rs. 200 per month; grand mother of the nawab: Rs. 100 per month; mother: Rs. 150 per month; Gohar Ali (uncle): Rs. 125 per month; other relatives: Rs. 1,031 per month. See NAI, Foreign Secret Consultations, nos. 204-7, 9 July 1857.
4. NAI, Foreign Secret Consultations, no. 71, 25 September 1857.
5. *Hisar District Gazetteer*, pp. 35-6.
6. NAI, Foreign Secret Consultations, no. 54, 31 July 1857.
7. *Hisar District Gazetteer*, pp. 35-6.
8. N.A. Chick, op. cit., p. 712.
9. Ibid.
10. Ibid., pp. 714-5; *Hisar District Gazetteer*, p. 36.
11. *Hisar District Gazetteer*, p. 36.
12. Ibid.
13. N.A. Chick, op. cit., pp. 714-16.
14. Ibid; *Hisar District Gazetteer*, p. 36.
15. See the battle of Narnaul above.
16. N.A. Chick, op. cit., p. 716; *Hisar District Gazetteer*, p. 36; PSA, File R. 268.
17. Ibid.

18. J. Cave-Brown (*Punjab and Delhi in* 1857, vol. II, pp. 275-6) says: 'In the neighbouring Districts of Hansi and Hisar were Mooneer Beg, one of the principal Mohammadans and Hookam Chand the chief banker, and one of the most influential Hindoos of Hansi, with Fuqeer Chand, his nephew, a youth of about twenty (who) had at the commencement of the outbreak conjointly drawn up a petition to the king of Delhi offering their services and undertaking to place Hansi and the district around it at his disposal. No sooner did General van-Courtland pour down his quickly raised levies into the district then these men were among the foremost to rally round him with profession of loyalty. Van-Courtland, only too glad, doubtless, to avail himself of their local influence, received them into favour, and gave them valuable appointments.'
19. *The Punjab Govternment Records*, vol. VIII, part I, p. 31.
20. Ibid. *Karnal District Gazetteer*, 1910, p. 40.
21. J. Cave-Brown, op. cit., vol. II, pp. 142-4.
22. Ibid., p. 143.
23. Ibid.
24. Ibid.
25. *Karnal District Gazetteer*, p. 40.
26. Ibid. *District Gazetteer*, however, does not give full account.
27. John Kaye, op. cit., vol. II, p. 107.
28. Wilson to Brandieth, 2 October 1857, vide NAI, Foreign Secret Consultations, nos. 440-52, 18 December 1857.
29. Capt. Hodson, who accompanied the column, described Tula Ram's position (in a written letter to his wife from Ballabhgarh on 3 October 1857) as follows: 'Go on tomorrow through Gurgaon to a place called Rewaree where one Tula Ram, a farmer of Government revenue in better times, but who now affectionates independent authority, has collected a force round his fortlet of some four to five thousand men and shows fight.' W. Hodson, *Twelve Years of a Soldier's Life in India*, p. 328.
30. Ibid.
31. See K.C. Yadav, 'Battle of Narnaul', *Journal of Indian History*, vol. XLIII, (August 1965), p. 658.
32. *Illustrated London News*, vol. XXXI (December 1857), p. 574.
33. W. Hodson, op. cit., p. 331.
34. Ibid.
35. Ibid., pp. 331-2.
36. *Illustrated London News*, vol. XXXI, 5 December 1857, p. 575.
37. NAI, Foreign Secret Consultations, no. 91, 27 November 1857.
38. Ibid.
39. For a detailed account of the activities of this column, see Mackenzie, *Mutiny Memoirs*, pp. 113-33.
40. *Records of Intelligence Department of the NWP*, vol. I, p. 216; NAI, Foreign Secret Consultations, no. 91, 27 November 1857.

41. *Illustrated London News*, vol. XXXI (19 December 1857), p. 603; *Records of Intelligence Department*, vol. I, p. 216.
42. N.K. Nigam, *Delhi in 1857*, pp. 166-9.
43. NAI, Foreign Secret Consultations, no. 91, 27 November 1857.
44. *Rohtak District Gazetteer*, pp. 41-3.
45. NAI, Foreign Political Consultations, nos. 145-53, 2 July 1858
46. W. Hodson, op. cit., p. 335.
47. *Illustrated London News*, vol. XXXI (5 December 1857), p. 603.
48. N.A. Chick, op. cit., p. 718. Hodson remarks regarding the fort: 'Took one of the strategist forts I have seen'. Hodson, op. cit., pp. 336-7.
49. *Illustrated London News*, vol. XXXI (5 December 1857), p. 603; N.A. Chick, op. cit., p. 719.
50. Ibid.
51. Ibid.
52. PSA, File 191.
53. C. Ball, *History of the Indian Mutiny*, vol. II, p. 59.
54. Ibid. NAI, Foreign Secret Consultations, nos. 21-7, 31 January 1858.
55. NAI, Foreign Political Consultations, nos. 51-5, 4 March 1859.
56. PSA, File R. 270.
57. *Illustrated London News*, vol. XXXI (19 December 1857), p. 503.
58. For his aims see NAI, Foreign Secret Consultations, nos. 145-53, 2 July 1857.
59. N.A. Chick (op. cit., pp. 718-19) says about them: 'Abdul Samad Khan, Tula Ram, Mohd Azim, the (ex) Kotwal of Meerut (Kishan Singh) are the brutes that serve as a nucleus to the mutiny of these Districts. These hell-hounds, with their followers fled a day before on hearing of our (Showers') approach to the villages of Singhana and Khetri and joined the Jodhpur Legion.'
60. It was a contingent force of Jodhpur. They broke out at Abu, etc., on 21 August 1857. They subsequently joined the Thakur of Awah who had a quarrel with the Maharaja of Jodhpur. On 8 September 1857 the Legion and the Thakur's troops jointly attacked and ruined the camp of the Maharaja of Jodhpur at Pali. Later they defeated a British contingent force led by General Lawrence. After this victory the rebel forces quarrelled with the Thakur of Awah and left his place. Their next destination was Delhi. But they had hardly reached Shekhawati when the city of Delhi fell to the British. They were disheartened and confused. But soon they got a new spirit infused in them by the joining of Rao Tula Ram of Rewari. NAI, Foreign Secret Consultation, no. 5, 29 January 1858. Also see *Narrative of Events regarding the Mutiny in India of 1857-58 and the Restoration of Authority*, vol. II, pp. 219-93.
61. NAI, Foreign Secret Consultation, no. 5, 29 January 1858; N.A. Chick, op. cit., pp. 718-19; Jwala Sahai, *The Loyal Rajputana*, p. 219; N.R. Khadgwat, op. cit., pp. 49-51, 156.

62. *Records of the Intelligence Department*, vol. I, p. 261.
63. G.B. Malleson, *History of the Indian Mutiny*, vol. II, pp. 110-1.
64. *Records of the Intelligence Department*, vol. II, pp. 272-3; G.B. Malleson, op. cit., vol. II, p. 109; Jwala Sahai, op. cit., p. 219.
65. Ibid., Holmes, p. 396.
66. G.B. Malleson, op. cit., vol. II, p. 110.
67. *Records of the Intelligence Department*, vol. II, pp. 272-3. Kaye and Malleson, op. cit., vol. IV, p. 76.
68. NAI, Foreign Secret Consultation, nos. 15-17, 29 January 1858.
69. Ibid., nos. 21-7, 28 January 1858.
70. Kaye and Malleson, op. cit., vol. IV, p. 72.
71. Jwala Sahai, op. cit., p. 219.
72. T.R. Holmes, op. cit., p. 397.
73. Ibid.
74. G.B. Malleson, op. cit., p. 319; Holmes and Jwala Sahai also agree with him.
75. G.B. Malleson, op. cit., vol. II, p. 113.
76. *Records of the Intelligence Department*, vol. II, pp. 272-3.
77. G.B. Malleson, op. cit., p. 319.
78. Ibid., vol. II, p. 114.
79. T.R. Holmes, op. cit., p. 397.
80. Kaye and Malleson, op. cit., vol. IV, p. 80.
81. G.B. Malleson, op. cit., vol. II., p. 115; NAI, Foreign Secret Consultations, nos. 21-7, 28 January 1858.
82. Ibid.
83. *Journal of Indian History*, vol. XLIII (August 1965), pp. 657-63.
84. T.R. Holmes, op. cit., p. 397.
85. Ibid.
86. *Illustrated London News*, vol. XXXIII (August 1965), pp. 272-3.
87. *Records of the Intelligence Department*, vol. II, pp. 272-3.
88. NAI, Foreign Secret Consultations, nos. 21-7, 29 January 1858.
89. G.B. Malleson, op. cit., p. 320.
90. *Records of the Intelligence Department*, vol. II, pp. 272-3, 277.
91. K.C. Yadav, *Rao Tula Ram*, p. 80.
92. Man Singh, *Abhirkuldipika*, p. 208.
93. Ibid.
94. *Records of the Intelligence Department*, vol. II, pp. 272-3.
95. Ibid.
96. Ibid.
97. *Illustrated London News*, vol. XXXIII, p. 18.
98. *Records of the Intelligence Department*, vol. II, pp. 272-3.
99. See *JHS*, vol. XVIII (1986), pp. 35-48.
100. Ibid.
101. NAI, Foreign Secret Consultations, nos. 21-7, 29 January 1858.

102. Ibid., *Records of the Intelligence Department*, vol. II, p. 220.
103. NAI, Foreign Secret Consultations, nos. 21-7, 29 January 1858.
104. Ibid., *Records of the Intelligence Department*, vol. II, p. 220.
105. NAI, Foreign Secret Consultations, nos. 21-7, 29 January 1858.
106. Ibid.
107. *The Punjab Government Records*, vol. VII, part II, p. 209; PSA, File R. 158; File R. 194.
108. PSA, Delhi Division Records, Military Department, Case no. 1 of 1858.
109. Ibid.
110. Ibid.
111. Ibid.
112. Ibid.
113. The Haryana region remained a part of Punjab till 1 November 1966, when the state was bifurcated and separate states of Punjab and Haryana were formed in accordance with the 'Punjab Reorganisation Bill' passed by the Indian Parliament on 10 September 1966.
114. PSA, File R. 199; *Settlement Report*, p. 158.
115. See Lapel Griffin, *The Rajas of the Punjab*, pp. 238-58 for details.
116. Ibid., pp. 393-408.
117. Ibid., pp. 465-8.
118. See *Report of the Haryana Development Committee*, Chandigarh.
119. This resulted in making this region backward in almost every field. See ibid.

8

The Wahabi Movement, 1858-1864

As noted in the preceding chapter, an unprecedented atmosphere of terror and awe prevailed in Haryana during the post-uprising (1857) period. There was a strange quietude—silence—all around which one usually noticed not in human habitates but in grave yards. So demoralized and dehumanized the local people had become that despite the worst type of tortures, sufferings and all that, no whisper was heard from any quarters. The European officials were '*hazur mai-baps*', '*next-to-Khuda*'. It is surprising indeed that a popular movement—the Wahabi Movement—opposing 'the *zalim* (tyrant), *be-iman* (irreligious) and *kafir* (infidel) *sarkar*' could come up in such an atmosphere.

The Movement

The Wahabi Movement[1] was started by Syed Ahmed (1786-1831) of Rae Bareilly in 1820s. In the beginning, it was a socio-religious movement aimed at improving the life of Muslims. After some time, however, it also acquired political content, emphasizing that every Wahab should try to establish Muslim raj. No true Muslim should live in a land ruled by a non-Muslim, they were told. It was but natural that Wahabs became enemies of the British raj.

Despite such political content, the Muslim populace responded to the movement with enthusiasm at a number of places. As a result, it soon developed into a powerful organization. Syed Ahmed was, as noted above, its 'Supreme Leader' (*Imam*) and 'Commander of the Faithful' (*Amir-ul-Muslimin*), with Muhammad Ismail as his deputy and organizer of military campaigns. Its centres were established throughout the country, especially in the North-West Frontier region. In 1826, Syed

Ahmed himself left for this place with a view to waging *jehad* (religious war) against the 'infidels'.

The reason why he shifted his headquarters to this distant land is not far to seek. North-West Frontier region, as we know, was 'still outside the influence of the British'. Its people were known for their valour and passion for independence. The situation of this area was also such that Syed Ahmed was free from the danger of hostile activity from his rear—behind it lay the uninterrupted belt of certain principalities with whose chiefs he had already been corresponding for the last several years. Again, in the case of his projected advance down the north-east, he could expect friendly cooperation from the states of Baluchistan, Bhawalpur and Sind, flanking his proposed route.

Clash with the British

Syed Ahmed's first clash was with the Sikhs whose 'country', Punjab lay between his 'place' and the British raj. Ranjit Singh, then Maharaja of Punjab offered them a resolute opposition—so much so that in one of the encounters Syed Ahmed lost his life (1831). But since Syed Ahmed had established a regular system of apostalic successors, the movement did not lose its vigour. It continued to retain its original force and vitality.

On the annexation of Punjab (1849) the fury of the Wahabis, which had formerly spent itself upon the Sikhs, was riveted to their successors, the British. The latter were also, it seems, prepared to meet any eventuality. The two sides were thus soon locked into a long, deadly strife.

From 1850 to 1857 the British despatched sixteen expeditions involving 33,000 regular troops against the Wahabis. But they did not attain any considerable achievement. After the uprising, they again picked up the thread by dispatching three expeditions (aggregating about 20,000 troops, besides irregulars, auxiliaries and police) to destroy their enemies. But still the Wahabis' might remained unbroken. So the fourth expedition was sent under Brigadier-General Nevile Chamberlain (commanding 7,000 infantry and a train of mountain artillery). The Wahabis met this force, too, right gallantly and compelled the British general to wire on 19 November, 1863: 'We much need reinforcements. I find it difficult to meet the enemy's attack. This is urgent.' The needful was done and in December when his position had improved, he defeated the Wahabis. The Punjab government summed up the result of the campaign thus: 'On no former occasion has the fighting in the hills been of so severe or sustained a character'.[2] After this campaign, the British decided to crush the Wahabis once for all. But for this it was necessary to go to the roots of the movement which lay not in the mountains in the north-west, but in the plains down below. Accordingly, a systematic campaign was undertaken for this propose, which gave meaningful clues of the existence of a network of organization of the Wahabis throughout northern India.[3]

The Movement in Haryana

Haryana was an important centre of the Wahabi activities, with its headquarters located at Thanesar (district Kurukshetra). One Muhammad Zafar, the head man of Thanesar, was the leading light behind the whole show. Thanks to his efforts, the organization had its branches opened at almost every big town in the region, viz., Karnal, Panipat, Jhajjar, and Hisar.[4]

It may be pretinent to know a little more about Zafar before we try to understand the movement. Who was this man? How did he join the movement? How did he carry on his work? Fortunately, we have full information about this man and his activities. He was born at Thanesar (Kurukshetra) on 23 February 1838 in a Muslim family of poor means. On the top of it, he lost his father, the only working hand in the family, when he was not yet 12. Though not a sapient boy, he learnt some Urdu from a local *maulavi* and took to the job of a petition-writer under the guidance of a relative (1856). He had a facile pen which made him successful in his avocation before long. He earned a lot of money and began to be counted among the wealthy persons in the town. After some time, he got official recognition, too, when he was made a *lambardar* (village headman).[5]

Zafar also had very strong streak of religiosity in him. He said his five *namazs* regularly and did other religious duties very carefully. He did not like corrupt and vulgar practices that had come to Islam. And probably this explains why he was attracted towards the Wahabi movement under the influence of an itinerant Wahabi preacher.

As Zafar was popular among his people, hundreds of people joined the new movement under his spell. Impressed by his organizational skill, piousness of life, singular sincerity, and 'burning zeal for the regeneration of the fallen community', Syed Ahmed appointed him *khalifa* or the official in-charge of the Wahabi activity in the north-western region upwards of Delhi.[6] Zafar, on his part, as already noted, spared no pains to justify his selection to this honourable post. He helped the 'freedom fighters' on the North-West Frontier by supplying them with men, money and material. Not only that, in some of the frontier wars he was personally present on the scene and fought in actions.[7] Surprisingly, Zafar's activities went on unnoticed by the British government for many years. But in 1863, as ill luck would have it, these were exposed.

There is an interesting story as to how all this came about.[8] One day, in May 1863, it so happened that one Ghazzan Khan, a junior police official, posted at Panipat (district Karnal), while on his 'rounds', found some strangers proceeding southwards along the Grand Trunk Road. Smelling something foul, the police official got into conversation with them, worked himself into their secrets, and elicited that they were Bengali luminaries on their way back to their native province to arrange for 'the forwarding of fresh supplies of money and men' to fight against the British infidels. The official at once arrested these men and took them to the police station. They were tried by the extra assistant commissioner, Ambala, who found nothing wrong with 'the peaceable wayfarers'. Consequently, they were set free.[9]

Ghazzan Khan chose to take the acquittal of these persons as an insult to his honour and he took a vow to prove the correctness of his charge. He at once sent a letter to his village committing his son in the name of family honour to go to the N.W.F. and to collect information pertaining to the network of the Wahabi organization which had spread throughout India. The faithfull son obeyed his father and at once set out to fulfil his mission. He joined the Wahabis at Sitana and remained there for some time (about five to six months). When his work was done he returned to Panipat, made a detailed report to the effect that there existed a widespread network for transmission of men and money from all over India to the frontier region. Thanesar was one of the main centres of the Wahabi activity and Zafar was one of its chief organizers.

Ghazzan reported the matter to the appropriate authorities with proof. Accordingly, the Punjab government appointed Parson, the superintendent of police, Ambala to make further investigations. Parson raided the house of Zafar (12 December 1863) after being supplied with the above information. He got some letters which referred to Muhammad Shafi, a contractor for supplying meat at Ambala cantonment, Yahaya Ali and some other persons from Bihar.[10] Zafar who could foresee the result of all these happenings did not think it wise to stay at Thanesar. He immediately left for Delhi and hid himself in the house of a Wahabi friend, Bashiruddin. After some time, he left this place also and moved eastwards along with Hosaini and Abdullah of Patna.

The Punjab police, meanwhile, moved earth and heaven to arrest

Zafar. They persecuted all the members of his family. His younger brother, who was built of a weaker fibre, disclosed the secret of his escape to Delhi. Parson at once went to Delhi and visited the houses of all the persons known to Zafar there. But Zafar, as noted above, had already left Delhi on his eastward march. Parson got this information also and he sent telegraphic messages to different stations on the highway leading to Bihar.[11] As a result, Zafar was arrested at Koil (Aligarh). Zafar's arrest was followed by that of many other Wahabi activists in Haryana, Punjab and Bihar. The chiefs of whom were Hussaini of Thanesar, Muhammad Shafi, a government contractor from Ambala (50), Abdul Karim (35), a relative of Shafi, Yahya Ali (47), Abdul Rahim (28), Abdul Ghaffar (25), Qazi Mian Jan (over 85) of Pabna, Abdul Ghafur (25), Hussaini and Ellahi Bux (28) all from Bihar.[12]

All the prisoners were put in the central jail at Ambala (March 1864) where they received third-rate treatment—they were kept in separate solitary cells measuring 8' x 4' with a small opening; the door of the cell was opened 'once in twenty-four hours when a *zamadar* gave the prisoners a pot of water and some bread and dal and the sweeper cleaned the commode'.[13]

The prisoners were charged of being guilty of waging war against the Queen (Section 121 of IPC) and were first put up before Tighe, the deputy commissioner of Ambala for drawing up committal proceedings. After that they were taken to the court of Herbert Edwards, the sessions judge, Ambala (April 1864). The trial went on for a couple of weeks. And then came the judgement: three persons—Zafar Khan, Yahya Khan and Muhammad Shafi—were sentenced to death (2 May 1864); others were given transportation for life; properties of all the eleven convicts were confiscated.[14] As we expected, the judgement was taken to the judicial commissioner, Punjab, the highest court in the province then for patent hearing in appeal. Much was said on both sides. The judicial commissioner, however, confirmed the judgement with a modification—the capital sentences on Jaffar, Yahya and Shafi were changed to transportation for life[15] (24 August).

With the exit of Zafar Muhammad, the leading light of the movement, and his associates, the Wahabi activities came to cessation in Haryana. Moreover, the attitude of the government was one of strict cautiousness; and nobody could dare take to the 'dangerous activity' in such circum—stances. Thus, the movement 'met its doom' after 1864.

Zafar spent about 18 years in the *Kalapani* (Andamans) and suffered a great deal in ways more than one. But as good luck would have it, the government of India released all the Wahabi prisoners in 1880. Zafar immediately rushed to his birth place—Thanesar—and was released from there in November 1883. He was accorded 'a warm welcome by his people'. After some time, he was shifted to Ambala where he served as a clerk in some office until his death.[16]

NOTES

1. For details pertaining to the movement see William Hunter, *The Indian Musalmans*, rpt. 1971; Q. Ahmed, *The Wahabi Movement in India*, 1969.
2. See William Hunter, op. cit., pp. 15-6, 19-30.
3. See the *Bengal Government Records*, vol. 45, pp. 120-40.
4. For Jaffar and his Wahabi activities see William Hunter, op. cit., pp. 77-9.
5. For details see Muhammad Zafar, *Kalapani*, pp. 80-1.
6. Ibid.
7. Ibid., pp. 79-82. Commenting on the fighting capability of Zaffar, Hunter says: 'Even in the unwonted work of fighting his force of character made him conspicuous' (p. 81).
8. For the story see Q. Ahmed, op. cit., pp. 107-10; William Hunter, op. cit., pp. 90-2.
9. Q. Ahmed, op. cit., pp. 233-8; William Hunter, op. cit., pp. 82-121.
10. Ibid.
11. Ibid.
12. Ibid.
13. Q. Ahmed, op. cit., p. 237.
14. William Hunter, op. cit., pp. 82-91; Q. Ahmed, op. cit., pp. 233-8.
15. Ibid.
16. See Muhammad Zafar, op. cit, pp. 104-5.

9

'*Nai Hawa*': Origin and Growth of Politico-national Awareness, 1885-1904

Every cloud, they say, has a silver lining. Though defeated, the people of India were benefited a great deal by the forces released by the uprising of 1857. For, the victors changed their strategies, methods and techniques to rule this country in the post-uprising days so that another catastrophe of the type would not come. And that brought renaissance—Indian renaissance to be exact. As a result, the country began to modernize. Happily, because of the '*nai hawa*'—winds of change—which began to blow, thanks to the factors given below, all over India at that time, Haryana also came to harvest the benefits of the new political developments.

Modern Education

The modern education played, as noted above, a substantially important role in improving the situation. The new education brought not only Shakespeare and Dickens to the people but also gave them liberal ideas of Locke and Russaou. They got an opportunity to study the histories of countries of Europe, America and Asia and acquired the knowledge of rise and fall of their fortunes there. This knowledge helped them comprehend the reasons as to what was wrong with them. Why could they not be like other independent countries there? And this comprehension led to the birth of the feeling of national awakening here.

Unfortunately, the people of Haryana were not as lucky as their countrymen elsewhere were, for, not to speak of colleges or universities, there were hardly any good schools here till 1870 where they could get modern education.[1] But, fortunately, the government's attention was attracted to this lack that year (1870). As a result, many schools were opened here, as Table 1 shows. But as far as colleges were concerned, the region continued to suffer neglect even during this period: it was only in 1926 that the first intermediate college was opened here.

Something is better than nothing, they say. The modern school education caused political awakening among the people. The students who passed out from the schools, though small in numbers, played a significant part in inculcating national awareness. Some of them produced good, modern literature and contributed to newspapers and periodicals. From among these scholars Deendayalu Sharma, 'a socio-religious activist from Jhajjar,' played a substantial role in the closing years of the century. He started two newspapers, *Haryana* and *Rifa-i-Am*, from his home town, Jhajjar. Babu Murlidhar started an important nationalist weekly, *Khair-Andesh*, from Ambala. Though useful, these newspapers were, however, short-lived.[2]

Babu Balmukund Gupta (1864-1907), was another great litterateur

TABLE 1: SCHOOLS IN HARYANA, 1870-1900[3]

Years	Total population	Population of schoolable children	No. of children going to schools	Total population	Population of schoolable children	No. of children going to schools
	Dist. Ambala			Dist. Karnal		
1870-1	10,35,488	86,290	4,929	6,10,927	50,910	1,399
1880-1	8,64,748	72,062	8,319	8,20,040	68,337	2,964
1890-1	8,63,641	71,970	—	8,61,160	71,763	2,483
1900-1	8,15,924	67,994	9,133	8,83,225	73,602	5,393
	Dist. Rohtak			Dist. Hisar		
1870-1	5,36,959	44,746	1,791	6,95,476	57,956	1,846
1880-1	5,53,609	46,134	3,562	6,71,569	56,047	4,189
1890-1	5,90,475	49,206	3,386	7,76,006	64,667	3,636
1900-1	6,30,672	52,556	5,097	7,81,717	65,143	5,085
	Dist. Gurgaon					
1870-1	6,96,646	58,054	2,224			
1880-1	6,41,848	53,487	3,807			
1890-1	6,68,929	55,744	4,693			
1900-1	7,46,208	62,184	5,139			

from the region. It is a matter of great surprise how this simple, straight lad from a small, obscure hamlet, Gudiani (district Rewari), who had the fortune of having his formal education up to the fifth standard only, came to occupy such a high place in the world of letters; and earned from the posterity an enviable epithet of 'the father of Hindi literature and journalism'. He was, in the every sense of the word, a sensitively enlightened man.[4] He wrote on national problems and freedom.

Perhaps no other man in India of his times has written so beautifully as Gupta has done on the hapless condition that this country was in owing to British slavery. He gave a scientific and objective critique of the British rule and exhorted his people to throw it off if they wanted to live happily as their forefathers lived in the *Ramarajya*, in the ages gone by. Some small excerpts from his writings to substantiate the above may be pertinent.

First, he took up poverty. India was a great country, he said, where once flowed the rivers of milk and honey. How has such a country, he then goes on to ask, became so poor now? Why have its great people become the wretched of the earth? Why there is nothing with them today except dearth and disease, suffering and scourge?

केहि कारण पावत नही आधे पेटहु नाज?
कौन पापसों बसन बिन ढकन न पावहिं लाज?
सीत सतावत सीत मँह अरू ग्रीसम मँह घाम।
भीजत ही पावत कटत कौन पापसों राम?
अब या सुखमय भूमि मँह नाहीं सुख को लेस।
हाड्-चरम पूरित भयो अन्न दूध को देस॥
बार-बार मारी परत बारहिं बार अकाल।
काल फिरत नित सीस पै खोले गाल कराल॥
यह दुर्गति नर देह की कौन पाप ते राम?
सच कहो क्या होइ है अब हमरो परिनाम?
बार-बार जिय में उठत अब तो यहै विचार।
ऐसे जीवन ख्वार पै लाख-लाख धिक्कार॥
फिरत पेट कै फेर मँह सुकर स्वान समान।
केहि कारन नर तन दियो कृपासिन्धु भगवान ?
हमने नर तनु ते भले कीट पतंग बिहंग॥
हमने नर तनु ते भले बानर भालु कुरंग।[5]

Who is responsible for this? Obviously, the exploitative colonial rule, says the poet; but we are also to be blamed for that:

कर्म–धर्म–संयम नियम जप–तप जोग–विराग।
इन सब को बहु दिन भये खेल चुके हम फाग॥
धन बल, जन बल, बाहु बल, बुद्धि, विवेक, विचार।
मान, तान, मरजाद को बैठे जुओ हार॥
हमरे जात न बर्न है, नहीं अर्थ, नहीं काम।
कहा पुरावै आप से, हमरी जात गुलाम॥
बहु दिन बीते–राम प्रभु खोये अपनो देस।
खोवत हैं अब बैठ कै भाषा, भोजन, भेस॥
नहीं गाँव में झोपड़ी, नहीं जंगल में खेत।
घरही बैठे हम कियो अपनो कंचन रेत॥
पशु समान विडरत रहें पेट भरन के काज
याही में दिन जात है सुनिए रघुकुल राज॥
दो–दो मुठ्ठ अन्न हित ताकत पर मुख ओर।
घर ही में हम पारधी, घर ही हम चौर॥
तोहू आपस में लडे, निस दिन स्वान समान।
अहो कौन गति होयेगी आगे राम सुजान?[6]

Is there any ray of hope for the submerged humanity? No, says Balmukund, unless our people, stand up and gird up their lions to get over their dehumanized state. Many years before Gandhiji, he asked them to create *Ramarajya* which, in the words of *'Tesu'* (a folk medium), was to be something like this:

टेसू आर लो असीस।
भारत जीवे कोटि बरीस॥
कभी न उस में पडे अकाल।
सदा वृष्टि से रहे निहाल॥
अपना कपडा आप बनावे॥
बढे सदा अपना व्यापार।
चारों दिस हो मौज बहार॥
माल विदेशी दूर भगावे।
अपना चरखा आप चलावे॥
कभी न भारत हो मुहताज।
सदा रहे राम का राज॥[7]

Balmukund criticized, in a series of articles entitled *Shivasambhu Ke Chitthe aur Khat*, the reactionary regime of Viceroy Curzon (1899-1905). This was probably the most powerfull attack on the mightiest in the land ever written in any language in India. The author posed as Shivashambhu, a poor Brahmana, addicted to *bhanga* and wrote nine powerful pieces (*Chitthe*) under the influence of the 'intoxicant'. He took up one by one all the reactionary activities of Curzon and exposed them in their true imperialist colours.[8] Likewise, he also took on Fuller, the then Lt. Governor of East Bengal, for his misdeeds, like creating communal tension between Hindus and Muslims and letting loose a reign of terror on peacefull students and agitators against the partition of Bengal (1905).[9]

When Minto replaced reactionary Curzon as Viceroy of India and Morley became Secretary of State, Indians were mighty pleased. For they thought the liberal duo would do something great for India. Balmukund, an astute judge of British character, told his countrymen through a satire, which is a powerful exposure of the realities of the situation, that there was nothing for them to be so happy about:

टोरी जावें लिबरल आवें, होली है भई होली है।
भारतवासी खैर मनावें, होली है भई होली है॥
लिबरल जीते टोरी हारे, हुए मार्ली सचिव हमारे।
भारत में तब बजे नकारे, होली है भई होली है॥
लिबरल दल की हुई बहाली, खुशी हुए तब सब बंगाली।
पीटें ढोल बजावें ताली, होली है भई होली है॥
नहीं कोई लिबरब, नहीं कोई टोरी, जो परनाला सोही मोरी।
दोनों का है पंथ अघोरी, होली है भई होली है॥
अब भी समझो भारत भाई, तुम्हें तुम्हारी दशा जनाई।
आप सहो जो सिर पै आई, होली है भई होली है॥
करते फुल्लर बिदेशी बर्जन्, सब गोरे करते हैं गर्जन।
जैसे मिंटो जैसे कर्जन, होली है भई होली है॥[10]

The salvation of India lay, said Balmukund, only in her own efforts. Neither Tories nor Liberals would give us anything.[11]

There were many other litterateurs who did almost the same job as Balmukund did to create political awareness and national consciousness among the people by their powerful writings in Hindi and Urdu, not only in Haryana, but elsewhere, too, in northern India.

The Middle Classes

The middle classes, too, played a significant role in creating national awareness in the region. But, unfortunately their contribution was not very substantial, for these were pretty weak here during the times under discussion. There were several reasons for this, the chief of which was unsatisfactory economic development. The people here were not lucky like their counterparts in Bengal, etc., and did not get opportunities like Banias and Duboises there to invest in the trade and commerce run by the western traders. Nor did anything like the permanent settlement take place here, so that the people could invest their capital like the Dev and Thakur families of Bengal and get zamindaris. Nor did they get the commercial opportunities which the Kavases, Tatas, etc., exploited in the Bombay presidency. There were hardly any big cities/towns here, where middle classes could take birth and flourish.[12] Surprisingly, however, like the birth of litterateurs in the region where no opportunities for higher education were available, some enlightened persons were thrown up by even these weak and underdeveloped middle classes.

The name of Babu Murlidhar from Ambala stands at the top of the list of such men. He had a good team of activists from the same class in Ambala who helped him in creating some institutions, like the Hindu Sabha, Rifa-i-Am, Indian Association, which played a substantial part in awakening the masses through various activities. In 1884, for instance, Murlidhar organized a historic meeting under the auspices of the Indian Association which was attended among others by the great nationalist Surendranath Banerjea from Bengal. He made a fiery speech in the meeting on the bad effects of the British rule in India. A resolution to increase the age limit for Indians in the Indian Civil Services (ICS) examination was also passed. Many rich persons gave huge contributions to the National Fund on the occasion. This was, however, not liked by the British bureaucracy which registered its annoyance. The Indian press—*The Hindu*, *Patriot*, *Indian Mirror*, *Bihar Herald*, *Indian Chronicle*, *Indu Parkash*, *Indian Spectators* and many other newspapers—criticized this action of the bureaucracy in strong terms.[13]

Though weak, the middle classes did bring some awareness to the people especially to the ones living in cities and towns.

Socio-Religious Reform Movements

But what about the villages, where about 90 per cent of the state's population lived? Was there no awakening there during this period? Far from it. Thanks to the efforts of the socio-religious reform movements, as indicated below, the national awakening had started taking its roots there, too.

Arya Samaj

Of all the socio-religious reform movements of the period, the Arya Samaj seems to have played the most important role in creating politico-national awareness here. The movement was started in Bombay by a great vedic scholar and social activist, Swami Dayananda Saraswati (1824-83), on 10 April 1875 with the object of eradicating social evils and creating a healthy society in India, especially among Hindus. The great reformer visited Haryana in 1880 and stayed here for several days at Rewari. He made some followers and established a branch of the Arya Samaj there. After some time, another branch of the Samaj was established at Rohtak. Subsequently, thanks to the efforts of a young man, Lajpat Rai, who, though a resident of Punjab (born at Jagaraon, 1865), had settled here in 1880s, a branch was also established at Hisar with the help of his friends like Chudamani, Chandu Lal, Hira Lal and Ramji Lal.[14] After sometime, the message of the Samaj spread to other

TABLE 2: SPREAD OF ARYA SAMAJ IN THE 19TH CENTURY

Established	City/Town	Members
1880	Rewari	21
1885	Rohtak	10
1886	Hisar	59
1889	Hansi	12
1890	Bhiwani	36
1890	Hathin (Gurgaon)	5
1890	Ambala City	14
1891	Jhajjar	13
1892	Sirsa	21
1893	Shahabad (Kurukshetra)	19
1894	Thanesar	15
1896	Ballabhgarh (Faridabad)	10
1897	Kosli (Rewari)	10
1900	Ladwa (Kurukshetra)	8
1900	Kaithal	30
1900	Pundri	20

districts—Ambala, Karnal and Gurgaon. A list of Samajas formed in Haryana in the nineteenth century is given in Table 2.[15]

In the succeeding century, the Samaj became still more popular. By 1920s we find Arya Samajas in almost every town and big village of the region. The membership, too, increased manifold. Simultaneously, the sphere of the activity of the organization also became very wide and comprehensive; the samaj activists fought serious battles against social evils, ignorance, illiteracy and orthodoxy.[16]

The Samaj also took to political work. This was owing to the inspiration from none other than their founder himself. Dayananda was the first social reformer who had made a forceful plea for political independence of the country. 'The swarajya was always the best thing', he said; a foreign government could not be beneficial even when it was free from religious bias, race prejudice and was just and symphathetic. He exhorted his followers 'to come out in the open to form your own government for that was God's dispensation'. In a religious garb the statesman Sannyasi gave an open message of an all out revolt against the British raj. 'Let no man abide by the law', he said, 'laid down by the men ignorant of the vedas'. And 'every man should use all his influence and power to destroy a sovereign who does not happen to be acquainted with the intricacies of the vedas'.[17]

These statements of Dayananda, said Mr. Grey, the public prosecutor in the notorious 'Arya Samaj Sedition Case, Patiala, 1910' and rightly of course, 'read as political speeches made by Tilak or Bipin Chandra Pal at a meeting or conference, except that they go further than any one dare go in lecturing to the public'.[18]

Arya Samaj was a modern organization. It took to all conceivable media for taking among other messages the above political dispensation of their guru to the people. As a result, hundreds of people were politicized. Thanks to the Samaj's efforts, nationalist winds began to blow in every nook and cranny of Haryana.[19]

Sanatan Dharma Sabha

The Arya Samaj, as noted above, attacked the Hindu orthodoxy while doing its work of reform. To save themselves from the onslaught of this organization effectively, the Hindu orthodoxy also made efforts to organize itself. The result was the Sanatan Dharma Sabha.

The Sabha had its beginning in Jhajjar, a small town in Haryana, owing to the efforts of Pandit Dindayalu Sharma on 22 August 1886.

After this the activities of the Sabha spread to Bhiwani (1890). Next year the Sabha made its influence on Hisar and the town had its branch opened there (1891). A branch came up at Sirsa about this very time. In 1892 Karnal had a branch opened. A little later the Sabha made its presence felt at Kurukshetra, Safidon, Rewari, Palwal, Kaithal, Panipat, Rohtak, Beri, Gurgaon and several other towns. Besides its religious work, the Sanatan Dharma Sabha, in order to compete with Arya Samaj, also advocated some reforms, like widow marriage, abolition of child marriage, refraining from drinking, gambling and such other vices. Some of its members also preached nationalist politics. But in this respect the Sabha was not a force to reckon with as the Arya Samaj was.[20]

Muslim Outfits

Like Hindus, the Muslims also founded several socio-religious reform societies in this period for their social and religious uplift. Though all these socities claimed to be non-political, they had politics in their programme of work. Of these societies (Table 3), the Central Mohammadan Association, which was founded by the Muslim leader Amir Ali at Calcutta in 1877, was the strongest of all in Haryana. Although its main centres were only at two places—Ambala and Hisar—its active members were there in other cities/towns and big villages. The Anjuman-i-Islamia had its branches in many cities. However, its membership was not as large as that of the Central Association. The Ithna had still less members on its rolls. But its political content was more than what the other outfits had. When Surendranath Banerjea visited Punjab, it was this outfit that welcomed him enthusiastically.[21]

TABLE 3: MUSLIM SOCIETIES IN HARYANA[22]

Name of society	Town where established	When established	Membership
Anjuman Ithna Ashahar	Ambala	1876	10
Central National Muhammadan Association	Ambala	1886	90
	Hisar	1888	
Anjuman-i-Islamia	Ambala	1884	45
	Jhajjar	1888	17
	Hisar	1888	29
	Sohna	1888	13

When compared with the Hindu organizations, these Muslim outfits were quite weak in almost every respect. As a result, they could not reach the Muslim masses effectively. Consequently, the Muslims remained for the most part apolitical.[23]

Sikh Organizations

Like Muslims, the Haryana Sikhs were also not as fortunate as their Hindu counterparts were in getting help from social reform movements during the period under discussion in their politicization. Except for one organization—the Singh Sabha—there was no other organization to do this work for them. And, unfortunately, even this organization could not, as Table 4 shows, spread itself beyond a few towns, and there, too, only a few persons came under its influence. In consequence, the political awakening came to the Sikhs very late—in the third decade of the present century, to be precise.[24]

The above discussion shows that in the period under consideration there was very little political awakening and national awareness among the Muslims and Sikhs.[25] This was so because the organizations which did this job elsewhere were not strong here. Unlike them, however, the Hindus were better off: the Arya Samaj did a great job in arousing politico-national awareness in its followers.[26]

The Indian National Congress

More than any other institution or organization, the Indian National Congress played a significant part in creating conditions for the development of politico-national consciousness among the people. Founded in Bombay on 28 December 1885, it had its feet planted here very early in the day, thanks to the efforts of Babu Murlidhar of Ambala, one of the founders of this all-India organization, and his friends like Madho Ram, Than Singh and Dwarka A. Dass. The Ambala branch (founded in

TABLE 4: THE SINGH SABHA IN HARYANA

Year of establishment	Place where established	No. of members
1886	Ambala city	10
1888	Ambala Cantt.	25
1890	Thanesar	05
1899	Kaithal	06

January 1886) was perhaps the first branch of the Congress in the country. It had a respectable following and had a newspaper, *Khair Andesh* to propagate its ideals and programme.[27] In 1888, Hisar, too, came to have a branch of the Congress, thanks to the efforts of Lala Lajpat Rai who, as noted above, was residing at Hisar then, and his associates, Churamani, Gauri Shankar and Chhabil Das. It was an active branch. In the words of Lala Lajpat Rai: 'Several public meetings were held in support of the Indian National Congress which were held and addressed by speakers from outside; hundreds of people attended these meetings, although Hisar was not a very big town and including its suburbs it did not contain more than 15 thousand souls.'[28]

Almost at the same time, the message of Congress also reached the neighbouring district of Rohtak. By the efforts of Babu Ram, Shamar Chand and Turrabaz Khan a branch of the national organization was set up there. On 12 October 1888, the Congress conducted its first historic public meeting at Rohtak.[29] The process of institutionalization of the nationlist politics in Karnal and Gurgaon districts was weak in the beginning. However, by the efforts of the leaders like Atma Ram and Chiranji Lal in Karnal, and Hait Ram, Lekh Ram and Dhani Ram in Gurgaon, branches of Congress were also established in both these districts in later years.[30]

It may be pertinent to ask such questions here as: who were these leaders who sowed the seeds and nurtured the sapling of Congress in Haryana in this period? What classes did they belong to? Where did they come from? Fortunately, we are in a position to answer all these questions.

The early leaders of Congress, as Table 5 shows, belonged by and large to the middle classes. They came mostly from urban areas. It were the pleaders who came first. Later on they were joined by the wealthy raeis, bankers, merchants, etc. But towards the end of the period (1918), some lower middle class rural leaders, mostly belonging to the peasantry, also came in.

It may also be interesting to know the religion-wise break-up of these early leaders. As shown in Table 6, an overwhelming number of leaders (91) came from among the Hindus (88.4 per cent). Next came the Sikhs. Forming 4 per cent of the population, they made only 4.8 per cent of the leadership. The Muslims were almost nowhere. Factors and forces like urbanization, education and socio-religious movements (like Arya Samaj) which contributed to national awakening among Hindus were not so strong among the Muslims. Hence this position.

A word about the social base of the movement at this point in time. Unfortunately, we do not have as adequate information on the subject as we have on the composition of the leadership. The relevant documents on the subject available tell us only so much that in the beginning 'nai hawa' of nationalism touched only cities and towns. But as time passed by, it reached villages, too, especially in Rohtak and Hisar where the Arya Samaj was strong. In other words it means that those who say the national awareness was restricted to only the middle classes in the urban areas during the period 1885-1918, are wrong. The movement had percolated to villages too—even among the illiterate persons there, especially owing to the efforts of the Arya Samaj and Sanatan Dharma Sabha, as the following account would show.

ACHIEVEMENT OF EARLY LEADERS

What was the programme of the early nationalists? Their programme was to highlight exploitation, oppression and dehumanization of the Indians

TABLE 5: CLASS-WISE BREAK-UP OF THE EARLY NATIONALIST LEADERS, 1885-1918[31]

Classes	Total no. of leaders	Leaders belonging to urban areas	Leaders belonging to rural areas
Pleaders	46	44	2
Raeis, Contractors, Bankers, Jagirdars, Merchants, etc.	32	32	–
Editors, Doctors, Teachers, etc.	13	13	–
Peasants	05	–	05
Miscellaneous	07	06	01
Total	103	95	08

TABLE 6: RELIGION-WISE BREAK-UP OF THE EARLY NATIONALIST LEADERS, 1885-1918[32]

Religion	Population percentage in Haryana	Total no. of leaders	Community-wise percentage of leaders
Hindus	70	91	88.4
Muslims	24	05	4.8
Sikhs	04	05	4.8
Others (Christians, etc.)	02	02	2.0

by the British, to suggest ways and means to meet this hapless situation, and finally to prepare the nation for *swaraj*. Great leaders living in cosmopolitan cities, like Dadabhai Naoroji, R.C. Dutt and others did make great contribution to expose the 'un-British rule and poverty' in India in the period under reference. Their reach and impact, was however, restricted to only the English-knowing middle classes in big cities who by all means did not exceed 0.5 per cent of the population. The Haryana writers of the day, however, reached and influenced millions of people as shown above, by writing on the same theme in the language understood by the masses. They formulated their theses in straight and simple idiom which the ordinary people could comprehend. They employed such tone and tenor in their writings which touched the right cord of the people and spread a powerful political message with huge nationalist content.[33]

The early leaders from the region exposed, as did their counterparts elsewhere, the so-called 'benevolent' British administration and portrayed it in colours true to history.[34] What precisely did they say may be seen from some excerpts from the speeches of one of them—Murlidhar. A critique of the police department, the so-called 'guardians of peace':

> One does not employ a cat to keep guard over his pigeons or to watch over his chickens. You can not place a cup of milk before a cat and ask it not to drink it in your absence. Wolves, tigers, hyenas and other ferocious beasts are either found in the jungles or kept in manageries. They are never allowed to roam at large and play havoc among the people. But these ferocious animals, even if let loose, cannot do that amount of harm to mankind as these wolves and tigers of the police in human shape do. One can shoot down a tiger with impunity but he cannot touch a hair of the head of this strange animal of the police, because he is a creature and pet of the mighty.[35]

Murlidhar had to pay a heavy price for this criticism. He was sentenced to jail on cooked-up charges. The Punjab authorities had thought that this would demoralize Murlidhar. But what happened was just the opposite of it. He went to attend the second session of the Indian National Congress held at Calcutta, in December 1886, straight from jail and made a powerful speech on the farce being committed in the name of justice by the Punjab judiciary. He suffered, he said, 'because I have my own opinion and speak what I think without fear. I was convicted not on weak evidence but on absolutely no evidence at all.[36]

After reaching home he criticized the 'amassing of judicial and non-judicial powers in the deputy commissioners-of police, the judges, the magistrates, the jury men, the counsel, the prosecutor, and everything.

Nothing more is desired, he said, 'to make him more formidable and irresistible. He is perhaps more irresistible than The czar of Russia himself. He should be made to part with these powers'. To serve the cause of justice effectively, he added, 'the executive and judiciary have to be independent of each other.'[37] Not only lower officials but even the Chief Court of Punjab was not spared by the fearless critic. He made scathing criticism of the highest tribunal in the Land of the Five Rivers at the annual session of the Indian National Congress in 1894.[38]

These developments seem to have demoralized the Punjab authorities, for we find them a great deal saner hereafter. Illustrations: Meredith, acting district judge of Ambala in late 1880s was an ill-tempered fellow. He used to misbehave with people. Once he insulted someone in his court in the presence of Murlidhar. The latter took him to task in a series of hard-hitting articles in his paper *Khair Andesh*. This annoyed Meredith and he sought government's permission to prosecute Murlidhar. The government, wiser as it had grown after the 1886 episode, dissuaded Meredith from doing so. Another senior officer, Gladstone, also indulged in almost similar type of activities. People were annoyed with him for his whimsical behaviour. Murlidhar also picked on him. The government saved him for some time, but eventually yielded: Gladstone had to leave Ambala.[39]

Chandu Lal, a semi-literate leader from Hisar, took on his deputy commissioner. The officer was in the habit of making undue interference in the municipal affairs of the city. Chandu Lal asked him to mend his ways, but to no effect. He, therefore, organized a hartal in the town (1888). This was a very big thing in those times. As a result, the administration was moved from top to bottom. The commissioner, Ambala Division came and had to yield before the semi-literate rustic man saying tauntingly: 'You are the Raja of the district.'[40]

These are just a few examples from the speeches and activities of one man to show as to how the early nationalists met with the situation in the last days of the preceding century. There were many more such activists who dared to call spade a spade, and were ready to take on the mightiest in the land, if he was in the wrong.

Conclusion

The post-uprising developments in our region were, as indicated above, of two types: one, the victors changed their framework of ruling us to some such extent that the catastrophe that overtook them in 1857 would not repeat itself. Two, our people took advantage of the opportunities that they got in the new circumstances. As a result, there came political awakening and national awareness among the people.

NOTES

1. See K.C. Yadav, 'A Brief History of the Development of Education in Haryana during the 19th Century', *JHS*, vol. 19, pp. 7-20.
2. Unfortunately, they did not go on for more than a few months.
3. K.C. Yadav (ed), *Haryana: Studies*, p. 107.
4. For Balmukund Gupta's life and achievements, see Jhabarmal et al., *Balmukund Gupta*, Calcutta, 1972.
5. *Bharatamitra*, 1 October 1900.
6. Ibid., 15 October 1904.
7. Ibid.
8. *Shivasambhu Ke Chitthe aur Khat* were serialized in *Bharatamitra* in 1905. These were later published in a book form. These were later translated into English and published in *Hindustan* (Lahore).
9. See *Bharatamitra*, 25 November 1905; 18 August 1906.
10. Ibid.
11. Even serious students of Indian politics did not think likewise in those days.
12. K.C. Yaḍav, *Haryana,* vol. II, pp. 156-71.
13. K.C. Yadav, *The Builder of Our Nation: Murlidhar* (hereafter *Murlidhar*) vol. I, pp. 57-8.
14. *JHS*, vol. XXIII, 1991, pp. 20-43.
15. Ibid.
16. Ibid.
17. Ibid.
18. Ibid.
19. Ibid.
20. Ibid.
21. K.C. Yadav, *Haryana*, vol. II, pp. 156-71.
22. Ibid.
23. Ibid.
24. Ibid.
25. Ibid.
26. Ibid.
27. See K.C. Yadav, *Murlidhar*, pp. 57-60.
28. K.C. Yadav, *Haryana*, vol. II, pp. 156-71.
29. For details about their lives see K.C. Yadav and Rameshwar Dass, *Rebels against the Raj: Who's Who of Freedom Fighters in Haryana* (hereafter *Who is Who*), vol. I, pp. 1-40.
30. *JHS*, vol. XXIII, 1991, pp. 20-43.
31. *Who is Who*, vol. I, pp. 1-40.

32. Ibid.
33. Ibid.
34. Ibid.
35. K.C. Yadav, *Murlidhar*, p. 78.
36. Ibid., pp. 16-17.
37. Ibid.
38. Ibid.
39. Ibid., pp. 60-1.
40. This remark, says Lala Lajpat Rai, 'was made tauntingly but it undoubtedly testified to Lala Chandu Lal's great influence and popularity', *JHS*, vol. XXIII, 1991, p. 29.

10

The Struggle for Freedom, First Phase, 1905-1914

We have seen in the preceding chapter how the seeds of politico-nationalist awareness were sown in Haryana in the later part of the nineteenth century and how the new factors and forces which came up then, like modern education, social reform movements, rise of new middle classes and new political organizations and outfits produced here what is popularly called '*nai hawa*'—the winds of change—which helped these seeds to become formidable saplings in no time. Because of these developments there came a crop of good leaders like Murlidhar, Balmukund Gupta, Madho Ram, and Lajpat Rai, who prepared strong ground for *swaraj* here by educating the people in many ways. Indeed it was a great time; and it should have been a really great experience for the people to live in it.

The Swadeshi Movement

Affected by the '*nai hawa*' of this great time the people could not sit and see things being mismanaged by the imperialists any more. Some of them, if not all, became restive and called for a change—right here and now. And they could not think of anything better than starting a movement for *swadeshi*, i.e. using of our own indigenous things in life and not the foreign goods and thus making a powerful blow at the colonialist who survived on our economic exploitation.The early leaders of Haryana did this work very ably. Their job was easy in villages where a vast majority of the population lived, for the rural folk, as we know, used clothes made by the village *julahas* (weavers), ate *swadeshi* things and kept *swadeshi* furniture in their houses. The panchayats still served a majority of them insofar as dispensing of justice was concerned. Very few people went to the British courts where justice was costly and mostly delayed beyond tolerable limits. And in large number of cases even the delayed justice was not available, for in 99 out of 100 cases truth did not prevail.

In the towns and cities, however, the situation was bad, especially among the upper and the middle classes who by and large opted for the western ways of life. Most of them used clothes made in England and ate foreign food and had foreign furniture in their houses. They had no respect for indigenous courts or schools. They considered British rule to be a blessing for them and had no positive feeling for anything like *swaraj*.

The early Haryana nationalists came very heavily on this element. Murlidhar provides a very good example of this. Speaking on the subject from the podium of the Indian National Congress in its annual conference at Nagpur, 1891, the Grand Old Man of Punjab made a beautiful speech. He began with a reprimand of his fellow delegates belonging to the middle classes for not adhering to the cult of *swadeshi.* He held them 'guilty of collaborating with cursed monsters fattening on the heart's of your brethren blood'. There were voices of 'no' 'no'. Murlidhar silenced them all by his impassioned, forceful words:

> I say, yes, look around, what are all these chandeliers and lamps, and European made chairs and tables, and smart clothes and hats and English coats and bonnets and frocks, and silver mounted canes and all the luxurious fittings of your houses, but trophies of India's misery; mementos of India's starvation? Every rupee you have spent on European made articles is a rupee of which you have robbed your poorer brethren, honest handicraftsmen who can no longer earn a living.[1]

Then he posed a very serious question in an admonishing tone:

> You cry that India is poor. Have you done your share of the work? Have you contributed anything towards reducing the poverty of the country? Have you established any manufacturies? Have you discarded European clothing? Have you shown to the world that you are really feeling and working for the poor? If you go to their houses and partake of their wretched food and lead life as they do, shivering with cold at midnight in those miserable huts with naked bodies, then you will feel the pinching poverty; then you will really feel the suffering of the people. Until you place yourselves in the position of the poverty-stricken people you will not be able to say that India is your motherland; that the people are poor and that you advocate their cause. Do advocate their cause sincerely. Pledge yourself to sit rather on the bare ground than to send for chair from Austria, three thousand miles away, which cost you Rs. 5000. Act as practical patriots and show by your life that you truly and sincerely feel for the poor; then the sympathy of all the poor shall be yours, and your names shall be placed in history and God will be immensely pleased with you for having done your work.[2]

TABLE 1: DECLINE IN THE PURCHASE OF FOREIGN GOODS IN HARYANA[3]

District	Foreign goods purchased in 1905 (*in Rs.*)	Foreign goods purchased in 1907 (*in Rs.*)
Ambala	25,000	10,000
Karnal	16,000	8,000
Rohtak	17,000	*
Gurgaon	11,000	*
Hisar	10,000	4,000

*Figures not available.

What impact the exhortations or the Haryana leader made on his countrymen is difficult to say but it did influence his own brethren in Haryana in a big way, especially after 1905 when the movement gained momentum in the wake of the partition of Bengal. As a result, the purchasing and consumption of the foreign goods dwindled here a great deal as is seen in Table 1.

Like *swadeshi* clothes, the Haryana leaders propagated in favour of *swadeshi* courts also. For instance, criticizing the British tribunals of justice, Murlidhar observed:

> Then there is the costly, utterly unsuitable foreign system (this, too, is important like so many of our other blessings) of civil and criminal so-called justice, I say our so-called courts of justices, are, too, generally dens of injustice, litigation is fostered and fomented by this system (A voice: But you are a pleader). And hence I thoroughly know what I am speaking about (cheers). Litigation, I say is the necessary result of this unsuitable and alien system of judicature, which has ruined large sections of the community morally and materially. Millions, who would otherwise have remained honest and truthful men are now rogues and professional liars. In old days, there was no tax on justice. You did not always get it, but when you did, it was free. Now I think you never get it, except by accident.[4]

Murlidhar and other Haryana leaders exhorted the people to go to national institutions for justice and other purposes. Their pleading and preaching had some impact on the masses, if not a particular class of westernized elite. In sum, thanks to the efforts of the early nationalist leaders, the *swadeshi* movement made good progress in Haryana during the period under study.

Institutional Infrastructure

The early Haryana nationalists pleaded vociferously for democratization of institutions. They began with the demand for a Legislative Assembly for Punjab. The Indian Councils Act of 1861 gave legislative councils to Bombay and Madras and authorized the establishment of similar councils in other provinces. In pursuance of this provision, Bengal and the United Provinces got councils in 1863. But it was in 1897, thirty-six years after the passage of the above Act, that Punjab got a legislative council comprising nine members and in a way what they got was just an eyewash, for there was no provision of election of the legislative council members. They were all nominated by the lieutenant governor.[5] Murlidhar raised great hue and cry to have a legislative council with duly elected members on it from different platforms. There was reason and force in what he said, as the following excerpt from one of his speeches on the subject made in Lahore in 1895 indicates:

> It was only in India that it was held that what was good for Allahabad, Madras and Bombay was bad for Lahore. What was nectar in one place was poison in another. When the people of this province went to Malta, China, Egypt, and other places to fight for the Empress, then they were the pillars of the Empire and poems were sung in praise of their valour and loyalty, but when they returned laden with material glories they were treated like children, not fit to have a Legislative Council. If Allahabad, Madras, Bombay and Bengal had Councils and profited by them why then the people of the Punjab should not have one.[6]

His efforts bore fruits and Punjab got a Council in 1905.

There was no High Court in Punjab. Initially, there was a Board of Judicial Commissioners. In 1866 a Chief Court was established which comprised two judges. The number of the judges was increased to six in 1886. The Chief Court did not work satisfactorily and objectively. For its judges were not appointed by the Crown, as was the case with the judges of high courts. Murlidhar raised powerful voice for it, again from the same platform—of the Indian National Congress—and that of the local conferences almost ad infinitum. What he spoke there can be known from the following excerpt from one of his speeches on the subject:

> We want a High Court. For who, but the High Court of Madras could have passed for the damages of Rs. 100 against its own Governor, Sir M. Grant Duff? Indeed, it was only the High Court that could take such a bold action. Hence this galladium of justice. We want the man of the calibre of Sir Barnes Peacock, Jr., Justice Ranade, Pandit Shambu Nath, Babu Dwarka Nath Mitter, Sir Richard Grath, we want men like Mr. Justice Straight, to be straight and honest and to be independent of the opinion of friends or foes, we want them to be appointed

directly by the Crown and not to be subordinate to Indian authority so as to be free from any bias or prejudice.[7]

Thanks to such efforts, Punjab got its High Court soon.

In sum, the early nationalists here had prepared the ground well for *swaraj* by creating necessary institutions during the period under reference.

REVOLT OF THE 10TH JAT

As indicated above, political awakening and national awareness had reached the masses even in rural areas during the period under study. They only needed an opportunity to join the struggle. And whenever that was offered, they seized it with both hands. Substantion: when the Bengal revolutionaries approached the Haryana soldiers in 1910, their response was warm.

These soldiers belonged to the 10th Jat Regiment. This regiment had been a mixed outfit of Hindus (Brahmanas and Rajputs) and Mohammedans, but in 1892 it was formed into a class outfit of Jats from Hisar, Rohtak and Jind. These districts were centres of Arya Samaj. As a result, a larger bulk of the sepoys in the regiment were either active Arya Samajists or they sympathized with the Samaj. This explains how in spite of opposition of their officers, these men held meetings under the auspices of the Samaj in their lines. This practice did not last long, however, because the authorities treated these meetings in the lines as highly objectionable and forbade the sepoys from holding them. The sepoys swallowed the bitter pill but found out an alternative to do their work. They started going out to the city to attend the weekly *satsangs* there. Even this was not liked by the authorities who forbade their attending the *satsangs* too. This was intolerable for the sepoys but they bore with it for the time being.[8]

In 1904, the regiment was shifted to Kanpur. Taking advantage of the engagements of their officers at the new station, the Arya activists again started the practice of holding weekly *satsangs*. But no sooner had they done that than the authorities forbade them to hold them. Not only that, the sepoys were ordered not to keep books like *Satyarthaprakasha*, etc., with them in the lines.[9]

The patriotic fire burning in the hearts of the sepoys was thus extinguished outwardly. But inside it was still smouldering. For example, in 1905 when the northern region came in the grip of the *swadeshi* movement, a number of sepoys took part in the meetings held to preach *swadeshi* in Kanpur. In September (1905) Sepoy Surajan Singh, their leader was reported by the police to be attending a *swadeshi* meeting and subscribing to its funds. He was punished for this indiscipline.[10] The following year meetings of the 10th Jat and 10th Hodson's Horse were held in infantry lines; books like *Satyarthaprakasha* and newspapers of a political character such as the *Kesari*, *Jat Samachar* and *Jat Hitkari* were read.[11] Lajpat Rai gave a lecture at Kanpur in the winter of 1907. Many sepoys of the Jat Regiment attended the lecture.[12]

This was a little too much for the authorities to bear with and they asked the Arya activists to leave the Samaj and part with sacred thread. Many obliged their officers. But there were others who were made of stronger fibre. They wrote anonymous letters to the commander-in-chief seeking his intervention against their religious persecution. When this did not yield any positive result, about a dozen of them came out in the open to oppose this arbitrary action of the authorities. Naik Jot Ram, the most vocal of them all, was court-martialled for insubordination and sent to jail. Ram Gopal, ward orderly, was discharged from service and ten others were 'suitably punished'.[13]

In February 1908, the regiment was shifted to Alipore. The local Samajists were very active at the new place and they formed links with the sepoys right at once. One Seth Chhaju Ram,[14] a Jat multi-millionaire businessman from Alakhpura in district Hisar, from where the bulk of the sepoys came, was the connecting chain between the two parties. Chhaju Ram says that the commanding officer of the regiment, 'not only entertained them, their wives and families but had also driven to the lines to visit them several times. The fact that this had not been reported made me suspicious, as the native officers generally like reporting the arrival of any influential friend.'[15] Chhaju Ram was reported to have impressed on the Jat junior commissioned officers that they should always keep in mind that when they were guarding prisoners of Alipur Jail, they were guarding their own brothers.[16]

After sometime, the Regiment went to Midnapore for training. As many as 39 detectives were posted by the local police to keep watch on them there. The Criminal Intelligence Department sent an extra detective for this purpose. Despite all this, however, the sepoys did their work, says Brigadier-General Cowans, who enquired into the matter later in this regard:

> Some men of the 10th Jats had been entertained in the houses of some extremists in Midnapore and shown an exhibition of sword-play; that some of the heads of the extremist party had been seen visiting the 10th Jats in their camp and that

some of the 10th Jats had been taken to see Khudiram Bose's house and had refused to give their names to a police sub-inspector who found them there.[17]

He further added that he was informed by the commanding officer of the Regiment that certain of his men were entertained by the Raja of Midnapore so notorious in the bomb case and who narrowly escaped transportation for life.[18]

The junior commissioned officers of the regiment were at least in sympathy if not in league with the seditious sepoys. This is borne out by the following observations of the brigadier which he made while discussing the regimental commanding officer's behaviour:

> On questioning him (Commanding Officer of the 10th Jat) regarding what was going on in the regiment, I ascertained that his Subedar-Major and other native officers were of practically no assistance to him in keeping him informed of anything undesirable (i.e. sedition in the lines) that was going on and he seemed to be entirely dependent for such information on a Muhammedan Hospital Assistant and his regimental School Master (a Havildar). This procedure seemed to me very unusual and I told him so and further that I considered that a Subedar-Major and native officers who so little fulfilled their duty were not worth keeping in the battalion.[19]

After the annual exercise were over, the regiment came back to Alipur, their headquarters in December 1909. Although the intelligence was not tightened around the regiment about this time yet the Arya activists did their job very efficiently. They visited the Arya Samaj *mandir* (temple) regularly and formed links with the Bengal revol-utionaries. The authorities had no knowledge of their doings. A few of them even went to the extent of joining a secret revolutionary society which had its branches at Kiddarpur and Shergarh (Calcutta). Sarat Chandra Mitter, Suresh Chandra Mitter, Bhuban Mohan Mukherji, Kristo Bhan (alias Bhu'an) Mukherji, Narender Nath Chatterji, Lalit Mohan Chakravarty had induced them to do so.[20]

What was this secret society like which the sepoys had joined? And what were its aims and objectives? Answer to these questions can be had from the following oath which the sepoys took on the occasion of joining the society:

(i) From today I am initiated to be a member of this society and so long as the liberation of the motherland is not effected, I shall continue to be a member of this society and work for the welfare of my country.

(ii) I do not become a member of this society under the influence of any evil motive.

(iii) If I have any ill-feeling or quarrel with any member of the society, I shall sincerely make that up as ordered by the leader and I shall look upon the other members of the society as my brothers.

(iv) I shall work under the orders of the leader. I shall obey him in whatever he orders without any questioning and take his orders to be such as can never be disobeyed.

(v) Without the permission of the leader, I shall not disclose any secret matter in connection with this society to any one, even to any other member of the society.

(vi) If I voluntarily do anything which is against the interests of the society, I shall gladly take any punishment inflicted by the leader, or by his orders.

(vii) I shall not marry so long as I shall be a member of the society.

(viii) After taking the *Gita*, fire, sword or dagger, and Ganges water I take this oath with God as my witness that so long as I live I shall continue to be a member of this society. If I voluntarily desert, then on the orders of the leader any member can take my life as a punishment. For that he shall not be responsible to God.

(ix) If I disobey any of these commandments, may my ancestors go to hell and may I be guilty of drinking my mother's blood.[21]

Before the sepoys and the revolutionaries could do anything worthwhile, one of the revolutionaries, Lalit Mohan Chakravarty, exposed a plot hatched by the men of the 10th Jat and the revolutionaries. The plot, one of the most dangerous conspiracies ever hatched by the revolutionaries, was as follows:

During the Christmas holidays in 1909 a ball was to be held at the residence of the Bengal Governor to which the Viceroy, Commander-in-Chief and all the high-ranking officers and officials of Calcutta were to be invited. The 10th Jat Regiment was to do sentry duty during the ball. The undercover patriotic organisation which had established contact with the soldiers decided to take advantage of this convenient ball to blow up the ballroom and thus destroy the colonial government.[22]

The police had suspected nothing and it is hard to say what the outcome would have been had the soldiers not been betrayed by the traitor who informed the authorities about the impending coup. The British government was shocked to hear of such a serious conspiracy and they at once took stringent measures against the culprits who were 42 in number. They were tried by a military court-martial whose proceedings were kept highly confidential. Surprisingly, however, these were leaked to the Russian Embassy which made them public through their paper *Zemachina* which wrote that the sepoys, said the paper, conducted themselves with great poise at the trial. They declared that they had joined a revolutionary union set up by Bengali patriots and were aware of the fact that this union wanted to overthrow British rule in India. They declared that they had taken an oath of allegiance to maintain unity and were duty bounds to help conduct revolutionary agitation among the troops. One of the accused told the judge. 'Don't think there are only 25 such sepoys. Oh no, there are many such sepoys and the fate of British domination in India is in our hands. The English court imposed severe penalties upon the arrested soldiers.[23]

The details of the punishment inflicted upon the revolutionary soldiers were as follows: by the order of the commander-in-chief, Hav. Chuni Lal and Sepoy Surjan Singh were dealt with summarily (summary court-martial under the Indian Articles of War) and were sentenced to be discharged from the service. Besides them, '43 non-commissioned officers and men out of 145 who might apparently have been implicated, or whose characters were doubtful, were summarily dismissed'. On 31 January the battalion was sent in the RIMS Northbrooke for Karachi. The constitution of the 10th Jat was changed. In the words of the Brigadier-General Cowans:

From all that I have heard recently, he said, the area of country from which they are recruited appears to possess an unusual number of leading members of the extremist or seditionist sections of the community and there is little doubt that these men are holding out large pecuniary and other inducements to men in the native army to join what is meant to be a serious movement to attempt the downfall of the British Empire in India.

A class regiment is peculiarly amenable to such attempts and one in which it is very hard to ascertain what is going on. With change of constitution would naturally come a transfer of certain of the British officers, some of whom cannot be altogether absolved of negligence in the matter of not keeping their native officers up to date. Especially in this so in the case of Lt. Colonel Pressey, who says little or nothing of what steps he took to keep himself informed of what was going on in a battalion which to his own knowledge, apparently had been toying with sedition for many years and which in the light of the many warnings issued to Commanding Officers from Army Headquarters during the years 1906-08, evidently required special attention. His complaint that the civil authorities did not inform him that outsiders were likely to attempt to tamper with the fidelity of his men can hardly be justified after receipt of these warnings, and after he himself had in 1908 to convict a Havildar clerk of insubordination due to outside influence of a political nature (vide his report dated 1908).[24]

Lt. Col. Pressey was sent in forced retirement for his negligent behaviour. The subedar-major was also sent on pension. All the subedars, i.e. company commanders, were summarily discharged from service with such pensions or gratuities to which they were entitled. The recruiting of the 10th Jat was confined to Jats enlisted under the recruiting officers for Rajputana and Central India with a view to introducing other classes than those which have lately shown sign of disaffection.[25]

That was not the end of the story, however. The problem of the 10th Jat was resolved, but the bug of the Arya Samaj was not killed. It was an 'immensely dangerous community' for which there could not have been any place at least in the Army. The commander-in-chief, therefore moved in the matter. He wrote a very strong note on 22 March 1910 on the question, recommending to the Army Department that notification be issued putting a blanket ban on the recruitment of Arya Samajists in the Army. But before that was done, he said, the permission of the governor-general of India be sought. In consequence, the matter was submitted to the Home Department.

The Home Department gave a serious thought to the question and advised against taking any such step in haste. There would be a lot of opposition to such a measure, they said. Representations would be sent to the government, memorials would be addressed to the secretary of state and questions would be asked in the parliament against such a measure. It was necessary, therefore, that before agreeing to such a proposal, they got hold of definite evidence supporting such an action. The Home Department it seems had grown wiser from their experience gained from Lajpat Rai's case. They had no sufficient grounds to deport the Lion of the Punjab and as such had to eat a humble pie when there were protests against their action in and outside parliament. They did not want to repeat the same mistake.[26]

To be on surer grounds before such an action was taken, the Home Department thought it proper to seek the opinion of the governments of Punjab and Uttar Pradesh on the question. In consequences, express communications were sent to them. The two governments took serious note of the problem and gave their considered opinion. The Punjab government said:

> Unless the Army authorities have very definite proof that Arya Samaj as a body is teaching sedition in the Army, the Lt. Governor would deprecate any direct action against the society as a whole and would deal with individual cases as they occur, i.e. anyone when found to be seditious, should be dismissed.[27]

The Uttar Pradesh government also thought likewise. It would be a mistake, they said, to proscribe the whole Samaj. The lieutenant governor expressed his inability to accept the proposal put forth by the commander-in-chief.[28]

The viceroy agreed with the observation of the Home Department and the governments of Punjab and U.P. He considered it inadvisable to proscribe the entire Arya Samaj for being seditious. It was left to the Army Department to tackle the problem of recruitment of undesirable elements in the Army thoughtfully. Accordingly, the commander-in-chief devised a novel remedy to the problem. Addressing an Army Order to all the general officers commanding divisions and independent brigades and all recruiting officers, he observed:

In view of the maintenance of discipline good order and loyalty in the Indian Army and to prevent discord and dissension arising among the native ranks: it is desired that all Commanding Officers and Recruting Officers to carry out the policy of Government in carefully restricting the enlistment in units to the classes duly authorised to form their composition. To illustrate this I am to point out that as in a Hindu Rajput Company Mohammendan Rajputs are not enlisted and as Brahmins who are Sikhs are not eligible for regiments enlisting Brahmins, so in the case of companies in which the Jats are authorised, steps should be taken to prevent the enlistment of Jats who have changed their religion to that of the Sikhs, Vishnois, Brahmo Samajists, Arya Samajists or any other sect and this rule should be applied to all classes enlisted in the Indian Army.[29]

Thus the enlistment of Arya Samajists was forbidden in the Army. This practice continued all through the period under study. No relaxation was made even during the first world war, 1914-18 when the British were in dire need of recruits as the following letter written to *The Tribune* by Sir Chhotu Ram, an eminent Jat leader of Rohtak, on 8 May 1917 shows:

The other day, an Arya Samajist offered himself for enlistment in the Army. He was asked to put off his sacred thread as a condition precendent. He refused to comply with his demand and was rejected in consequence.[30]

In sum, the above account should negate the hypothesis advanced by some people that there was no politico-national consciousness in Haryana during the period under study, and the people here played no role whatsoever in the struggle for freedom at this time. Conversely, there was a lot of awakening, political awareness and nationalist consciousness in them and they, like their brothers and sisters elsewhere, played a part in the struggle for freedom in its earliest phase, 1905-14.

NOTES

1. K.C. Yadav, *Murlidhar*, pp. 16-17.
2. Ibid., p. 72.
3. K.C. Yadav, *Haryana*, vol. II, pp. 172-82.
4. K.C. Yadav, *Murlidhar*, p. 79.
5. K.C. Yadav, *Elections in Punjab, 1919-1947*, Tokyo, 1981.
6. See K.C. Yadav, *Murlidhar*, pp. 73-4.
7. Ibid., p. 17.
8. Ibid.
9. Ibid.
10. Ibid.
11. Ibid.
12. Ibid.
13. Ibid.
14. He was treasurer of the Calcutta Arya Samaj.
15. NAI, Home Political (Conf.), Deposit no. 7, August 1910.
16. Ibid.
17. Ibid.
18. Ibid.
19. Ibid.
20. Ibid.
21. Ibid.
22. R.C. Majumdar, *Freedom Movement in India*, vol. II, p. 290.
23. Ibid.
24. NAI, Home Pol. (Conf.), Deposit no. 7, August 1910.
25. Ibid.
26. Ibid.
27. Ibid.
28. Ibid.
29. Ibid.
30. *The Tribune*, 8 May 1917.

11

The First World War and its Impact

Many countries in Europe had made tremendous, but unequal progress by the beginning of the twentieth century. As a result, they were indulged in a fierce competition for increasing their production of food grains, minerals, and industrial products for establishing their monopoly over the world trade and ultimately over the world market. The task being pretty difficult, it proved unaccomplishable for any single country on its own strength. Hence several like-minded countries joined hands to do what they could not do single-handedly. In consequence, several blocks came into existence.

But even this did not satisfy the ambitions of these countries for long. They dismantled their existing outfits and regrouped themselves. As a result, the 'bipolar world' or 'two-groups arrangement' came into being. Expectedly, there was mad race and cut-throat competition between the two blocks for supremacy in trade and monopoly over the world market. This eventually culminated into a World War on 4 August 1914. At the start 'the conflict' involved seven countries, but later some thirty countries joined it. It was the most bloody affair where world's entire resources were used to produce death and destruction. Nothing like it had happened before.[1]

Being an integral part of the British Empire, India was pushed into the 'bloody affair' immediately. Interestingly, the British did not think it necessary to take Indians into confidence before doing this. Nor did the other side protest. Thousands of Indian soldiers went to the war fronts in distant lands for defending 'honour, freedom and justice' all over the world. The rich opened their coffers and contributed lakhs 'to fight the war properly'. The Indian leadership, comprising such greats as Surendranath Banerjea, Sir Ferozeshah Mehta, Lala Lajpat Rai, Gandhiji, etc., not only thanked the Government but also expressed great pleasure in giving them an opportunity 'to serve a cause', and made a fervent appeal to their countrymen not to hesitate 'to give their last paisa and last drop of blood to the Government in their hour of sore-need'.[2]

HARYANA'S RESPONSE

How did the people of Haryana respond? Not very differently from their countrymen elsewhere. The Hindus, Muslims and Sikhs vied with each other to help the *Sarkar Bahadur* in their 'bad times' (*bura waqt*). The Jats, Ahirs, Rajputs, Gujars, Pathans, Ranghars, almost every one who considered oneself to be a part of the so-called 'martial races', came forward to join the army with great enthusiasm, and in pretty large numbers, as Table 1 shows. District Rohtak was, for instance, asked to give ten thousand recruits and it gave more than twice this number in no time. The story was more or less the same in other districts also.[3]

Like the youth, the urban middle class elite and the village leaders also made substantial contribution to the War effort. They joined the 'War Leagues', 'Recruiting Committees', 'Publicity Committees', 'Red Cross Societies', etc., and exhorted the people to help the government in every conceivable manner.[4] The following persons earned special gratitudes of the government for these services: Ch. Lal Chand, Ch. Rati Ram and Pt. Prabhu Dayal (Rohtak); Rao Balbir Singh (Gurgaon); Ch. Lajpat Rai, Ch. Bans Gopal and Pt. Janki Prasad (Hisar); and Rai Bahadur Seth Sukh Lal (Sirsa). Interestingly, even Haryana women made special efforts in collecting war loans and making contributions to the Red Cross Societies.[5]

The wealthy persons from the region contributed liberally to the war

TABLE 1: DISTRICT-WISE ENLISTMENT, 1915-18

District	1 Jan. 1915	4 Aug. 1914- 31 March 1916	1 Jan. 1917- 30 June 1917	1 July 1917- 31 Dec. 1917	1 Jan. 1918- 31 May 1918	1 June 1918- 30 Nov. 1918	Total upto Nov. 1918
Hisar	3,046	2,795	1,438	4,589	1,251	3,698	15,461
Rohtak	6,245	5,025	3,014	3,361	1,546	3,950	22,144
Gurgaon	2,481	3,440	2,241	4,048	2,184	4,869	18,867
Karnal	6,33	532	635	1,463	683	3,005	6,553
Ambala	17,55	1,256	482	989	1,893	2,070	8,241
Princely States	12,89	–	703	783	1,049	1,515	8,566

funds, as Table 2 shows. Rai Bahadur Seth Sukh Lal stood on the top of the list of donors to the Imperial Relief Fund (IRF) in the whole of Punjab (including Haryana). As indicated below, he gave Rs. 10 lakh. Rai Sahib Tara Chand (Bhiwani) gave Rs. 4.5 lakh. R.B. Sukh Lal's wife occupied, as noted, the first position among the women donors: she gave Rs. 1 lakh. Among the cities/towns, Bhiwani topped the donors' list—the town was allotted Rs. 15 lakh but it gave Rs. 25 lakh instead.[6] Besides this, the Haryana villages also made liberal contributions.[7]

TABLE 2: DONORS TO THE WAR FUND[8]

Name of the donor	Amount (*in Rs.*)
District Hisar	
Seth Sukh Lal (Sirsa)	10,00,000
Ms. Ramnarain - Jailal (Bhiwani)	5,59,750
L. Tara Chand (Bhiwani)	5,40,250
L. Jagan Nath Balu	1,41,100
Ch. Chhaju Ram (Alakhpura)	1,40,000
Ch. Sher Singh (Hansi)	1,35,000
L. Raghu Nath (Hansi)	1,15,000
L. Ram Sahay family (Sirsa)	1,06,000
L. Ballu Ram (Hetampura)	1,04,000
Ms. Narsingh Bhuramal (Bhiwani)	1,02,000
Ms. Sukh Lal (Sirsa)	1,00,000
Khan Yakinuddin (Sirsa)	66,000
Ms. Ramnarani (Bhiwani)	56,000
Ms. Tara Chand (Bhiwani)	55,000
Ch. Sodhekhan (Shekhpura)	55,000
Ms. A. Lalit	52,000
L. Chhabil Das (Hisar)	50,000
K. Abdul Gaffur Khan (Hisar)	50,000
District Rohtak	
L. Lachhmi Narain (Beri)	55,000
Mahant Puran Nath (Asthal Bohar)	51,000
District Gurgaon	
L. Behari Lal (Rewari)	65,000
L. Jagan Nath (Gurawara)	55,000
District Karnal	
Seth Jwala Singh (Jharoli)	1,21,400
Seth Lakhmi Chand (Panipat)	1,21,400

Why, one may ask here, the people of Haryana behaved this way? Were they inspired by the thought of protection of the British Empire? Or were they touched by the fact that the British government were fighting the war to save and safeguard the nobler things like 'honour, freedom and Justice'? Not, precisely: none of these things was there. The Haryana elite, like their counterparts elsewhere, were not so naive as to believe that it was 'their War' or the British were fighting it for safeguarding great values—'honour, freedom and justice' world over—when they had robbed them of all these things.[9] They were, in fact, helping them for serving their own interests: the nationalist leaders for getting something like 'concessions' or reforms' for the country, other elites for personal favours, like *Rai Bahaduri*, *Khan Bahaduri*, *Sardar Bahaduri* or membership of the councils of the governors/viceroy; and 'non-classmen'—peasants, etc.—for monetary gains, for most of them were awfully poor and unemployed.[10]

This was one side of the coin bearing pro-government disposition. But on the other side of the coin, astoundingly, an altogether different scribbling—an anti-Government, anti-war scribbling—which said in so many words 'fight, not for the government, but for *swaraj*—self or Home Rule', as advised by the 'extremist' nationalist leader Lokamanya Bal Gangadhar Tilak.

Home Rule Movement

In Haryana, the leader of the above mentioned movement was Pt. Neki Ram Sharma—'a rebel with a cause'.[11] He was born on 8 December 1877 in a Brahmana family of Kelanga, a small village in district Bhiwani. His father, Pt. Hari Prasad was an erudite scholar of Sanskrit. Small wonder then, the sapient child was given good education in the ancient language, first at home, and then at Sitapur (Oudh) and Benaras.

Neki Ram became interested in nationalistic politics while studying at Benaras. However, as time passed this interest changed into a passion with him.[12] He wrote a very strong indictment of the British government on Lala Lajpat Rai's deportation in 1907. The government took a serious note of it and marked him as 'a dangerous man' in their records. This had, however, no effect on the young man who kept the flame burning. He had a special liking for Lokamanya Bal Gangadhar Tilak and took to his programme of Home Rule in a big way, first in Madhya Pradesh and then in Haryana (1917).

This being the war time, the deputy commissioner of Rohtak warned Neki Ram 'not to do any such thing in his district'. Neki Ram refused to oblige the officer and kept his activities going. The officer tried another trick: this time he offered him 25 acres of land, should he mend his ways. 'No way', replied Neki Ram, 'not even 25,000 acres, or even more would satisfy me. I want the whole of India, its entire land, for it belongs to me. Unhappy and enraged, the district chief asked him to leave his office which he did at once.[13]

The deputy commissioner wanted to take serious action against Neki Ram. But his superiors did not allow. For they knew that Neki Ram had no following at that time, in the war days, in Haryana and, therefore, he could hardly create any problem for them. The district chief had no other alternative but to agree to the sane advice. And Neki Ram was left where he was. He tried to arouse the masses for *swaraj* (Home Rule). Unhappily, however, there was no response. The British bureaucracy was right: the rebel from Kelanga could not do anything worthwhile.[14]

War Impact on Haryana

The above discussion shows that every caste, class and collectivity in Haryana supported the war efforts to the best of their abilities and means. The peasants gave men; the wealthy traders, bankers, *zamindars* and other rich men gave money, material and other services. But what did the government give these people in return of their services and help? Many persons were given titles—*Rai Bahaduri*, *Khan Bahaduri* and *Sardar Bahaduri*, *Kurshinashini sanads*, *jagirs*, recruiting badges, etc., as Table 3 shows.

Who were these lucky persons who were rewarded by the government? Were they the ones who had fought bloody battles at the front and humbled their deadly foe? Were they the ones who had given everything

TABLE 3: REWARDS FOR WAR SERVICES[15]

District	No. of awards	Sword of honour	Seat in durbar	Jagirs	land (rectangles)	Recruiting badge
Hisar	12	2	3	4	18	7
Rohtak	14	6	2	4	28	13
Karnal	6	2	3	–	19	6
Ambala	12	3	4	–	34	12
Gurgaon	5	6	2	2	13	20
Total	49	19	14	10	112	58

TABLE 4: CLASSIFICATION OF REWARDEES[16]

Category	Titles	Jagir	Land (rectangles)	Seat in provincial or dist. durbar
Rajas, Nawabs and Jagirdars	6	–	16	–
Landlords	29	9	102	9
Traders	13	1	8	3
Other Upper Middle Classman	5	2	6	3

that they had got—even their precious lives—to win the war? Were they the humble peasants from villages who parted with their most precious assets—their young, newly wedded sons—smilingly for a cause? No, none of these was there the receipens and awards were those who contributed small fraction of money which they had amassed by indulging in foul trade, black-marketing etc. to the war Fund they were those who helped in the recruitment drive. They were the so-called class people, as shown in Table 4.

What a justice! What a reward! Surely, the non-class people were wronged. But that was not the end of it. There were many more sufferings in store for these neglected people. Soon after the war was over, the government took to demobilization in the army which rendered thousands of able-bodied young, poor soldiers jobless. They got no pension or any other means for subsistence[17]. There was shortage of everything. Prices, even of essential commodities, went sky-high. As a result, the poor suffered a great deal in both the villages and towns. And so did the petty shopkeepers, businessmen and traders who were over-taxed in many ways to overcome the financial strain of the war. Some new industries[18] which came up then to meet the war needs of the Army hit the poor artisans, who lived on small scale, industries and traditional crafts. They became jobless and paupers.[19]

In a way, the post-War conditions made almost every section of our population, excepting of course the upper middle classes of collaborators to the raj, unhappy with the government. Gandhiji, who had come on the Indian political scene by now, capitalized on this situation and started an all-India movement against the government, as we shall see in the next chapter.

NOTES

1. L.E. Snellgrove, *The Modern World Since 1870*, p. 81.
2. See K.C. Yadav, *Haryana*, vol. II, pp. 183-99.
3. M.S. Leigh, *The Punjab and the War*, pp. 119-26.
4. K.C. Yadav, *Haryana*, vol. II, pp. 183-99.
5. Ibid.
6. Ibid.
7. Ibid.
8. Ibid.
9. Ibid.
10. Ibid.
11. See *Pt. Neki Ram Sharma Abhinandana Grantha*, pp. 122-40.
12. Ibid.
13. Ibid.
14. Ibid.
15. K.C. Yadav, *Haryana*, vol. II, pp. 186-96.
16. Ibid.
17. Ibid.
18. For instance, cotton industries at Bhiwani and Hisar and metal industries at Rewari.
19. Jagdish Chandra, *Freedom Struggle in Haryana*, pp. 108-9.

12

The Struggle for Freedom, Second Phase, 1919-1928

As noted in the preceding chapter, the people of India had stood by and large by the British in their hour of great crisis during the war, 1914-18. They spared no effort and grudged no help. They gave them men, money and material generously and even extravagantly, thinking that after the War was won and the British honour and glory restored, the grateful nation would give them their legitimate rights. Surprisingly, however, what they got instead was demobilization which threw thousands of people out of employment, scarcity and black-marketing, dearth and diseases which took heavy toll of life. Such a situation as this was bound to create considerable resentment and disaffection in the country. And it really did: the townsfolk and villagers, the traders and peasants, the rich and the poor, almost everyone, experienced a feeling of having been cheated by the government.

Was the government ignorant of all this? Not exactly; they saw the crisis written on the wall and planned to arrest if it could not be averted. As early as 20 April 1917 Montague, the secretary of state for India tried 'to apply balm over the lacerated Indian wounds' by his famous declaration—'We are soon going to take an effective step towards the progressive realization of responsible government in India as an integral part of the British Empire.' This was followed by the reforms of 1918-19 which gave, among other things, 'a bicameral legislature with elected majorities chosen by enlarged electorates but without having any power to control the ministry or stand against the Viceroy empowered with a veto at the centre'; and a dyarchy where 'the ministers responsible to the legislature were given departments with less political weight and little funds as against the officials who controlled important departments, like law and order and finance, and provincial governors, armed with veto and immense power' at the provincial level.[1]

The Rowlatt Act Agitation

Simultaneously, a step was also taken in other direction. In December, 1917, a committee headed by Sir Sidney Rowlatt was appointed to investigate the causes of the rising tide of militant nationalism in India and to suggest ways and means to check it.[2] By December 1918, the committee had completed its work, when it submitted a 22-page report on the subject, suggesting among other things passing of two bills 'to curb the menace of terrorism'.[3] Consequently, the government of India presented to the central legislature two bills—the Criminal Law Emergency Powers Bill and the Criminal Law Amendment Bill. There was stiff opposition to the bills on the part of the public, and it was perhaps owing to this that the first Bill was withdrawn by the government on 18 March. Now only the second Bill remained which *inter alia* provided for several highly objectionable provisions, the chief among which were as follows:

(a) If the government so desired, it could order the arrest of any politically dangerous person without warrant;
(b) the government could effect the confinement of any such person in such place and under such conditions and restrictions as specified; and
(c) the government could conduct the search of any place mentioned in the order.

The Bill also provided for keeping in jail the political persons arrested under the Defence of India Rules even after the expiry of the time limit of the DIR. No order under this Act could be called in question in any court, and no suit or prosecution or other legal proceedings could lie against any person for anything done under this Act. Any person actively concerned in any movement which, in the opinion of the government, were likely to lead to the commission of offence against the state, could be given all or any of the following directions:

(a) That such person shall execute a bond for good conduct for a period not exceeding one year;
(b) shall remain or reside in any area specified in the order;
(c) shall notify his residence and any change of residence as ordered;
(d) shall abstain from any act which in the opinion of the local government was calculated to disturb public peace or was prejudicial to the public safety; and
(e) shall report himself to such police officer and at such periods as may be specified in the order.

This order 'could continue in force for a period of one month only but if a person was found guilty by an inquiry committee which would carry out its work in camera not being bound to observe the rules of the law of evidence, the period could be extended to one year and even more'.[4]

The Bill was considered as 'unjust, subversive of the principle of the liberty of the subjects, and destructive of the elementary right of an individual'. Gandhiji, therefore, gave a call to his countrymen to challenge it with all the strength that they could muster, for submitting to such laws 'was like forfeiting one's humanity and accepting slavery'.[5] Victorious in the war, the government, however, did not bother about the criticism or public opposition to the Bill and passed it on 18 March 1919.

As a reaction, Gandhiji asked his countrymen to observe hartal on 30 March 1919 throughout the length and breadth of the country, observing fast, offering prayers, and holding meetings and passing resolutions against the 'black law'. As the notice period was thought to be too short to reach every part of India properly, the dates were changed to 6 April 1919.[6] The people of Haryana took the message pretty seriously and observed hartals from 30 March to 6 April as shown in Table 1.

The above account shows that hartals were observed in almost all the cities and towns in Haryana. According to official records, the hartals were held in most of the cases without any persuasion. The meetings were well-attended—some of them having as big an audiences as 10,000. The people wore black clothes or *matmi-kapre* (black mourning clothes) from top to bottom. On being asked as to why did they do so, their reply invariably was: 'The king has died. Hence the mourning dress.' Hindus and Muslims showed remarkable unity. And so did the people of different classes—even the lowest among the low seemed to have been fired with patriotic fervour. For instance, Rev. Carylon, a missionary died at Rohtak. No carpenter came forward to make his coffin and no labourer was available to dig his grave. The district authorities had to make strenuous efforts for six long hours to get some men from outside the town to do the work.[8] Not only the towns but even the villages were astir. There the peasants stood up in arms against the *zalim* sarkar in a big way. The artisan, and other, too, stood up with them. It is amazing that a good number of women in towns, especially in Hisar and Bhiwani, came forward and worked to make the agitation a grand success. Illiterates, prisoners of *purdah*, *burqa* and *ghunghat*, who hardly stirred out of their homes were the active soldiers of freedom now!

A pertinent question arises here: How could the anti-Rowlatt Act agitation become so popular in Haryana? Educated people in cities and

TABLE 1: ANTI-ROWLATT ACT HARTALS OBSERVED IN HARYANA, 30 MARCH-6 APRIL 1919[9]

Date	Place	Hartals	Nature of meetings	Speeches/ Resolutions, etc.
30 March	Rohtak	Partial	–	–
	Karnal	"	–	–
	Ambala	"	–	–
	Panipat	"	General meeting	Speeches and resolutions
2 April	Ambala City	"	"	"
	Rewari	"	"	"
4 April	Karnal	Partial	"	"
5 April	Bahadurgarh	Complete	"	"
6 April	Ambala City	Partial	"	"
	Ballabhgarh	Complete	"	"
	Faridabad	Complete	"	"
	Palwal	"	"	"
	Rewari	"	"	"
	Gurgaon	Partial	"	"
	Bhiwani	Complete	"	"
	Hisar	"	"	"
	Hansi	Partial	"	"
	Karnal	Complete	"	"
	Panipat	Partial	"	"
	Bahadurgarh	Complete	"	"
	Rohtak	Partial	"	"
	Sonepat	Complete	"	"
	Satrod	"	"	"

towns might have known a bit about it but not the illiterate, rustic mass of people living in villages. How did they join the movement? The explanation in simple terms is that local leaders sold the Act differently to different people.[10] For those who were Arya Samajists, it was a sacred *yajna* to undo the shackles of bondage of *Bharatamata* (Mother India). Each Arya was duty-bound, therefore, to put his *ahuti* (offering) into it[11] (*yajna*). For some rich or middle peasants the Act was an instrument to make them part with their land in excess of 30 *bighas*. For others it had something to do with the government sharing 1/2 of their produce or taking away food grains in excess of 9 maunds per family. And so forth.[12] The women activists were active, for they had taken a vow—at the time of their marriage—to lend their hand to their spouses in whatever work they did. For some others it was a some sort of a religious duty given by a *Mahatma*. An example: a sweepress at Hisar gave notice to his officer that she would not come on duty on 6 April (1919) as that was 'a sacred day of fasting'. On being questioned as to what the fast was about, she could not say anything. The officer then explained everything to her in very simple terms. Nothing could convince her, however, and she did not attend to her duty on 6 April.[13] Thus different persons took to the agitation for different reasons.

The agitation ran its course very effectively. However, to add more fuel to it, Swami Shraddhananda and other leaders invited Gandhiji to visit Delhi and Punjab (including Haryana). Gandhiji accepted the invitation. The Punjab government, however, banned Gandhiji's entry into the province (9 April). Gandhiji defied the order. In consequence, he was arrested at Palwal (10 April). This was his first arrest in India.

The people reacted sharply to the arrest of their beloved leader. Hartals were promptly observed in almost every city and town throughout Haryana. Even villages were astir. The Hindus and Muslims vowed to fight their battle together.[14] On 13 April yet another dastardly tragedy—Jallianwala Bagh massacre—occurred which shook the people's faith in the government. Some of them lost control over their saner nerves. In consequence, the agitation turned violent at a number of places[15] as shown in Table 2.

Unnerved by these activities, the Punjab government placed the districts of Karnal and Gurgaon under the Police Act.[16] Rohtak and Hisar were already covered by the Seditious Meetings Act (1907). Thus the entire region came under the tight control of the police. Meetings were banned, Congress and Arya Samaj activists were harassed. The loyalists were encouraged to counteract the movement by hook or by crook. For instance, on 22 April a meeting was organized at Rohtak by some Muslims who opposed the movement. Two days later, a similar meeting was held in the Jama Masjid at Hisar. On 26 April, a similar meeting was called at Hansi. The same day, some loyalist Muslims took a vow at Sirsa

TABLE 2: VIOLENT INCIDENTS IN HARYANA

Nature of incidents	No. of incidents
Railway stations attacked/damaged	2
Telegraphs wires cut	4 places
Post office attacked	1
Govt. buildings burnt	2

to support the government at every cost. Similar thing happened at Hodel, district Gurgaon, next day. The Municipal Committee, Palwal passed a resolution to remain loyal to the government (30 April). Some Hindus did so at Hisar the same day.[17] These measures, however, had little effect on the movement. Almost all towns and cities were under its influence. And so were most of the villages in Rohtak and Hisar districts where Arya Samaj was strong. But elsewhere—in districts of Gurgaon, Karnal and Ambala—the villages remained in most of the cases uninfluenced, thanks to the efforts of their traditional chaudharis who were loyal to the Raj.[18]

The Khilafat Movement

Meantime, another powerful all-India agitation, popularly called the Khilafat Movement was started. The Muslims all over the world accepted the Sultan of Turkey as their *khalifa* (religious teacher) and held him in high esteem. He was opposed to the British during the first World War and as such the former treated him shabbily after the war. According to the treaty of Serves, 1920, the office of the *khalifa* was virtually extincted and his entire empire dismembered. This infuriated Muslims in India who started the Khilafat agitation in support of their *khalifa.* Gandhiji gave his blessings to the movement and asked his Hindu brethren to side with the Muslims in their moment of crisis.[19] The 10,33,530 Muslims in Haryana had by and large, like their counterparts elsewhere, great sympathy for the Khilafat. They waged *jehad* (religious war) against the British. Ambala, Karnal, Panipat, Rohtak, Jhajjar, Hisar and Sirsa became the main centres of the *jehad* in no time. Hundreds of people came forward and joined the movement under their leaders (Table 3) who belonged to different classes. Most of them came from urban centres.[20]

The movement was quite successful throughout the state. The government felt unnerved and they launched a double-pronged attack on the agitators. To begin with, they asked the loyal element to educate their misguided brothers. There was prompt obedience and a Khairkhawah Majlis was formed with its branches at Bhiwani, Rohtak, Gurgaon and Karnal.[21] Simultaneously, the government took to strong arm methods. Almost all the leaders, referred to above, were arrested and their followers warned of serious consequences should they not pay heed to the voice of peace.[22]

The efforts of the government bore the desired fruits. The leaderless

TABLE 3: PROMINENT KHILAFAT LEADERS IN HARYANA

District	Leader	Position
Ambala	1. Abdul Rashid	Lawyer
	2. Ghulam Bhik Nairang	Lawyer
	3. Khan Abdul Gaffar Khan	Landlord
	4. Hanif Khan	Businessman
	5. Shaminullah	Businessman
Karnal	1. Laqnullah Khan	Landlord
	2. Sufi Iqbal	Landlord
	3. Usmani	Landlord
	4. Sanaullah	Landlord
Gurgaon	1. Mohd. Yasin Khan	Landlord
	2. Abdul Ghani Dar	Businessman
	3. Yaqub Khan	Ex. J.C.O. (Army)
Rohtak	1. Bashir Ahmad	Haqim
	2. Zamin Ali	Businessman
	3. Alauddin	Businessman
	4. Abdul Aziz	Shopkeeper
	5. Khair Mohd. Khan	Businessman
	6. Mohd. Shafi	Businessman
	7. Habibul Khan	Landlord
	8. Jan Muhammad	Municipal Commissioner
	9. Mustaq Hussain	Lawyer

movement began to peter out. But fortunately, another powerful movement—the Non-Cooperation Movement, took over it before it could die down.

The Non-Cooperation Movement

In view of the government's failure to listen to the voice of sanity to undo the Punjab wrongs and to solve the Khilafat problem, the Indian National Congress blared the bugle of non-cooperation against the government in August 1920. Gandhiji, the supreme leader of the move-ment, set the following programme to be followed to make the Non-Cooperation Movement a success:

(a) surrender of titles, honorary offices and resignation from seats in local bodies;
(b) refusal to attend government and other official and semi-official functions held by the government;

(c) gradual withdrawal of children from schools, colleges owned, aided or controlled by government and their sending to national schools and colleges;
(d) boycott of British courts by lawyers and litigants and establishment of private arbitration courts by their aid for the settlement of private disputes;
(e) withdrawal of candidates for elections to the reformed councils; refusal on the part of the voters to vote for any candidate who might stand despite the Congress advice;
(f) boycott of foreign goods and adoption of *swadeshi* revival through hand spinning and hand weaving;
(g) collection of a crore of rupees for the Tilak Swaraj Fund; and
(h) enrolment of Congress members.[23]

The movement became popular in Haryana. A political conference was held at Panipat on 10 October 1920 under the chairmanship of Lala Lajpat Rai. Thousands of people took the vow of non-cooperation here.[24] On 22 October, the first Ambala divisional political conference was held at Bhiwani. Mahatma Gandhi along with Ali Brothers, Maulana Abul Kalam Azad, and Swami Satyadeva attended the conference. It was presided over by Babu Murlidhar, the Grand Old Man of Punjab. About 15 to 20 thousand persons were present in the conference. Gandhiji made a historic speech on the occasion, *Hamari yah saltanat shaitan ki saltanat hai* (This government of ours is a satanic government). To deal with the satanic government they hit upon the remedy of non-violent non-cooperation. He then explained the programme of non-cooperation to the people and exhorted them to suppress their anger and refrain from violence and make self sacrifice. If 33 crore Indians, said the Mahatma, adopted non-cooperation, the Khilafat and the Punjab wrongs could be righted and *swaraj* attained within a year.[25]

On 6-8 November 1920 Sham Lal of Rohtak organized another political conference at Rohtak to strengthen the movement. It was in this meeting that the Jat leader Chhotu Ram left the Congress, for he had no faith in the scheme of non-cooperation.[26] Elsewhere, however, things moved smoothly. Resolutions supporting the programme of non-cooperation were passed almost at every town. Villagers too came in thousands to make the movement a success'. A large number of students left colleges and schools. The Jat and Vaishya Schools, Rohtak and Hindu High School, Sonepat, disaffiliated themselves from the Punjab University. Students left Bahadurgarh High School, Rohtak Gaur School, Kalanaur School and Jhajjar School in large numbers.[27]

The elders, too, behaved well. The honours provided by the government were given up. Murlidhar (Ambala) renounced his title of *Rai Sahib* conferred upon him in 1989. He also surrendered his *sanads*, badges, and *Kaiser-i-Hind* silver medal (of 1904) on 16 August 1920. Mirza Nazir Beg, Ganapat Rai, Gokal Chand, Nainsukh Das threw away their *kursi-nashini* medals and certificates. Jem. Akhe Ram of Mitathal (Bhiwani) returned his recruiting badge and *sanads*. About a dozen of lambardars and zaildars renounced their posts. In January 1922, about 14 persons tendered their resignations from government jobs. An activist preached to the recruits who were about to be sent to their respective posting centres by the assistant recruiting officers at the Hisar railway station platform and succeeded in inducing one recruit to leave the newly acquired post.[28] There was boycott of courts by lawyers. Duni Chand of Ambala gave up his practice at the High Court at Lahore;[29] Abdul Rashid, Gulam Bhik and Durga Charan did that in Ambala. In Hisar Sham Lal left his lucrative practice.[30] His friends and followers followed him. Sham Lal a leading advocate of Rohtak, and Ram Chander Vaid, Dwarka Das, Abdul Majid and Jugal Kishore of Karnal also did likewise.

There was boycott of government courts by litigants.[31] The cases were taken to national courts (*rashtriye nayayalaya*) of which the one at Bhiwani inaugurated by K.A. Desai on 26 May 1921 was quite popular. This court had eight benches. Elsewhere, the programme was not successful, however.[32] And so was the case with the Municipal Committees. Except for the Jhajjar Municipal Committee,[33] no other committee came forward to nationalize itself. The programme of boycott of elections to the Punjab Legislative Council held this time was successful in towns. But not in villages where the Unionists had their hold over the voters.[34]

The boycott of foreign goods was, however, successful. Murlidhar and his friends Duni Chand and Abdul Ghaffar Khan made it in Ambala. In Karnal the visit of Swami Shraddhananda made great impact. Gurgaon district, too, did not lag behind in the propagation of the *swadeshi*. A wedding ceremony in Rewari was postponed as the bridgegroom refused to marry the bride clad in foreign clothes.[35] In the district of Rohtak splendid work was done by Sham Lal, Shri Ram Sharma and other members of the District Congress Committee. Bonfires of foreign clothes were the most usual scenes in the city these day.[36] To hot up the agitation further, the programme of mass satyagraha was launched on 2 January 1922. By a rough estimate, about 500 persons—400 in Haryana and 100 outside the state (in Delhi and Dharsana-Gujarat)—courted arrest from Haryana during the movement.[37]

Surprisingly, despite these facts, a general notion persists that the people of Haryana did not play any part in this struggle. The reason given for their 'apathy' is that during the period, i.e. from 1885 to 1922, the people here were backward in almost every walk of life. They had no political awareness. Hence this state of affairs. The people here were backward no doubt. But still they had political awakening and awareness, for the reasons explained elsewhere. Not only that, they took more active interest in the movement than their counterparts in the better placed parts of Punjab, is evident from the fact that out of the total arrests of 719 in Punjab, Haryana's share was about 500. Haryana constituted about 18.8 per cent of Punjab's population then. Because of this position its share of arrests should have been 135 only. In other activities also, like leaving of schools, and colleges by students, boycotting of courts by lawyers and litigants, going for *swadeshi*, etc., their contribution was equally significant. Nowhere in Punjab, the villagers and women participated so enthusiastically and in such a large a number as is in this region. In Bhiwani, for instance 10,000 women gathered in a political meeting on 16 February 1921. They took out processions there and at Hisar.[38]

On 4 February 1922, a violent tragedy took place at Chauri Chaura in Gorakhpur—the non-cooperators burnt alive 23 policemen there. Gandhiji was moved by this violent incident and he at once withdrew the movement.

New Political Developments

As elsewhere, the withdrawal of the movement gave a sort of setback to the movement in Haryana also. The Congressmen were divided into two camps: (i) Swarajists who wanted to give up non-cooperation (also called pro-changers); and (ii) non-cooperationists (also called non-changers) who pledged to stick to the earlier programme. In Haryana the former were in great majority. And they made quite some effort to put the national movement back on the rails. A young man, Shri Ram Sharma of Rohtak deserves special mention here. He played a very significant role in revitalizing the movement. He started a newspaper, *Haryana Tilak,* from Rohtak in 1923 and took the message of his party to the masses.[39] He looked after the organizational aspect of the movement effectively. As a result, he came in direct clash with Ch. Chhotu Ram who had formed the Unionist Party by then (1923). But he did not bother and did his work effectively.[40]

The Congress-Unionist clash was sharpened still further during the

TABLE 4: ELECTION RESULTS, 1923[41]

Constituencies			Party position	Seats won
Central Assembly		1	Congress	1
Punjab Council				
Non-Mohammedan	Towns	1	Congress	1
	Rural	5	Congress	1
			Unionists	4
Mohammedan	Towns	1	Unionists	1
	Rural	2	Unionists	2

elections of 1923. Both the parties did their best to win the elections. They put up good candidates and did a lot of propaganda. But the results were in no way different from what the anticipations were. The Congress won most of the urban seats where its social base was wide. The Unionists won all but one rural seats. The entire position has been statistically explained in Table 4.

In the new Punjab ministry formed after the elections, Rai Bahadur Lal Chand from Rohtak was made a minister of cabinet rank. Lal Chand's stars did not favour him, however, for no sooner he occupied the ministerial chair than he was unseated by an election petition. But his loss was Chhotu Ram's gain: the lieutenant-governor offered the ministerial *gaddi* to the young friend of Lal Chand.[42]

Chhotu Ram was intelligent, resourceful and dynamic. He was also an organizer *par excellence*. He injected a part of his personality into his party's body-politic and made it a first rate organization.[43] Besides this, fate also favoured this man. His opponents, the Swarajists suffered many a setback in quick succession. On 16 June, the leading light of Swarajists, C.R. Dass died. This led to a split in the party which weakened it a great deal. After some time, another split came. Lala Lajpat Rai, Gopi Chand Bhargava and other so-called responsivists and independent Congressmen formed a coalition party known as the Independent Congress Party (ICP). Many Congressmen in Haryana led by Neki Ram Sharma joined the ICP.[44]

In the meantime elections came again (1926). The Swarajists were demoralized, whereas their opponents—the Unionists—were on the top of the world. The contest was indeed uneven. And the result was again what was expected—the Unionists won five seats, the Hindu Mahasabha bagged two, and the Swarajists could snatch only one.[45] Sir Malcolm Hailey, the then lieutenant-governor of Punjab was not well disposed towards Sir Chhotu Ram. He, therefore, did not appoint him minister in his new cabinet. This was a setback for the Unionist Party, especially in Haryana.[46] The Congress which was demoralized took courage and re-organized itself. It got a shot in its arm on the advent of the all white Simon Commission in 1928 for reviewing the progress of the working of the 1919 reforms in India.[47] The Congress leadership regarded the exclusion of Indians from the Commission as a direct insult to the intelligentsia of this country and they proposed its boycott. The people of Haryana endorsed the decision with one voice.[48]

On 30 October (1928), the Simon Commission went to Lahore, where it was opposed by a huge crowd headed by Lala Lajpat Rai. The police lathi-charged the crowd, not sparing even Lajpat Rai. This hurt the old lion and he passed away on 17 November. As elsewhere, there was genuine sorrow throughout Haryana. Condolence meetings were held at almost every town and business was suspended as a mark of respect to the great leader. The villagers, too, did not lag behind. There, too, the crime was condemned.[49]

The blood of the martyrs, it is said, and rightly of course, gives life to a movement. Lalaji's blood gave life to the nationalist movement, as also to the Congress which was in bad shape in 1928. Substantiation: in its 1929 session at Lahore the Congress felt so strong as to pass a resolution for *purana swaraj* (complete freedom), as we shall see in the next chapter.

NOTES

1. For details see Sumit Sarkar, *Modern India*, pp. 167-8.
2. The other members of the Committee were: Sir Basil Scott, the Chief Justice of Bombay High Court; Sir Verney Loyatt, Member of the U.P. Board of Revenue; Dewan Bahadur C.V.K. Shastri, Judge of the Madras High Court; and R.C. Mitter, Vakil of the Calcutta High Court.
3. The Committee submitted its report on 15 April 1918. After much deliberations the Government drafted two bills and presented them to the Central Legislative Assembly on 18 January 1919.
4. For details see M.K. Gandhi, *The Collected Works*, vol. XV, pp. 110-18.
5. Ibid., p. 110.
6. For details see Jagdish Chandra, *Freedom Struggle in Haryana*, pp. 26-7.
7. Ibid.
8. Ibid.
9. K.C. Yadav, *Haryana*, vol. II, pp. 200-22.
10. A general notion persists that the anti-Rowlatt Act agitation did not touch villages. Its social backward base was restricted to the towns alone. Nothing could be farther from truth than this.

11. See, for instance, the exhortations of Swami Shraddhananda, Swami Satyadeva, Indra Vidyavachaspati and other Arya leaders.
12. Based on a poster of 17 April 1919 entitled 'Galat aur Bebunnyad Afwaon Ki Tardid', issued by Ch. Lal Chand, a loyalist activist of Bhalaut (Rohtak).
13. NAI, Home Ministry, File no. 1416, 24 May 1919.
14. NAI, Home Political Proceedings, nos. 114-62, April 1919.
15. Ibid.
16. Based on confidential files relating to the movement in April 1919 in different districts of Haryana.
17. Ibid.
18. For these loyalists see NAI, Home Political A, Proceedings, nos. 86-92, January 1921.
19. For details about the movement see A.C. Niemeijet, *The Khilafat Movement in India*; R.C. Majumdar, *History of the Freedom Movement in India*, vol. III.
20. For details see Jagdish Chandra, op. cit., pp. 37-8.
21. Ibid.
22. Ibid.
23. For details see NAI, Home Political A, no. 106, July 1920.
24. Jagdish Chandra, op. cit., pp. 36-40.
25. See NAI, Home Political A, nos. 183-6, December 1920.
26. For details see *The Tribune*, 13 November 1920.
27. K.C. Yadav, *Haryana*, vol. II, pp. 200-22.
28. Ibid.
29. Ibid.
30. Ibid.
31. Ibid.
32. Ibid.
33. This was done with great effort. The government came very heavily on the agitators and jailed their leader Pt. Shri Ram Sharma.
34. In the towns 6 to 17 per cent of people voted. But in villages the percentage was higher—53 per cent in Gurgaon and 32 per cent to 48 per cent in other districts.
35. AICC Papers, Report of the Work done by the Congress in Punjab, 1922, part III, p. 145.
36. *The Tribune*, 6 August 1921.
37. Estimate based on official records and information given by freedom fighters.
38. *The Tribune*, 18 February 1921: The ladies donated their ornaments after the meeting.
39. K.C. Yadav, *The Builders of Our Nation,* vol. II: *Shri Ram Sharma*, for details.
40. Ibid.
41. See K.C. Yadav, *Elections in Punjab, 1919-1947* (hereafter *Elections*), pp. 52-60.

42. See K.C. Yadav, *Haryana*, vol. II, pp. 200-22.
43. Ibid.
44. Ibid.
45. Ibid.
46. Ibid.
47. Ibid.
48. Ibid.
49. HSA, Conf. files of DC Rohtak, no. 118: Civil Disobedience Movement.

13

The Struggle for Freedom: Third Phase, 1929-1936

The year 1929 had opened on a very disturbing note. The death of Lala Lajpat Rai about this very time worsened the situation still further. The Indian National Congress made the fullest use of the situation and passed a historic resolution in its historic meeting on the banks of the river Ravi at Lahore on 31 December 1929: We want *purna swaraj*[1] (complete freedom), here and now! Soon after, as the night fell and the clock struck 12, they unfurled the flag of liberty. It was the beginning of a new year—1930—and a new era—of freedom, peace and prosperity!

This was a glad tiding for the entire Indian nation. The people—a large number of them, if not all—welcomed the decision. On 26 January 1930, they, as directed by the Congress High Command, passed the following resolution:

> The British Government in India has not only deprived the Indian people of their freedom but has based itself on the exploitation of the masses and has ruined India economically, politically, culturally and spiritually. We believe, therefore, that India must severe its connection with the British and attain complete independence and take a solemn pledge to do their very best to transform the resolution into a working reality.[2]

The people in Haryana, especially those who were under the influence of the Congress, also behaved likewise. The Government, too, took the matter pretty seriously and came very heavily, especially in district Rohtak, on the nationalists. The Congress leaders were arrested and jailed for no offence. Baba Kashi Ram, a member of the Municipal Committee, Sonepat was, for instance, removed from the membership of the Committee and put behind the bars for singing a patriotic song in a *purna swaraj*[3] meeting. Lala Ramsaran Das from Bahadurgarh was sentenced to three years rigorous imprisonment for a 'rebellious speech'.[4]

Many other nationalists were also arrested and jailed for years on very minor or concocted offences. Surprisingly, the oppression had no effect on the people who continued their fight for *swaraj*.

The Civil Disobedience Movement

Gandhiji warned the Government to give at least some concessions to the people which would make their lives worth living, if not the *purna swaraj* that they have pledged to go for. The government turned down Gandhiji's offer with all the contempt at their command. Now the only course open for the Mahatma was to launch a civil disobedience movement to dislodge the government. And that he did by breaking the government's salt laws at Dandi, a village on the sea coast in Gujarat, about 240 miles from his Sabarmati Ashram.

It was a signal to the nation to defy the greatest imperial power in the world by breaking its laws. The Haryana nationalists had made elaborate plans to break salt laws in a grand manner at a village called Zahidpur (also called Wahed Pur) near Jhajjar where they had taken on lease brackish water wells. What these plans were like can be seen from the following excerpt from an intercepted letter of Sham Lal, President, DCC, Rohtak, to Dr. Khan Chand Dev, Secretary, PCC, Lahore:

> The first batch of 10 volunteers will start under my supervision at 4 p.m. on the 6th April. Passing through various villages and preaching propaganda it will reach Zahidpur on the evening of the 15th April. The Deputy Commissioner will be informed on the Ist April. We have chalked out a programme. We shall go on foot (to prepare salt on 16 April).
>
> If some other leading gentlemen of the province intend to join this Civil Disobedience they can do so by all pleasure. It would be better if you appeal to other Districts of the Ambala Division to join the Rohtak District Civil Disobedience and to send the names of volunteers to the Secretary, District Congress Committee. Please, render all help in this matter which you can. Please, send instructions, if any, and inform us if there is any other programme for the province.
>
> If you think proper, you may make this place as a centre for Civil Disobedience for the whole province or at least for the Ambala Division. In that case you will have to do all work. We shall do what duty is assigned to us. In that case the first *jatha* should be led by the President of the Provincial Congress Committee. We shall not do anything without your sanction. Please write soon.[5]

The government took the whole thing very seriously—so much so that they fraudulently cancelled the lease of the salt wells and arrested Lala Sham Lal, President, DCC, Rohtak and Pt. Shri Ram Sharma and others proceeding to Zahidpur for breaking salt laws. But this could not check the breach of salt laws at other places. The District Congress Committee, Rohtak manufactured salt near Kalalan Mohalla temple at Rohtak on 10 April. It was done openly. The crowd was big and defiant. The police, too, was in large numbers but they preferred to witness the law-breaking ceremony in silence rather than taking any action in the matter.[6] The process was repeated at Jhajjar on 13 April, again openly and defiantly. Here, too, the police watched the spectacle silently. The same thing happened at Sonepat, Beri, Sanghi and in many other big villages in the district.[7]

Like Rohtak, Gurgaon was also active. Salt was prepared here at Rewari on 20 April. It was a tedious work: the law-breakers could prepare only about 10 gram salt after a good deal of efforts. But when auctioned it brought a good amount—Rs. 1,040. On 23 April, a big meeting was organized at this very place which was attended among others by Pt. Neki Ram Sharma and Kharak Bahadur, a special representative of Mahatma Gandhi. They congratulated the people of Rewari for defying salt laws and exhorted them to be ready to make greater sacrifices. The government did not like these 'seditious activities' and they arrested Mahashe Bhagwan Das and 13 other activists who were running the show in the town. But it hardly made any impact on the movement which went on unabated.[8]

The next to catch the contagion was Hisar. Here the people organized a very big meeting at Bhiwani on 13 April to prepare salt. It was presided over by Pt. Neki Ram Sharma. As many as 5,000 persons attended the meeting. The salt was prepared—about 3/4 pound. When auctioned it fetched Rs. 250. Hisar was touched on 27 April. About 1,000 persons prepared salt openly in a public meeting.[9] The people of Sirsa, Hansi and Fatehabad also behaved likewise.[10]

The salt laws were torn into a hundred pieces at Ambala too. Astoundingly, the activists who did it were women. Led by Vidyavati, the daughter of Dunichand Ambalavi, they did the job right heroically. Their men folks also stood by them.[11] Similarly, salt was prepared at Karnal, Shahabad, Ladwa, Thanesar and Pundri also. Public meetings were also held and resolutions passed in favour of the movement at almost all these places.[12]

It may be interesting to note that the movement had remarkable transparency in every respect. Nothing was secret or confidential here. Even the details of salt-making meetings and satyagraha were communicated to the 'enemy' well in advance. Contextually, the following letter from Ganpat Ram Talwaria is worth noticing:

To
The Deputy Commissioner,
District Hisar, Hisar.

Dear Sir,

I beg your leave to inform you that as per the directions given by the Congress, a batch of *Satyagrahis* under my command will march for preparing salt at Bhiwani on the 13th. We will start from here on the 12th by the 1.15 a.m. train. Being a humble disciple of Gandhiji and a non-cooperationist, I consider it my duty to inform you well in advance so that you may take appropriate action in the matter.

Yours: Ganpat Ram Talwaria[13]

Apart from breaking salt laws, the agitationists also resorted to the campaign of boycott of foreign goods. Gopi Chand Bhargava, Neki Ram Sharma, Suraj Bhan, Abdul Gaffar, etc., toured the whole of the state to make the campaign a success. There were bonfires of foreign clothes at many places. The traders from Rohtak, Ambala and Bhiwani took a vow not to purchase foreign goods. In Ambala ladies picketted temples and allowed only people wearing *khaddar* to enter into them. About 5,000 people took a solemn pledge to wear *khaddar* only.[14] Likewise, the wine shops were also picketed. People exhorted not to drink or take drugs.[15] The government run institutions were boycotted. Some peasants who participated in the movement refused to pay land revenue to the Government.[16]

Interestingly, even the lower castes joined the movement in pretty good numbers. The lead was given by the people of Puthi Mughalkhan in district Hisar who did an unheard of thing: they assembled in a Panchayat and resolved (on 10-13 March 1930) not to extend any help whatsoever to those who were opposed to the nationalist movement. In the words of C.N. Chandra, deputy commissioner, Hisar:

Because of these Panchayats, half of the village Chamars have resolved not to work for Non-Congressmen. All the Dhanaks, Barhis, and Nais have also avowed not to give any service to these men. They have given a written undertaking that if they broke these promises, they would pay Rs. 500 as fine.[17]

The students also made substantial contribution to the movement. The students of the Ahir High School, Rewari took very active part in picketing wine shops and in bonfires of foreign clothes. The deputy commissioner of Gurgaon was very much annoyed with the school management headed by Rao Bahadur Capt. Balbir Singh and he reprimanded him on 25 May 1930, saying: 'Neither you, nor your men helped us in this hour of need. Conversely, your school students took part in picketing, etc. The head master was told to ask these students to offer apologies. But to no avail.'[18] Similarly, the students of Vaishya and Gaur Schools, Rohtak played a good role in the movement. In Hisar, a naughty boy did a 'strange drama'. He got hold of a donkey and made him wear a pant each on his front and back legs, coat on its back, a tie on its neck and a spectacles on his eyes. Having a placard with the word 'Englishman' inscribed on it in its neck, the donkey was taken in a procession through the streets of Hisar with great fanfare. The students at Bhiwani were also quite active. Especially, the students of the Chandu Lal Vedic School played a leading role there. Some students of the Government School also joined them.[19] The students of the DAV School Shahabad (Kurukshetra) were also active. They.prepared salt and took out processions. Astoundingly, a small boy (aged 12-13) was their leader. Can you guess who this boy was? No, no one can guess, for he was the son of the man (SHO Bichattar Singh) whose duty it was 'to stop such unlawful activities'. His name was Rajendra Singh. The father snatched the tricolour from his hands but he could not close his mouth. The boy continued to shout defiantly: 'Inquilab, Zindabad', 'Angrezi Sarkar, Hai, Hai', 'Gandhi Maharaj Ki Jai', etc. These students also went to the nearby villages and gave the message of 'revolt' to the farmers there. In the words of the Deputy Commissioner, Karnal:

> The Zaildar of Thol, Ch. Pritam Singh, told me that on 2 May 1930 some 30-40 students, mostly about 15 years old, visited Nishangarh village. They had the tricolour in their hands. They incited the farmers not to pay land revenue and join the Civil Disobedience Movement. After doing their work there, they went to village Kewari. There, too, they did the same thing. Thereafter they visited several other villages and gave the message of the Civil Disobedience.[20]

The deputy commissioner took a serious note of these 'rebellious activities'. He asked the head master of the school to ask students to write the following sentence one thousand times: 'It is the duty of every student to pay attention to his studies instead of politics'. None obliged the Head Master.[21]

Like their brothers, the girls of the DAV School, Shahabad also came forward and joined the movement in some numbers. And so did the students of the DAV School, Karnal. Surprisingly, some students from the local Government High School also joined them. The story was repeated at several other places in the state but we do not have exact details with us.[22]

TABLE 1: *SATYAGRAHIS* FROM HARYANA, 1930-1[23]

District	No. of *satyagrahis*
Rohtak	610
Hisar	380
Gurgaon	90
Ambala	67
Karnal	33
Total	1,180

The government was alarmed by these developments and it took strong measures to arrest the movement. To begin with, the Congress was declared an unlawful organization. A large number of Congressmen were imprisoned (as Table 1 shows), the chief among whom were: Ramsharan Das, Kanshi Ram, Sultan Singh, Shri Ram Sharma, Daulat Ram Gupta, Sham Lal, Ramphal Singh, Rao Mangli Ram, Mohan Swami, Kasturi Bai, Darka Devi, Nanki Devi, Shiv Chand, Nanhu Ram, Jug Lal, Asha Ram, Chandu Lal, Kanshi, Ram Chander, Harphool, Lalmohan, Trilok Singh, Agrasen, Man Singh, Sukhdev, Shivbaksh Singh, Bharat Singh, Baldeo Singh, Khair Mohd., Atmanand and Mehar Singh from Rohtak; Neki Ram, K.A. Desai, Ram Kumar, Ram Kishan, Shishpal Singh, Ganpat Ram, Pat Ram, Jagdish Ram, Mange Ram Vats, Hamir Singh, Jati Purnanand, Ram Chander, Mela Ram Moda, Nunkaran, Gokal Chand, Vidhi Chand, Chand Bai, Rohini Devi, Ram Chander, Raghu Nath, Parshu Ram, Chandrajit, Gangadhar, Hardev Sahai, Sham Lal from Hisar; Duni Chand, Mangat Ram, Bhagat Ram Shukla, Abdul Gaffar Khan, Durga Charan, Raja Ram, Radhe Shyam, Suraj Prakash, Nohariya Ram and Aryanand Sharma from Ambala; Ghulam Hussain, Mula Singh, Kaka Ram and Hiranand from Karnal; and Bhagwan Das, Phool Chand, Charanji Lal, Ramji Lal and Dhanpat from Gurgaon.[24]

On 5 March 1931, when the movement was going at full speed, it experienced a sudden break. Two warring powers sat on a table and signed the Gandhi-Irwin pact. As a result, the Civil Disobedience Movement came to an end. The nationalists got a chance to rehabilitate themselves. But this was not to be. Soon after the pact became a reality, the government began breaking it into pieces. Lord Willingdon, the viceroy who replaced Lord Irwin seemed to be in no mood to honour the pact signed by his predecessor. The Congressmen were harassed and their sympathisers penalized. Many lambardars were, for instance, dismissed in the state for having 'pro-Congress bias'. The political activists were not allowed to organize meetings/conferences.

The district officials spared no pains to make the Congress ineffective in their districts. A document listing the efforts of the deputy commissioner Rohtak makes a very interesting reading:

1. A Dehati League comprising representatives of all the castes in the District has been formed. Its main aim is to keep the people away from the Congress. The League has organized meetings in many villages to wash off the impact of the Congress on the people. Similarly, an Aman Sabha has been formed in Sonepat, which is doing this very work.
2. Zaildars and other important persons in the villages have been asked to oppose the Congressmen so that nobody in the villages gives them food and shelter when they visit their villages.
3. A meeting of the District Soldiers Board was held a few days ago. All the members were instructed, then, to dissuade ex-soldiers from joining the Congress.
4. If any Lambardar, Safedposh, Zaildar or Patwari is found having sympathy for the Congress, action is taken against him.
5. The Congressmen are fully watched. Their speeches are noted by the police and revenue people and action is taken against them under Section 108 CrPC.[25]

TABLE 2: THE CONGRESS GOVERNMENT IN DISTRICT[26] ROHTAK

Tehsils	Tehsildars	Thanas	Thanedars
1. Rohtak	B. Anad Sarup	1. Rohtak	Ch. Amar Singh Saini (Rohtak)
		2. Kalanaur	Swami Nizanand (Kalanaur)
		3. Sampla	Ch. Garib Ram (Kharar)
		4. Bahadurgarh	Pt. Kshma Dutt (Subana)
2. Jhajjar	Rao Mangli Ram	1. Jhajjar	Ch. Juglal (Achhej)
		2. Beri	Ch. Maya Ram (Beri)
		3. Salhawas	Ch. Laiq Ram (Marut)
3. Sonepat	L. Ram Chander	1. Sonepat	Ch. Dharmvir
		2. Rai	Ch. Chand Ram (Nahari)
		3. Ganaur	Ch. Chhaju Ram (Chimni)
4. Gohana	Ch. Bharat Singh	1. Gohana	Ch. Baru Singh (Chhatera)
		2. Baroda	Ch. Chandgi Ram (Nuran Kheri)
		3. Meham	Ch. Sheokaran (Mokhra)

Amazingly, the measures taken by the government to suppress Congress and Congressmen did not yield any appreciable result. Conversely, their 'opponent' accepted the challenge and stepped up their activities to spread their influence to all nooks and crannies. The Rohtak District Congress Committee did a really remarkable job in this direction. It cast its net far and wide covering a huge mass of people. They established a parallel government in the district of which Lala Sham Lal was the executive head (DC) and Pt. Shri Ram Sharma police chief (SP). The entire district was divided into tehsils and thanas and put under tehsildars and thanedars respectively as given in Table 2.

The people were exhorted to go to their own *sarkar* (government) in place of the *videshi sarkar* (alien government). Some people did listen to them but not the majority of them.[27] The government viewed these activities with concern and understandably, they came very heavily on the 'undesirable elements.' Surprisingly, however, the nationalists, instead of being demoralized showed fight. They launched frontal attack on the government and spoke a language which the people had not heard before. For instance, Mula Singh, a Congress activist from Kaithal made a fiery speech at a meeting held in the town on 13 April 1931, exhorting the people to learn to die like Bhagat Singh.[28] In another meeting at Salwan, a village near Kaithal, Ghulam Husain of Udalane asked the people to be bold and learn to live without fear. 'As far as I am concerned', he said, 'if I find Lord Irwin standing before me and I have Gandhi's permission to shoot him, I will do it at once'.[29] While addressing a meeting at Bahu Akbarpur (Rohtak) on 23-4 April, Swami Bhagwan Das Sanyasi said: 'Get together like grasshopers and eat away this government of tyrants. Treat these monkeys (Englishmen) as a potter treats his donkey'.[30] On 26 April, Hira Nand Swami spoke the following while addressing a meeting at Panipat: 'Don't fear anything not even death and get freedom. Finish off your enemies'.[31] Sheo Chand, said at Bahu Akbarpur about this very time: 'You have to make sacrifices for freedom. Take up your arms. The Government dogs—Zaildars and Safedposhes—will be set right'.[32] On 31 May, Lala Shamlal roard at Ambala: 'There is no place for an alien Government in India. The Congress will not let it rule the country'.[33]

Understandably, the powers that be were greatly annoyed with the nationalists. They resorted to strong arm methods to quell all rebellion against the Raj. The nationalists also reacted manfully. As a result, the Civil Disobedience Movement was again started on 4 January 1932. The *satyagraha* was resumed as before. People offered themselves for arrest

TABLE 3: ARRESTS IN PUNJAB, 1932[34]

Year	Arrests
1932	1797
1933	175
1934	10
Total	1,982

in good numbers, but, as Table 3 shows, their strength began to dwindle very fast after the initial success.

Assessing the situation correctly, Gandhiji withdrew the movement on 7 April 1934. As in other states, the Haryana *satyagrahis* from this region, were also released from jails.[35]

A general notion persists that the people of Haryana did not take any effective part in the Civil Disobedience Movement. This is wrong. As noted above, during the period under study, the Haryana region was very backward as compared to Punjab. Despite that, however, it gave more than its quota of arrests. A good number of lawyers gave up their practice. More shopkeepers boycotted foreign goods and more people came forward for boycotting and picketing of liquor shops than their well-off Punjabi counterparts. The Haryana students were more active in the movement than their counterparts in Punjab. And same was the case with our womenfolk. Surprisingly, a good number of them, who lived in *ghunghat* and *purdah*, came in open and fought the greatest imperial power in the world with confidence and courage. They inspired their menfolks to do the same.[36]

The withdrawal of the Civil Disobedience Movement was followed by elections to the Central Legislative Assembly in October-November 1934, and to the Council of States a little later in 1935. Although Congress bagged both the seats, their performance in the Haryana region was far from satisfactory. Here the Unionists ruled the roost.[37]

There was no political activity after this for quite some time except for making preparations for the elections of 1937, as provided for in the Government of India Act, 1935.

NOTES

1. The session was presided over by Pt. Jawaharlal Nehru. A large number of delegates from Haryana participated in the session.
2. Pattabhi Sitaramayya, *History of the India National Congress* (ab. ed.), pp. 177-8.

3. HSA, Confidential, File no. 177, 1930.
4. *The Tribune*, 8 March 1930; 17 March 1930.
5. HSA, Conf., File no. A 13, 1930.
6. Ibid.
7. Ibid.
8. Ibid., File no. A 12, 1930 (part 1).
9. Ibid.
10. Ibid., File no. A 11, 1930 (part 1)
11. *The Tribune,* 1 March 1930.
12. *JHS*, vol. XXII, 1990, pp. 22-51.
13. HSA, Conf., File no. 118, 1930.
14. *JHS*, vol. XXII, 1990, pp. 22-51.
15. Ibid.
16. Ibid.
17. HSA, Conf., File no. D 3, 1930.
18. Ibid., File no. A 11, 1930; A 12, 1930; A 14, 1930.
19. Ibid.
20. Ibid.
21. Ibid.
22. Ibid.
23. *JHS*, vol. XXII, 1990, pp. 22-51.
24. Ibid.
25. Ibid.
26. Ibid.
27. Ibid.
28. HSA, Conf., File no. A 14, 1930 (part 1).
29. Ibid.
30. NAI, Home Pol., File no. 33, 1931, p. 167.
31. HSA, Conf., File no. A 13, 1930.
32. NAI, Home Pol., File no. 33, 191, p. 167.
33. Ibid.
34. *JHS*, vol. XXII, 1990, pp. 22-51.
35. Ibid.
36. Ibid.
37. Ibid.

14

From Autonomy to Swaraj, 1937-1940

The 1937 Elections

The year 1937 opened on a very hectic note owing to elections to the Punjab Legislative Assembly, as provided for in the new constitution (1935), which granted autonomy to the people at the provincial level. Almost all the major political parties joined the fray. First they formed their election boards, as Table 1 shows, and then moved earth and heaven to achieve success at the hustings.

TABLE 1: ELECTION BOARDS IN HARYANA, 1937[1]

Party	Head of the Board
Congress	Pt. Shri Ram Sharma
Unionist Party	Sir Chhotu Ram
Hindu Mahasabha	Rao Bahadur Balbir Singh
Congress Nationalist Party	Pt. Neki Ram Sharma
Muslim League	Ghulam Bhik Nairang
Majlis-i-Itihad	Zafar Ali Khan

Top leaders of all the political parties, like Jawaharlal Nehru, Sarojini Naidu and Satyadeva of the Congress; Sir Sikander Hayat Khan, and Chhotu Ram of the Unionist Party; Raja Narendra Nath and Rao Balbir Singh of the Hindu Mahasabha; and Pt. Madan Mohan Malviya and Neki Ram Sharma of the Congress Nationalist Party, toured the region and addressed hundreds of meetings. There was some heat and acrimony, too, in the air but no untoward happening took place.[2] The elections were held on 18 January (1937). The Congress registered its victory in the Hindu urban segment—it bagged one out of two general-urban seats. The Unionists proved strong in the rural areas. The Congress could only snatch one (Ambala-Shimla) seat out of thirteen from them. In the Mohammedan constituencies, the Unionists performed still better. They captured both the urban as well as all the five rural seats. In the Sikh constituencies, the Akalis and the Khalsa National Board came out victorious.[3]

In 1923 and 1926 elections the Congress had not fared so bad. How come that the Unionists made a clean sweep, especially in rural areas, in 1937? There were several reasons for this. First, the Congress was a badly divided house now. The Unionists, on the other hand, were a cohesive, well-knit group. Secondly, the Congress did precious little for the rural masses. The Unionists did, or at least pretended to be doing some good work for these neglected people. Thirdly, being collaborators, the Unionists were helped by the government and other loyalist elements who had voting right, in winning the elections. Besides this, the Congress leadership in 1937 was weak as compared to the Unionist leadership. Hence the resounding victory for the Unionists.

The Unionist also fared well in the rest of the Province. The Congress came next. The Khalsa Nationalist Party and Hindu Mahasabha bagged the third place. Astoundingly, the Muslim league occupied the last place. Statistically the overall position of different parties in the Punjab Legislative Assembly (PLA) was as follows (Table 2).

In view of the above position, the lieutenant-governor invited Sir Sikandar Hayat Khan, the leader of the Unionists, to form the government. He accepted the offer right at once and formed a six-member cabinet in which Sir Chhotu Ram was the Development Minister. Chhotu Ram, as noted above, was a traditional rival of the Congress. His appointment as a minister, was therefore, a serious setback to the Congress in Haryana.

TABLE 2: PARTY-WISE POSITION IN PLA, 1937[4]

Party	Strength
Unionists	99
Congress	18
Khalsa Nationalist Party	13
Hindu Mahasabha	12
Akalis	02
Itihadi-Millat	02
Ahrass	01
Muslim League	01
Congress Nationalist	01
Total	175

THE CONGRESS-UNIONIST CONFLICT

But it must be said to their credit that the Congressmen did not lose heart and following the old adage, they went for defiance in their hour of defeat. They arranged a series of meetings in the villages which were strong bastions of the Unionists. Intoxicated by victory and power, the Unionists did not take any note of these activities, however, until the Punjab Provincial Conference was held at Madina (Rohtak) on 26-7 March 1938. This was a big affair. Eminent leaders like Bhula Bhai Desai, N.V. Gadgil, C. Prakasha, Satyamurthy, Dr. Satyapal, etc., participated in it. The crowds at the conference numbered more than 20,000.[5]

This conference pricked the swollen ego of the Unionists, and they held a counter-conference at Rohtak on 7 October, where Premier, Sir Sikandar Hayat Khan came. The crowd was large, as well as unruly. They attacked the houses of prominent Congressmen, like Lala Sultan Singh, Secretary, City Congress Committee, Rohtak 'pulled down national flags and badly hurt his relatives'. Shops were looted and property damaged. The local police, apparently under the influence of Sir Chhotu Ram, did not act swiftly in the matter. Pt. Shri Sharma, a dynamic Congress activist from Rohtak, made scathing criticism of the *goondagardi* of the Unionists in the columns of his paper *Haryana Tilak* and denounced it in the Legislative Assembly. At one point he went even to the extent of saying: 'Is the Parliamentary Secretary aware that the Hon'ble Premier and Development Minister (Sir Chhotu Ram) were in league with the hooligans who entered the house of Lala Sultan Singh and inflicted injuries to his relatives?' The government was forced to start criminal proceedings against the goons.[6]

These things, however, did not dishearten the Unionist goons. Nor did the Unionist leadership seems to have improved their conduct to any extent. Rather they went down. Earlier they had taken only the police support. Now they took the bureaucracy and even judiciary with them in their nefarious game of *goondagardi*. This was proved to be so by what happened at a Congress meeting held at Asaudha (Rohtak) on 18 December 1938. As Pt. Shri Ram Sharma was the moving spirit behind the Asaudha Conference, let us hear the story in his own words:

> In order to educate the rural population the Congress is carrying on propaganda in rural areas so that its message may reach the remotest corner. We in the Rohtak district are doing the same in our own humble way in order to acquaint the poor and ignorant people of that *ilaqa* with the agrarian problems. We hold meetings in different villages and people come to those villages to hear what we have to

say. One of these periodical meetings was held at Asaudha (18.2.1938). This village is situated in the Jhajjar Tehsil which the Hon'ble Minister for Development represents. I might also mention here that this *ilaqa* is inhabited by people belonging to his caste. 'The position that emerges from the evidence of witnesses produced by the complainant is that while some of the owners of the land were in favour of the meeting being held there, the accused persons were opposed to it and, as stated by the complainant, they said that they would not permit the meeting to be held there. As co-owners of that land, the accused persons have a right to say that they would not permit the conference to be held on that land but use of provocative language does not justify the institution of proceedings under Section 107, Criminal Procedure Code, against them.'

Now coming to the actual happenings, I will narrate only one incident. Two aged women Congress workers who had been undergoing hardship in the cause of freedom of the country and had also to their credit the sentences of imprisonments came to attend this conference. The *goondas* and *badmashes*, who had collected there to commit all sorts of hooliganism and lawlessness, addressed the following words to these aged ladies:

'You both are *badmash* women. Could you not get stronger men to satisfy your passions at your homes? Why should you stay at your houses when there are so many stout men in your group? Here you are two and they so many.'

I had brought all these shameful matters to the knowledge of the Honourable Premier, the Inspector-General of Police, Commissioner and the Deputy Inspector-General of Police. One cannot imagine a more shameless and immoral attack on the patriotic women of the Province. This hooliganism was organised by the local Zamindara League which left no stone unturned in committing all sorts of lawlessness with the help of the *goondas*.

I want to sound a note of warning to the Unionists that if they think that they can defeat the Congress by these low tactics, they are seriously mistaken. If the Government believes in these tactics, the Honourable Premier and the Development Minister should be honest and courageous enough to come and beat drums themselves at Asaudha, instead of enjoying it to be done by hirelings and bad characters through their party organisation.[7]

The Congressmen were not unnerved by the nefarious activities of the Unionist goons. On 3 January 1939, they again held a meeting there. But the same old story was repeated. The Congressmen did not yield even now and they held the third meeting on 19 February. It was an impressive show—thousands of people came to hear the Congress leaders. This was, however, too much for the Unionist goons—they attacked the peaceful crowd in a savage manner.[8] About 60 persons were badly injured. They had to be hospitalized at Bahadurgarh and Rohtak for long, as given in Table 3.

The Congressmen did not yield even in the face of such a grave situation. Rather they showed greater determination to fight the savage

TABLE 3: INJURED PERSONS HOSPITALIZED AT BAHADURGARH AND ROHTAK[9]

No. of injured persons	No. of days spent in hospitals
14	1 day
13	2 days
25	3 days
1	7 days
1	11 days
2	12 days
1	13 days
2	18 days
1	25 days
1	35 days
1	36 days
1	37 days

force. Hundreds of people came to Asaudha from all parts of Haryana and sat on *dharna*. When the Unionists saw that there was a likelihood of the *satyagraha* spreading to other parts of India, they yielded. They would allow the Congressmen to hold their meeting, they said, provided Shri Ram Sharma did not attend it. The Congress leadership did not accept this, but Shri Ram did. As a result, a meeting was held on 3 March 1939. Thousands of people attended it. Master Nanhu Ram, a prominent Congressman from Jasrana, a village in close proximity of Asaudha, presided over the meeting and eminent leaders like Mrs. Sarojini Naidu participated. The meeting ended peacefully. It was a great victory for the Congress.[10]

After this, several other political meetings were organized in the villages. The Unionist goons had no guts to disturb them. As a result, some more rural masses were drawn to the Congress.

THE CONGRESS REORGANIZES ITSELF

In the fall of 1938, Subhas Chandra Bose, the then president of the Indian National Congress, visited Haryana to supervise relief work going on in the region for the famine stricken people here under the auspices of the Indian National Congress.[11] The Congress president also studied the problems of the party in Punjab in general and the Haryana region in particular during his visit and advised the local leadership to vitalize the

TABLE 4: CONGRESS COMMITTEES IN HARYANA, 1938-9[12]

District Congress Committees	No. of Comts.	Tehsil Congress Committees	No. of Comts.	No. of Town and Village Congress Committees
Ambala	1	Ambaḷa	1	40
		Kharar	1	
		Jagadhari	1	
		Naraingarh	1	
Karnal	1	Karnal	1	35
		Panipat	1	
		Kaithal	1	
		Thanesar	1	
Rohtak	1	Rohtak	1	50
		Jhajjar	1	
		Gohana	1	
Hisar	1	Hisar	1	50
		Hansi	1	
		Bhiwani	1	
		Fatehabad	1	
Gurgaon	1	Gurgaon	1	30
		Palwal	1	
		Rewari	1	
		Nuh	1	
		Ferozepur-Jhirka	1	

party. He met several delegations, visited many villages and addressed a number of political meetings where he exhorted people to fight for *swarajya* instead of fighting among themselves.[13] The exhortations of the dynamic *Rashtrapati* gave added strength and vitality to the party.[14] It reorganized itself and spread a network of Congress Committees from district to village level.

Table 4 shows that the Congress had five district branches, 20 tehsil branches and 205 town and village branches in Haryana in 1938-9. There is no evidence to suggest the number of primary and active members associated with these committees, however.

THE WORLD WAR

On 3 September 1939, Britain declared war on Germany. Soon after the governor-general of India made a simple proclamation: 'War has broken out between His Majesty and Germany', and India was at once engaged in a deadly strife doing her 'duty to king and country'. Elsewhere, excepting Eire, the member states of the Commonwealth had taken this decision on the advice of ministers responsible to their own parliaments. In Australia and New Zealand, the declaration was confirmed by parliament. In Canada and South Africa it was not made till parliament had approved of it. This was not to happen in India, however.

The Congress resented the way India was dragged into War. They passed a lengthy resolution (on 15 September) taking the grave view of the viceroy's proclamation of War without the consent of the Indian people, protesting against the exploitation of the Indian resources for imperial end and declaring emphatically that 'India cannot associate herself with a War said to be for democratic freedom when that freedom is denied to her'.[15]

How did the people of Haryana react to the War situation? The loyalists came forward to help the government's War-efforts by men, money and material. But Congressmen opposed it. The Government took stern measures against those who in any way put any spoke in the smooth prosecution of War. It let loose a reign of terror in the region. Several leaders, like Murlidhar (Hisar), Maru Singh (Madina-Rohtak), Shri Ram (Jhajjar), Risala, Kisan Lal and Guljar (Rurki-Rohtak), Mange Ram Vats (Rohtak), Gabdu, Chhote, Bhoja, Mohd. Yusuf (Gurgaon), Jyoti Prasad (Ambala) and Jagadish Chander (Karnal) were arrested under the DIR.[16]

Gandhiji tried his very best to impress upon the government to see the reason but all in vain. The Mahatma, therefore, launched an all-India *satyagraha* movement on 17 October 1940, the details of which are given in the next chapter.

NOTES

1. See K.C. Yadav, *Haryana*, vol. II, pp. 253-63.
2. Ibid.
3. Ibid.
4. K.C. Yadav, *Elections*, p. 134.
5. Jagdish Chandra, op. cit., p. 104.
6. *PLA Debates*, vol. VIII, no. 7 (1939), pp. 433-7; vol. IX, no. 3 (1940), p. 203.
7. Ibid., vol. VIII, no. 6 (1939), pp. 395-400.
8. For other details see Shri Ram Sharma, *Asaudha Ka Satyagraha*, pp. 1-20.
9. *PLA Debates*, vol. X, no. 1 (1939), p. 9.
10. Shri Ram Sharma, op. cit., pp. 1-20.
11. For details see *The Tribune*, 29-30 November 1938.

12. See K.C. Yadav, *Haryana*, vol. II, pp. 253-63.
13. He addressed meetings at Hisar, Satarod, Bhiwani, Palwal, and Rohtak and visited many villages like Meham, Sarakara, Bahu Akbarpur and Kalanaur.
14. Subhas Chandra Bose also laid the foundation stone of the Congress Bhavans at Hisar and Palwal on this occasion.
15. See K.C. Yadav, *Haryana*, vol. II, pp. 253-63
16. Ibid.

15

The Last Struggle for Swaraj, 1941-1947

The Individual Satyagraha

We have seen in the preceding chapter how Gandhiji was forced to launch an all-India movement against the Raj in 1940. The movement was styled as Individual Satyagraha by Gandhiji, for it was not a mass movement of civil disobedience, but an individual movement of protest under which only selected persons were allowed to defy the government and court arrest, shouting slogans against the War efforts. Here anybody who had firm faith in *ahimsa*, etc., and plied *charkha* daily, could offer himself for *satyagraha* after obtaining prior permission from Gandhiji.

The Individual Satyagraha was conducted into the following four stages in Haryana:

(1)	Stage I	17 October 1940 to 15 January 1941
(2)	Stage II	27 January to 15 April 1941
(3)	Stage III	16 March to 15 April 1941 and
(4)	Stage IV	16 April to 31 December 1941[1]

During the first phase of the *satyagraha* the top leaders, like Dr. Gopi Chand Bhargava, Duni Chand, Mrs. Duni Chand, Shri Ram Sharma, Sham Lal, Sahib Ram (all MLAs), Sham Lal (MLA Centre) and eminent leaders in the organization, like Neki Ram Sharma, courted arrest.[2]

The second phase was a bit bigger affair when a good number of the second line of leadership, like Balwant Rai Tayal, Madan Gopal, Hardwari Lal, Jugal Kishore, Chand Ram, Chand Bai, Kasturi Bai, Bhagwan Das and others offered themselves for arrest.[3]

The third phase was still bigger when the activists like Mul Chand Jain, Ranbir Singh, Nanhu Ram, Aryanand Sharma, Pat Ram, Ram Kumar, Man Singh, Madho Ram and many others courted arrest.[4]

TABLE 1: DISTRICT-WISE ARRESTS (1940-1)[5]

District	1940 Oct.	Nov.	Dec.	1941 Jan.	Feb.	Mar.	Apr.	May	Jun.	Jul.	Aug.	Sept.	Oct.	Nov.	Dec.	Total
Hisar	2	–	1	7	8	17	33	19	5	3	–	1	–	2	–	98
Rohtak	–	–	–	2	12	40	91	45	1	–	–	2	4	4	1	251
Gurgaon	1	1	–	–	6	7	9	2	–	1	1	–	2	–	–	30
Karnal	–	–	1	4	9	8	10	3	2	–	–	–	–	–	2	39
Ambala	–	1	–	2	7	6	38	16	1	4	18	2	2	–	–	97.
Total	3	2	2	15	42	78	181	85	9	8	71	7.	7	3	2	515

Lastly, in the fourth phase, ordinary Congressmen, a large number of people, went to jail (Table 1). In all, about 500 persons courted arrest during the movement.

One fine morning the movement came to a grinding halt in December 1941 when Gandhiji withdrew it on account of its making little impact on the powers that be. Some critics say that, like other movements, the Individual Satyagraha was also far from satisfactory in Haryana for the simple reason that the region was in the tight grip of the Unionists who were opposing the movement. The Table 2 given below would perhaps clear the position better than any debate on the point.

The above figures speak for themselves. In the entire Punjab, Rohtak district topped the list in offering arrests. And surprisingly a vast majority of the Rohtak *satyagrahis* who went to jail belonged to villages—and they were peasants (Jats). Hisar occupied the second place. The position was equally good in other districts also. Thus there is no truth in the assertion that the Unionists had held back the peasants from the movement and that the Individual Satyagraha was not a success in Haryana.

The Quit India Movement

Gandhiji, as noted above, realized after about fifteen months that the Individual Satyagraha was not serving the purpose well. So he launched a powerful mass movement on 8 August 1942. The Britishers were

TABLE 2: DISTRICT-WISE ARRESTS IN PUNJAB DURING THE INDIVIDUAL SATYAGRAHA[6]

District	Total arrests	District	Total arrests
Hisar	98	Sialkot	28
Rohtak	251	Gujranwala	39
Gurgaon	30	Sheikhpura	12
Karnal	39	Gujarat	22
Ambala	97	Shahpur	11
Kangra	17	Jhelum	13
Hoshiarpur	72	Rawalpindi	12
Jullundur	64	Attock	5
Ludhiana	164	Montgomery	36
Ferozepur	73	Lyallpur	80
Kasur	52	Jhang	21
Lahore	49	Multan	35
Amritsar	80	D.G. Khan	2
Gurdaspur	35	Simla	2

asked to a quit India lock, stock and barrel right at once.

These were war days and understandably the government took the challenge very seriously. To begin with, it arrested all the important nation leaders, including Gandhiji on 9 August. A reign of terror was let loose on the entire nation. There was, however, no effect on the people who also reacted with full force. In consequence, a spontaneous revolution burst forth, and almost the entire country came out to fight the British imperialism. In the struggle, it is heartening to note, the people of Haryana did not lag behind. Despite large scale arrests of leaders, police *zulam* and all sorts of repressive measures, they offered resistance to the *sarkar* and its collaborators.

District Karnal took the lead. The moment the news of the arrest of national leaders reached Karnal, hundreds of people came out on the streets, took out processions and shouted anti-government slogans. In the evening, they held a meeting under the leadership of Shanti Swarup, Sardar Man Singh Rahi and Dr. Krishna (Panipat) who made forceful speeches. They exhorted the people to throw out the British from India in a non-violent manner.[7]

These developments unnerved the district authorities. They arrested Rahi, Krishna and other leaders and *lathi*-charged the peaceful crowd in the meeting. Many persons were injured. Heavy arrests were made. A reign of terror was let loose on the Congressmen and their sympathisers.[8]

These tough measures had, however no impact on the people, especially on the youth who decided to give a befitting reply to the oppressive government. They organized a first rate outfit to do their job, Nathi Ram, a young man form Karnal was their leader. Munshi Ram, took care of the organizational machinery. Ram Prasad, Atma Ram, etc., from Alhar were deputed to make arrangements to set government offices on fire and uproot railway tracks. Vishnudatt Ashri and some other young men were assigned the most dangerous task of killing the governor of Punjab who was going to visit Karnal in the second week of August.

This 'work' was to start with hurling a bomb on the governor. But as ill-luck would have it, the bomb which Ashri and his associates had made for this purpose exploded before it was to be used. The police got alerted. Ashri gave up the assignment.[9] But not the work. They acted elsewhere; as the following excerpt from a policeman's account shows:

16 August, 1942. The sun had just set. Police station, Karnal received the information that Deputy Commissioner's Office was afire. A lot of records were burnt. The fire was hardly extinguished there that Sessions Judges' Office started

burning. After some time, the Post Office also met the same fate.[10]

The whole thing was seriously investigated. One Somnath, revolutionary, turned approver and gave full information. As a result, Nathi Ram, the leader of the revolutionary party, was arrested. He was tortured for 1104 hours at a stretch. He did not break however.[11]

Some young men produced anti-government literature. District Ambala played a leading role in this matter. Balmukund and Kalicharan Das, proprietor and manager respectively of the *Khaddar Bhandar* in the Ambala Cantonment prepared and distributed 'seditious literature' for the soldiers in the cantonment. The police viewed the whole thing very seriously and arrested the 'seditionists'. There was a quick trial and each of them got 10 years rigorous imprisonment. Some young men uprooted railway tracks near Jagadhari.[12] The people of Rohtak also played a prominent role in the movement. They organized meetings and took out processions. Some young men uprooted the railway tracks near Ganaur, cut telegraph wires at Rohtak and Bahadurgarh and burnt a train at the Rohtak railway station.[13] The angry men at Hisar also behaved likewise. They uprooted the railway tracks near Sirsa and damaged the Hisar railway station. Seditious literature was also distributed there.[14] Gurgaon also did not lag behind. Meetings were organized and processions taken out at Gurgaon and Rewari on 9 August. The students of the Government High School, Rewari were at the forefront of these activities.[15]

There was trouble in the princely states also. The people there uprooted railway tracks, cut telegraph wires and damaged railway stations at a number of places. A bomb was hurled at the police station, Narnaul. The bomb was not of high quality, and therefore it did not cause much damage. The Patiala state authorities took action and arrested a number of revolutionaries. They were tried and given punishment as under:

1.	Ram Kishore	10 years (r.i.)
2.	Bhagwat Prasad	8 years (r.i.)
3.	Ayodha Prasad	8 years (r.i.)
4.	Harikishan	6 years (r.i.)
5.	Munshi Lal	5 years (r.i.)
6.	Duli Chand	4 years (r.i.)

The resolutionaries went in appeal against the dicision. The Punjab High court gave them the benefit of doubt, however, and let them off.[16]

There was some violence at other places, too. The whole picture was as follows (Table 3):

TABLE 3: VIOLENT ACTIVITIES IN HARYANA, 1942[17]

Particulars	No. of destructive activities
Stations attacked	4
Post Offices attacked	11
Telegraph wires cut (at places)	12
Police stations and other govt. buildings attacked	8
Railway lines demaged by scrapping fish-plates	6

During the War days, these were very serious happenings. The government's reaction was, understandably, quite forceful. The Congress party was declared an unlawful organization and its offices, etc., were locked. There were indiscriminate *lathi*-charges and firings for suppressing the movement. Men or women having even the slightest sympathy with the Congress were harassed. A large number of persons were put behind the bars, as Table 4 shows. However, Gandhiji withdrew the movement in May 1944. It came to a grinding halt in Haryana, too, right at once.

Before we close, it seems pertinent to know as to how did this movement compare with the movement in other parts of Punjab and elsewhere? Broadly, the movement here was, for obvious reasons, which have already been noted above, was weak when compared with the movements in Uttar Pradesh, Bombay and other provinces. But not so when compared with the movements in other districts in Punjab as is evident from Table 5. The Haryana districts compared very well with other districts in the number of arrests given during the movement. For instance, Rohtak occupied third position after Lahore and Rawalpindi. Gurgaon, Hisar and Ambala are also high in the list. Karnal is a bit low—but still it is better than many other districts.

TABLE 4: DISTRICT-WISE ARRESTS, 1942-3[18]

District	No. of arrests
Ambala	61
Karnal	49
Gurgaon	111
Rohtak	225
Hisar	76
Total	522

TABLE 5: DISTRICT-WISE ARRESTS FROM PUNJAB DURING THE QUIT INDIA MOVEMENT, 1942-43[19]

District	Total arrests	District	Total arrests
Hisar	76	Gurdaspur	86
Rohtak	228	Sialkot	39
Gurgaon	111	Sheikhupura	38
Karnal	49	Gujranwala	53
Ambala	61	Gujarat	75
Kangra	15	Shahpur	70
Hoshiarpur	68	Jhelum	88
Jullundur	60	Rawalpindi	188
Ludhiana	82	Attock	23
Ferozepur	120	Montgomery	11
Lahore	826	Multan	36
Kasur	28	Lyallpur	57
Amritsar	90	Muzzafargarh	11

THE INA AND HARYANAVIS

After the fall of Singapore (1942), during the Second World War—a large number of Indian soldiers were taken prisoners. Capt. Mohan Singh, a p.o.w., along with an enlightened Japanese officer, Maj. Fujiwara (later Lt. General), formed a revolutionary army (INA) from out of these p.o.ws. for liberation of their motherland. For about a year the army did not or could not do anything to achieve its aim. Things improved in 1943, however, when Netaji Subhas Chandra Bose came and assumed its command.

In this revolution army—INA of Netaji—Haryana's share was 398 officers and 2317 other ranks (see Table 6).[20] These Soldiers gave very

TABLE 6: SOLDIERS FROM HARYANA IN THE INA

District	Officers	Other ranks	Total
Ambala	1	30	31
Karnal	14	105	119
Gurgaon	106	580	686
Rohtak	149	724	873
Hisar	61	478	539
Jind	53	296	349
Mahendragarh	14	104	118
Total	398	2,317	2,715

good account of themselves in the several actions against the mighty Allied Forces in the eastern sector. Many of these brave soldiers received most enviable awards and decorations. For instance, Maj. Khazan Singh and Maj. Surajmal got *Sardar-i-Jang* medals. Naik Molar Singh got *Shahid-i-Bharat*, the highest gallantry award. Responding to Netaji's call 'Give me blood, I will give you freedom', 346 brave sons of Haryana gave their blood-life-for the noble cause.[21]

The INA failed to win the war, but it succeeded in getting us freedom. After the war was over, despite the government's firm resolve to punish the INA soldiers, it had to release them. Each one of these soldiers was a part of Netaji—always ready to sacrifice everything for their motherland. On reaching their villages, they jumped into the fray and worked for freedom. The national movement gained fresh blood from them. The struggle for freedom turned into a real mass movement.[22]

Praja Mandal Movement

The national struggle for freedom also made deep impact on the people living in the princely states of Pataudi, Dujana, Loharu, Jind and the present Mahendragarh district which formed parts of Patiala and Nabha states. The princes who ruled over these states collected exorbitant revenue and taxes. They took *begar* (*haq-ul khidmat*) without paying any remuneration. There was no say of the people in administration. There were no good roads, no hospitals, or good dispensaries, no colleges or good schools anywhere.[23]

In the mid-1930s, the awakened state subjects appealed to their rulers to ameliorate their condition. The arrogant princes did not listen to them. In consequence, the suffering people formed Praja Mandals in the states to fight injustice being done to them. The rajas and nawabs came heavily on them. The people did not yield. The struggle went on for quite sometime. It was weak in the beginning, but in the forties it became very potent and forceful and forced the princes to yield as given below.

Post-war Developments

After the war (1945), the national movement gained immense popularity. The reasons for this change were many. Although the British had won the war, yet they were badly beggared. There was unrest in the armed forces which conveyed them (the British) that the cry for freedom was now too loud to be ignored. Hence the Labour Party, which had come to power in England by then, saw the shadow of the coming events clearly.

Consequently, it took no time in deciding to leave India. But how? In what form? United or divided? Let this question be decided, said the imperial masters, by the elected representatives of the people. Hence the elections of 1946.

Sir Chhotu Ram had died last year, and his party had gone very weak. As such, there was no party in 1946 which could have opposed the rising tide of the Congress. In consequence, the Congress won the elections with thumping majority, as the following Table (7) would show:

TABLE 7: RESULTS OF THE PLA ELECTIONS, 1946[24]

General Urban	
Southern Towns	
Pt. Shri Ram (Cong)	8,858
Suresh Chandra (Ind.)	980
Hardwari Lal Sharma (Ind.)	994
Madan Gopal (Ind.)	375
General Rural	
Hisar South	
Capt. Ranjit Singh (Cong)	10,118
Ch. Man Singh (Union)	5,886
Hansi	
Ch. Suraj Mal (Union)	7,223
Ch. Lajpat Rai (Cong.)	5,782
Hisar North	
Ch. Sahib Ram (Cong.)	7,957
Ch. Ramji Lal (Ind.)	4,403
Ch. Ram Lal (Union)	1,585
Rohtak North	
Ch. Lahri Singh (Cong.)	1,4235
Ch. Tika Ram (Union)	1,2137
Pt. Hira Lal (Indp.)	11
Rohtak Central	
Ch. Badlu Ram (Cong,)	9,338
Ch. Ram Sarup (Union)	6,668
Ch. Man Singh (Indp.)	4,157
Jhajjar	
Ch. Sher Singh (Cong.)	11,866
Capt. Dalpat Singh (Union)	6,873
North-West Gurgaon	
Rao Mohar Singh (Union)	8,956
Rao Guajrat Singh (Cong.)	8,725

South-East Gurgaon	
Jiwan Lal (Cong.)	10,063
Ch. Sumer Singh (Union)	2,750
Ch. Prem Singh (S.C.) unopposed	
Karnal South	
Chander (Ne Sumer) (Cong.)	10,964
Dhan Singh (Indp.)	7,238
Ch. Ram Chandra (Union)	4,013
Ch. Multan Singh (Indp.)*	—
Karnal North	
Jagdish Chandra (Cong.)	13,232
Narsingh (Indp.)	11,782
Ch. Rampat (Union)	6,512
Sunder Singh (Indp.)	13,136
Ambala-Shimla	
Ch. Rattan Singh (Cong.)	20,708
Pirthi Singh Azad (SC)	10,503

* Not available

The above account shows that Congress fared well in the 1946 elections in Haryana. But when we look at the entire state of Punjab, the situation was bad. There the Muslim League was the single largest party—they won 73 of 175 seats. Congress bagged 51 seats, whereas Unionists got only 19. The Akalis snatched 21 seats and independents got 11. As no party was in a position to form the government on its own, the Congress, Unionists and Akalis did it jointly. The Unionist leader Sir Khizr Hayat Khan Tiwana was made the Premier. Ch. Lahri Singh from Haryana was appointed a minister. This was done for combating the old Unionist propaganda that when in power the Congress would not accord any ministry to a Jat.[25]

In the new Assembly, the Muslim League, as noted above, was in formidable strength. They abused their position in the Assembly to such an extent that there was demoralization all around. Pt. Shri Ram Sharma and other Haryana MLAs showed ample guts on the floor of the house and fought the League manfully.[26] But this could not continue for long. The League went out for direct action and forced Khizr to resign. There was breakdown of the law and order machinery. It was free for all until 15 August 1947 when freedom came.

The people of Haryana, though backward in ways more than one during the period under study, still they made substantial contribution to the struggle for freedom from 1937 through 1947.

NOTES

1. For details see K.C. Yadav, *Haryana*, vol. II, pp 262-82.
2. The account is based on data contained in confidential files of district officers, Haryana State Archives, Panchkula.
3. Ibid.
4. Ibid.
5. Based on the NAI, Home Dept., Political Proceedings of these months.
6. See S.L. Malhotra, *From Civil Disobedience to Quit India*, pp. 180-1. Some figures have been corrected here and there on the basis of district records and other contemporary papers.

7-16. K.C. Yadav, 'Haryana's Role in the 1942 Movement', *Harigandha*, August 1993, pp. 55-60.

17. Jagdish Chandra, op. cit., p. 111.
18. Ibid.
19. S.L. Malhotra, op. cit., p. 183. Some figures have been corrected here and there on the basis of district records and other contemporary papers.
20. See K.C. Yadav, *Haryana*, vol. II, pp. 264-82.
21. A district-wise break-up of these martyrs was as follows:

District	Officers	Soldiers	Total
Ambala, Panchkula and Yamuna Nagar	–	–	–
Karnal, Panipat and Kaithal	–	5	5
Gurgaon and Faridabad	5	72	77
Rohtak, Jhajjar and Sonepat	12	126	138
Hisar, Sirsa and Bhiwani	2	51	53
Jind	2	53	53
Mahendragarh and Rewari	1	17	18
Total	22	324	346

22. Ibid, pp. 264-82.
23. Ibid.
24. K.C. Yadav, *Elections*, pp. 106-21.
25. Shri Ram Sharma, *Meri Ramakahani*, pp. 94-5.
26. Ibid.

16

Formation of the State

The Problem

The distribution of provinces in India by the British had no rational basis. It was merely 'due to accident and the circumstances attending the growth of the British power in India'.[1] Haryana region was one of the worst sufferers in this historical process. It was made to change its shape, size and position every now and then. In 1803, they made it a part of the Bengal Presidency. It was called 'Delhi Territory'. In 1834, it became a part of the North-Western Provinces as 'Delhi Division'. Then after 1857, it became a part of Punjab (6 February), though known as 'Haryana region'.[2]

The people of Haryana had played an important part in the uprising of 1857. This was, understandably, not liked by the British. They wanted the people of Haryana 'to be taught a lesson for their misbehaviour'. Accordingly, they were treated shabbily. The doors of government services were closed upon them; they were denied other benefits of the raj, like education, health and social welfare measures, irrigational facilities, etc., for a pretty long time. As a result, the people here became literally the hewers of wood and drawers of water.[3] They were a 'colony' of Punjab.

Passive Development

The Haryanavis were not the only ones to have suffered like this at the hands of the colonial masters. The Biharis and Oriyas suffered in Bengal; Telugus and Andhras suffered in Madras; the Marathas suffered in the Central Provinces and so on. Some of these suffering people gave vent to their feelings which, fortunately for them, caught the attention of some thoughtful Englishmen like Henry Bright, Herbert Risley, etc. They studied their problems in all seriousness and suggested that the only way to improve the situation was to redistribute provinces on rational basis of language and culture. Henry Cotton agreed with this fine idea in his presidential address to the AICC at Bombay (1904). G.K. Gokhale said the same thing the very next year in his presidential address at Benaras. Enlightened Biharis, Andhras, Oriyas, Marathas took inspiration from these utterances and raised their voice for justice. But we did not hear anything from the people of Haryana, the reason being the backwardness of the people. Secondly, the Congress leadership was helping the suffering people elsewhere for raising their voices. But in Punjab, of which Haryana formed a part then, the Congress leadership was in the hands of the Punjabi Hindu bourgeoisie which was not interested in the separation of the Haryana region from Punjab for the reason that that would have reduced their communal strength in the Punjab.[4]

The Haryanavis' suffering was, however, immense. Their economy was in bad shape; their cultural development was next to nil. The people over here stood reduced, as noted earlier, to the status of the hewers of wood and drawers of water. They had wounds inflicted upon them, but their wounds had no tongue. They felt very strongly that separation from Punjab was necessary so that they could be saved from this situation. But they could not give expression to their feeling in this period. This period is, therefore, designated as a period of passive developments.[5]

Congress Too Neglects

Impressed by the popular demand for formation of provinces on socio-linguistic basis, the Indian National Congress passed in 1920 a resolution for redrawing the map of India on socio-linguistic basis. The government, however, took no note of this suggestion. In 1921, the Congress on its part gave a concrete shape to its resolution by setting up linguistic provinces for its own organizational purposes. Surprisingly, Haryana did not figure even in the list of 18 Congress provinces. It was clubbed with Punjab, although its existence was implicitly accepted by accepting that Punjab was a bilingual province, Punjabi and Hindustani being the languages of its people.[6]

Besides this, the Congress emphasized the need of redrawing the map of India on socio-linguistic basis on several occasions. It supported the cases of several suffering people. But never was a word uttered about Haryana. Surprisingly, when the organizational map of Congress was redrawn in 1939 and the strength of its linguistic provinces was raised to 20, Haryana's separate existence was again negated. Punjab, which was bilingual in 1921, became unilingual in 1939. This strange phenomenon can be easily explained if we throw a glance over the Congress leadership of Punjab at that time. It comprised by and large of the Punjabi Hindus. The backward Haryana region had hardly any leader there who could speak on their behalf.[7]

The New Era

Unlike, Congress, however, the Muslims League took an interesting stand in this matter. Pirzada Muhammad Hussain, chairman, reception committee of the All-India Muslim League session held at Delhi in 1926, advocated the separation of Haryana from Punjab.[8] In 1940, Sir Muhammad Iqbal also spoke in the same vein during the course of his speech propounding his so-called Allahabad theory of 'Muslim India within India'.[9] Similar statements were made by some Muslim League activists on other occasions also.[10]

Here a pertinent question may arise: Why did of all the parties the Muslim League hold such a view? Was it moved by the sad plight of the Haryanavis? The answer in one word is 'no'. The League did it in its own interest. In Punjab, Muslims constituted 55.3 per cent of the population. The Hindus were 31.8 per cent. The Sikhs counted for 11.1 per cent. In other words, the Muslims here had a majority of a little over 5 per cent over others—not a comfortable majority by all means. But if the Hindu-dominated Haryana region was gone, then Muslims would form 61.8 per cent of the Punjab population. The Hindus and Sikhs would be just 23.6 per cent and 12.6 per cent respectively. Secondly, Haryana's separation would force the Unionist Party (the then ruling party in Punjab), to change its secular outlook. With no supply of Hindu MLAs from Haryana, it would be a Muslim party or in other words Muslim League. In Haryana, too, the Muslims who went for the Unionist Party would perforce opt for Muslim League. It was for these reasons that the Muslim League had been all along for advocating separation of Haryana from Punjab. But whatever the reasons or motives, a right demand was being voiced insofar as the interest of the suffering Haryanavis was concerned.[11]

In 1931 the demand found a great supporter—surprisingly an English man—Sir Geoffery Corbett, ICS. On the occasion of the second Round Table Conference, in England, Sir Geoffery circulated a memorandum on 12 October which enjoyed the blessings of Mahatma Gandhi,[12] setting out that

> the existing provinces though possibly convenient for the purposes of British rule, are not necessarily suitable units for responsible self-government. For

instance, historically the Ambala Division (Haryana) is part of Hindustan, its inclusion in the Province of the Punjab was an incident of British rule. Its language is Hindustani, not Punjabi. It is fair to assume, therefore, that in any rational scheme for the redistribution of provinces, the Ambala Division less Simla district and the north-west corner of the Ambala district would be separated from the Punjab.[13]

The new Punjab and Haryana, would, according to Sir Geoffery, have the following population[14] (see Table 1).

Gandhiji gave his blessings to the scheme, for in the newly created Punjab the provision of joint electorate would be acceptable to the Muslims. This would have created positive repercussions elsewhere and the communal tangle would have eased. The Sikh and Hindu representatives from Punjab did not accept this proposal, however.[15]

Encouraged and inspired by Gandhiji's blessing to Sir Geoffery's scheme, Desh Bandhu Gupta, a prominent Congress activist from Haryana, made a public statement in favour of the separation of Haryana from Punjab on 9 December 1932:

> The Ambala Division, excluding Simla district, has never been a part of the Punjab throughout Indian History and is distinct from Punjab in all respects. Tagged to the Punjab by accident of the haphazard growth of the province, it has been misfit and owing to wide differences of language, culture and tradition and history, and mode of life, no less than ethical distinctions, the population of Ambala has remained un-assimilated in the Province.[16]

The proposal was disliked by the Congress and the Unionists alike in Punjab. Nor did it suit the British imperial interest, for separation of Haryana would have, to some extent, solved Punjab's communal tangle and might have had wider repercussions, too, in this sphere.

In this situation, there came the freedom on 15 August 1947 and also partition of Punjab and the country. At this point, I venture to make a bold

TABLE 1: COMMUNITY-WISE POPULATION IN THE PROPOSED BIFURCATED STATES, 1931

Community	Present position		New Punjab		Haryana	
	Total	%	Total	%	Total	%
Muslims	11,444,000	55.5	10,45,000	61.3	999,000	26.4
Hindus	6,579,000	31.8	3,997000	23.6	2582000	68.3
Sikhs	2,294,000	11.1	2,137,000	12.6	157,000	0.4.2
Others	367,000	1.8	324,000	02.0	44,000	01.1

guess. If the nationalist forces in India had accepted the existence of distinct cultural groups and had worked for getting them separate provinces and full chances to develop themselves culturally, economically and politically, the partition might have been averted. The two nations theory of Jinnah was a falsehood. But existence of many distinct linguistic-cultural groups was a fact. Denial of a fact led to the acceptance of a falsehood.

Post-Independence Developments

After independence, the demand for Haryana's formation gained momentum. The reasons were: (i) politicization of Haryanavis, (ii) the Congress manifesto of 1845-6 which promised to give linguistic provinces, and (iii) the fall of the Unionist party which was opposing the separation of Haryana from Punjab, fearing its own fall owing to loss of Haryana MLAs.

In the meantime, the Sikhs also raised their demand for a Punjabi suba by excluding the Hindi-speaking areas of Haryana from Punjab. So far they were opposed to the separation of Haryana from Punjab. But they wanted it now for the simple reason that if Haryana was separated then Sikhs would be 52.8 per cent and Hindus 31.8 per cent. They would be able to rule the state after division, they thought.[17]

After a while the two demands of Haryana and Punjabi Suba for the bifurcation of the state got linked together. The Punjabi Hindus for their fear of being reduced into a minority opposed both the demands. And so did the government. A question may arise here, however: What precisely were the reasons which made the government change its old stand of forming states on linguistic-cultural basis? Obviously, the partition of the country which had created such a fear in the minds of the leadership that any demand for a separate state was also looked upon as endangering the national unity still further. More so in the case of Punjab where religion was mixed up with a linguistic-cultural question.[18]

Instead of accepting the demand for bifurcation, the Punjab government took some measures to assuage the feelings of both the groups voicing the demand. The Education Department, Punjab ordered, for instance, in June 1948 that 'all education in the schools of the East Punjab shall be given in the mother-tongue of the children'. This did not satisfy the people, however. The Punjab government took another bold step. On 1 October 1949, they gave what is known as 'the Sachar Formula' according to which the state was divided into two regions: (i) Punjabi-speaking region; and (ii) Hindi-speaking region. Punjabi in Gurmukhi script was made the official language in the Punjabi region, and Hindi written in Devanagari script in the Hindi region. Even this medicine did not cure the disease.[19]

As in Punjab, so in other parts of India, there was popular demand for fulfilling the promise to give linguistic provinces made before independence. As a result, there came the States Reorganization Commission (SRC), 1955. Both the parties—the protagonists of the Punjabi Suba and Haryana, as also the antagonists to the demands presented their cases very forcefully before the Commission. The Commission was, however, not convinced by the arguments of the 'separatists'. It gave its verdict (10 Oct. 1955) against any division of Punjab for the following reasons:

> We are convinced that the separation of the so-called Hariana areas of the Punjab which are deficit areas, and are according to the memorandum submitted by the Akali Dal, only a liability which can be better borne by their neighbours with whom they have greater affinity in language and culture will be no remedy for any ills, real or imaginary from which this area at present suffers.[20]

The Regional Formula

The SRC report caused great resentment among the supporters of the two subas. As expected, there was agitation on the part of both the parties. Surely, the agitation of Akalis was much more forceful and dynamic than that of their Haryanavi counterparts. However, to assuage the agitated feelings of the people, the government came with a new formula—the so-called Regional Formula, on 27 July 1956, according to which

(i) the state of Punjab was made bilingual, with Punjabi (in Gurmukhi script) and Hindi (in Devanagari script) as the official languages of the state;
(ii) the state was divided into two regions—Punjabi and Hindi regions;
(iii) the official language of each region at the district level and below was to be the respective regional language;
(iv) for each region a Regional Committee of the members of the State Assembly belonging to each region was formed which was supposed to legislate on specified matters relating to their respective regions;
(v) the state was to continue to have one legislature for the whole of the state, however, and one governor aided and advised by the Council of Ministers.[21]

TABLE 2: DISCRIMINATION AGAINST HARYANAVIS[22]

Subject	Punjab (six districts) Measure	Haryana (six districts) Measure
Food grains (thousand tonnes)		
Wheat	768.6	400.7
Rice	129.6	41.3
Irrigation (lakh acres)	22.0	05.0
Factories (regd.)	3,526.0	959.0
Shops/hotels, etc.	1,33,883.0	57,892.0
Vehicles (jeeps, trucks, etc.)	1,9431.0	9,525.0
Banks (cooperative, etc.)	335.0	171.0

This formula also failed to satisfy either side. The protagonists of the demand for separate Haryana kept on voicing their demand, though their voice was feeble. But this was not the case with the Akalis. They took the government bull by its horns. By 1960, their agitation became a bloody struggle. The government reacted strongly and put 50,000 Akalis behind the bars. There was lull in the storm for some time. But the demand was again revived in 1965.

The protagonists of the demand for separate Haryana also intensified their agitation. They spoke and brought out literature to convince the masses that they were great sufferers in Punjab. A specimen of this literature may be of interest (see Table 2).

Birth of the State

After some time, the agitation for Punjabi suba took a new turn. The Akali leader Fateh Singh threatened to immolate himself if the suba was not conceded by 25 October 1965. This moved the government into action. There was an announcement in the Lok Sabha on 6 September that a 'cooperative solution of the problem agitating the minds of the people of Punjab will be discovered on goodwill and a reasoned approach'.[23]

Shortly afterwards, a Parliamentary Committee of twenty-two members belonging to different parties and from both the Houses of Parliament[24] was appointed to recommend a solution to the problem. The Committee looked into the matter and recommended bifurcation of the state of Punjab. On 21 March 1966, the Minister for Home Affairs made a statement in the Lok Sabha that 'the government had given careful thought to the recommendations made by the Committee of the members of the Parliament and had decided to accept in principle that the present state of Punjab be reconstituted on linguistic basis'.[25]

On 3 April 1966, the Punjab Boundary Commission consisting of Justice J.C. Shah, S. Datt, and A.M. Philip was constituted to draw the boundary line dividing the two states.[26] The Commission submitted its report in May 1966, recommending the inclusion of the following areas in Haryana: Hisar district, Mahendragarh district, Karnal district, Gurgaon district, Rohtak district, Narwana and Jind tehsils of Sangrur district and Naraingarh, Ambala and Jagadhari tehsils of Ambala district.[27] The rest of Punjab constituted the Punjabi suba. The parliament accepted the report and passed the Punjab Reorganization Bill on 18 September 1966: it became the Act 31 of 1966.[28] In consequence, the seventeenth state of Haryana was born on 1 November 1966.[29] A long cherished dream of the people was fulfilled. They were happy.

NOTES

1. *Indian Round Table Conference (Second Session) Report*, p. 108.
2. For details see K.C. Yadav, *Haryana*, vol. II, pp. 331-52.
3. Ibid.
4. K.C. Yadav, 'Language, Religion and Politics: A Study of the Formation of the State of Haryana', presented at the SALA Roundtable (1984), University of Texas at Austin (USA).
5. Ibid.
6. Ibid.
7. Ibid.
8. Ibid.
9. Ibid.
10. Ibid.
11. Ibid.
12. Ibid., *Indian Round Table Conference (Second Session), Report*, pp. 107-13.
13. Ibid.
14. Ibid.
15. Ibid.
16. *Hindustan Times*, 9 December 1932.
17. For details see Baldev Raj Nayyar, *Minority Politics in Punjab*, New Jersey, 1966.
18. Ibid.
19. For the Sachar formula see *The Punjab Boundary Commission Report*, 1966, pp. 62-3.
20. See the *States Reorganization Commission Report*, 1956, pp. 140-56.

21. Ibid., pp. 65-82.
22. To make the comparison straight and meaningful six districts from each region were selected here as follows: (i) Punjab: Jullundar, Ludhiana, Hoshiarpur, Ferozepur, Amritsar and Gurdaspur; (ii) Haryana: Ambala, Karnal, Hisar, Gurgaon, Rohtak and Mahendragarh.
23. *The Punjab Boundary Commission Report*, pp. 55-6.
24. Ibid., p. 57.
25. Ibid., pp. 58-9.
26. Ibid., pp. 60-1.
27. Ibid.
28. See *Gazette of India (Extraordinary)*, part II, section 1, no. 39, dated 18 September 1966, Bhadra 27, 1888 Saka.
29. The newly born state had an area of 43,887 sq. km. and population of 75,99,759 persons living in 6,690 villages and 62 towns. Its headquarters was placed in Chandigarh.

Part Three

CULTURE

17

Religion, Caste, Class and Social Institutions

RELIGION

To begin with, the Haryana society was uni-religious, the people professed Hinduism. A little later, about the sixth to third century BC, two reformed forms of the old religion, namely the Jainism and Buddhism came to have their hold over the people. Several centuries later—in the medieval times, to be precise—there came Islam, closely followed by Sikhism (eighteenth century) and Christianity (nineteenth century). Today, people here follow all these religions, as shown in Table 1.

HINDUISM

The majority of the people, as shown in Table 1, follow Hinduism (89.4%). This ancient religion is, as in olden times, divided into several well-marked sects, like Shaivism, Vaishnavaism, etc. Surprisingly, however, the people here do not belong to any particular sect now, as their, ancestors once did. They have faith in all the sects—of course in varying

TABLE 1: MAJOR RELIGIONS IN HARYANA[1]

Religion	Population	Percentage of total population
Hindus	1,46,86,512	89.4
Sikhs	9,56,836	6.2
Muslims	7,63,775	4.0
Jains	35,296	0.3
Christians	15,699	0.1
Buddhists	2,058	neg.
Other religions	156	neg.
Religion not stated	3,316	neg.
Total	1,64,63,468	100.0

measures. They hold the old Triad, Brahma, Vishnu and Mahesha in esteem. Lord Rama and Krishna, are also worshipped with equal if not more veneration. Then come Ganesha, Hanumana and Bhairon. They are also worshipped like the Triad at several places.[3]

Besides these, some benevolent gods are also worshipped with devotion. Of these *Suryadevata* or the Sun God is the main. On Sundays, the *bhaktas* worship him by abstaining from salt, and doing some rituals. Then comes *Dhartimata* or the Mother Earth. Most of the people do obeisance to and invoke her as they slip out from beds in the morning. The peasant, the labourer, the shopkeeper almost everybody begins his work by a *namaskara* to her. The planets like Saturn, Mercury and Mars are also worshipped. While building a house, nine planets are invoked together. During an eclipse, people bathe in a sacred stream or pool and repeat the *mantras* which 'release the Sun or Moon from Rahu's and Ketu's persecution'.[3] Occasionally, river goddesses, the Yamuna and the Ganga are also worshipped. People go to Delhi and Hardwar to bathe in them to earn *punya*. Mother goddess is worshipped in numerous and diverse forms: as the goddess of learning, she is Saraswati; as the goddess of destruction, she is Kali; as genetrix, she is symbolized by the Yoni; as a type of beauty, she is Uma; and as a malignant being, she is Durga. She is Sati, Ambika, Gauri, Bhawani, Tara and Paravati—the faithful spouse of Shiva living in Kailasha, the sacred mountain.[4] In villages they are *Mata*, however. The women, who are their devout devotees, can hardly identify them in any other form.

The animals, birds, etc., are also venerated. For instance cow is worshipped on the eighth of the light half of *Kartika* on the occasion of the *Gopashtami.* During nine days in the month of *Bhadon*, the snake is worshipped. The shady *peepal* tree, the village well (*kuwan*) and the pond (*johar*) are worshipped on special occasions.[5]

The people here—almost without an exception—believe in God. They believe in heaven and hell. They believe in transmigration of soul, in theory of *karma* (effort) and *bhagya* (fate).

Muslims

After Hindus come the Muslims. They were a numerous community before partition. But a large majority of them have gone to Pakistan (1947). Now they form, as noted above, only 4.05 per cent of the population. As most of them are converts from Hinduism, so they have a large number of common religious beliefs and practices with Hindus. They have, like Hindus, raised the prophet to the status of the Lord of the

Universe, *Sarwar-i-Sainat.* The deification is extended to the saints, too, who also stand raised to the level of minor or major deities. Take, for instance, the cases of Sheikh Abdul Qadir, Sheikh Muinuddin Chisti and Syed Salar Masud. They are all worshipped in a spirit that could be called distinctly polytheistic—circumambulation of the shrine, tying of threads in the *dargah* with the expectation of fulfilment of a desire, gift of money for the *urs* as well as offering of flowers and scents, lighting of lamps at the graves, all bear testimony to this fact.[6] The degree of 'sub-conscious influence of Hindu beliefs and practices is too pervasive to be precisely stated—even the most orthodox could not escape it. A large number of Muslims believe in omens and consult astrologers for something or the other. Many of them worship, of course with a little variation, earth, water and air, the trees, rivers and mountains, and so on. The old practice of snake worship seems to have taken the form of veneration for Guga, who has been believed to be a Chauhan chief by the Rajputs, and a *pir* by the Muslims. Khwaja Khizr, the god of water is also venerated like that. We have it on the testimony of the author of *Siyar-ul-Mutakhirin* that this practice is of Hindu origin.[7]

Besides this, in the villages where the bulk of the population lives, both the Muslims and Hindus worship several common village deities. Women in general play an important part in this respect. A Muslim woman who has not offered her respects to the small-pox goddess (*Sitala*) would feel that she has deliberately risked her child's life. On special occasions she feeds Brahmana priests. Similarly, a Hindu woman would regularly make offerings at the shrines of Muslim saints every thursday, and at the time of a marriage in the family.[8]

Other Religions

The Sikhs, Jains and other communities also show great deal of similarity with the Hindus in their religious beliefs and customs. This explains why we have been witnessing communal homogeneity in the state since time immemorial.[9]

THE CASTE

As elsewhere, the caste is, and has always been, for centuries out of number, a very powerful social institution in Haryana. It seems relevant, therefore, that in what follows a detailed discussion of its origin, and structural and functional aspects may be attempted.

First the origin. This is an exceedingly difficult problem and scholars feel at loss to say anything definite about it. We often hear some of them repeating what an old agnostic said while summing up his philosophy: 'The only thing I know is that I know nothing, and I am not quite sure that I know that.'[10] I wish to shed some light on this otherwise complex problem by studying the past with the present day or later evidence. This method may, at its face, appear to be non-scientific. But it is not so, obviously for two reasons: (i) old evidence is not available, and (ii) the caste, though an ancient institution, is still living in the present as alive as it was in the days gone by. So if a living plant cannot be studied from its roots down below for some reason or the other, we can do it from the top, taking branches, etc., first.

The caste, studied from this approach, seems to have its origin in purely economic sphere. Later, some other factors also contributed to its making. In the vedic period the caste was not there. Then, there were four *varnas* or classes determined on a person's merit and qualifications. Two heads may be equal, says the *Rig*, 'but their work is not equal; the cows born of the same mother do not yield the milk in equal proportion, twin from one mother are not equal in their strength and capacity and the two individuals of society have not the equality in giving alms'.[11] Therefore, men stand divided into 'four classes by their worth': 'Some are selected for the administration (Kshtriyas), some for the performance of grand *yajna* and intellectual feats (Brahmanas), some for the finance and trade (Vaishyas), and some for the labour and service (Shudras).'[12]

The *varna* system seems to have worked well for some time. But when population increased and economic necessities in the changed circumstances compelled people to change their economic pursuits, it failed. Under compulsion, the Brahmanas took to Kshtriyas' professions and Kshtriyas went for agriculture and trade. The traders thrown out of the profession took to services, and dynamic Shudras turned agriculturists and traders. And thus came the castes. Examples from later history will, I suppose, bring home this truth more clearly. Some Brahmanas, despite religious sanction that a man born of a Brahmana parentage would remain a Brahmana, were not accepted as such because they had abandoned (*tyag dena*) the priestly profession. They became Tyagis. Likewise the Brahmanas who took to handicrafts became Thavis. They were also no more Brahmanas. The Mahabrahmanas, who performed the last rites of persons to earn their livelihood, became so impure that in many villages they were, until the other day, not allowed to enter the temples. Similarly, the Dakauts and Gujratis who took to non-Brahmanical professions also fell from 'the sacred order' and became separate castes.[13] 'Some Tarkhans, Lohars, and Nais of Sirsa, known to have been Jats or Rajputs within quite recent times, have taken to the hereditary occupations of these castes; and some of the Chauhans of Karnal, whose fathers were born Rajputs, had taken to weaving and became Sheikhs.'[14]

Besides economic factor, two other factors, namely artificial social rules and political dominance also played some role. Sir Denzil Ibbetson has given examples to substantiate this contention. 'In Sirsa,' says he, 'we have instance of clans who were a few generations ago accounted Jats being now generally classed as Rajputs, having meanwhile practised greater exclusiveness in matrimonial matters, and having abandoned widow marriage; while the reverse process is no less common.' Some Rajputs—'Cauhans on the Haryana-Delhi border are no longer recognized as Rajputs since they have begun to marry their widows.' Besides this, 'one and the same tribe is often known as Rajput where it has and as Jat where it has not risen to political importance'. 'A few decades ago,' says Sir Denzil, 'Apharias, a clan of Ahirs in Rewari, began to seclude their women and abandon widow marriage; they no longer intermarried with the other Ahirs, and were about to be reckoned a separate caste, but other Ahirs rose up and frustrated their aims.'[15] This is how castes have been formed in the past.[16]

Even in deciding exact position in the scale of social hierarchy, the three factors referred to above played a vital role. The stamp of ritual purity—impurity is only a show off. Some sociologists/anthropologists have, on the other hand, attached greater importance to this factor than it really deserves. For instance, if we accept their position, then a caste should hold the same position everywhere throughout India. But actually it is not so: a caste may occupy different positions at the same time. For instance, an Ahir in Haryana occupies the same position as is done by a Rajput, but not in U.P. or Bihar. Similarly, Jat is as high in social position as a Rajput in Haryana, but not in some parts of Rajasthan; there Rajput claims superiority. This can be explained in the light of what has been said above, namely, the true basis of caste has not been religious but economic. Two other factors, political dominance and artificial rules confirm this factor. We can safely say that religious and ritualistic plastering on the castes which has been made to appear as their creator and preserver is in fact only an outer coating—just a show off.

Now a word about castes in Haryana—their general description, settlement and functioning.

The Hindu Castes

Among the Hindus the priestly castes occupy important position. Obviously, the Brahmanas stand at the highest rung of the social ladder. They are divided into five main groups: the Gaurs, Saraswats, Khandelwals, Dhimas and Chaurasias. The Gaurs believe that they came originally from Bengal, but it is much more likely that they came as *purohitas* or family priests of the various immigrant agricultural tribes among whom they were settled at various places. The Saraswats were, however, the original settlers of the region (the Saraswati valley). Earlier they 'were of high rank but since medieval times they are being treated apparently below the Gaurs who until recently neither ate, drank nor intermarried with them'. The Khandelwals and Dhimas, who in all probability migrated from Rajasthan in the early medieval times, are ranked a little below the Gaurs and Saraswats. The Chaurasias, so says the tradition, are so named because they assisted at Janamejaya's holocaust of snakes, and received a gift of *chaurasi* (84) villages. The Brahmanas have hundreds of genets (*gotras*), the most common ones being the Bhardwaja, Vashishtha, Gautama, Parashra, and Sandalya.

The Brahmanas live in every village and town, working as *purohitas*, though some of them have also adopted agriculture and other professions and are not directly engaged in religious functions. But priest or peasant or anything else, the Brahmana is held in esteem by Hindus everywhere. Out of respect for his socio-religious status, he is called *dada* (like grandfather) in the countryside.

There are some castes which, though belong to the Brahmana fold, have come to have separate identity of their own. Of these the most important are the Gujrati or Vyasa Brahmanas,[18] who came from Gujarat several centuries ago and settled here. They consider themselves higher than other Brahmanas. They are always fed first; and they bless a Gaur when they meet him. The latter do not accept them superior, however, for they take inauspicious offering also. Another caste—Dakuts[19]—are also treated like that. They claim to have come from Agroha in Hisar. They are pre-eminent as astrologers and soothsayers. They receive even 'unlucky offerings', such as 'black things and old clothes'. They number only a few thousand in Haryana and are poor and backward. Another such caste is of the Tyagis.[20] They are found in Karnal and Kurukshetra districts in some numbers. Ask them, says Sir Denzil, and they will claim to be Gaur Brahmanas by origin, and to have acquired their present name because they abandoned priestly functions and took to agriculture. Elliot, in his *Races of the North-West Provinces* has identified them 'with the Takkas of the Scythian race who had the snake for their totem, and whose destruction by Raja Janamejaya is supposed to be commemorated in the tradition of that monarch's holocaust of serpents'. The Tyagis, however, deny Elliot's contention. They are probably the oldest inhabitants of the upper Yamuna Khadar.[20]

The next position in the social hierarchy is occupied by the trading castes, obviously due to their better economic status. Of these castes the Banias are the most important, They are divided into three main divisions: Agrawals, Oswals and Maheshwaris. These three divisions 'appear to be real tribal divisions, because none of these inter-marry, eat or smoke with each other'. All the three divisions claim their origin from Rajasthan and it does not seem unlikely that they migrated from there in the early medieval times. Like Brahmanas, the Banias also live in almost every village and town in Haryana, controlling business, trade and banking. They are mostly well-off and for that reason, as already indicated, command respect in the society.[21]

Another trading caste is of Khatris. They live mostly in towns. Though mainly engaged in trade, they are also largely employed in the services. And same is the case with Aroras, another trading caste.[22]

The third position in the social hierarchy is claimed by some peasant castes. Among them the Jats are important. They are for the most part concentrated in Sonepat, Rohtak, Bhiwani, Sirsa, Hisar and Jind and some parts of Gurgaon, Karnal, Kurukshetra and Ambala.[23] They are divided into clans, the chief among them being the Gathwala whose members trace their origin from Ghazni. Their headquarters is at Ahulana, a village in the Gohana tehsil of Sonepat. They are numerous in this region and are also found south of Karnal. They are also called Maliks.[24]

Another important clan is of the Dalals who live in Rohtak and in the adjoining territory of Sonepat, Bhiwani, Hisar and Jind. They were settled in Rohtak some 30 generations back. Their ancestor had four sons from whom the Dalal, Deshwal, Mann and Suhag (Deswal) *gotras* sprang up. That speaks why these four tribes do no intermarry.[25]

Then there are the Dahiyas found on the north-eastern border of the Sampla tehsil and the adjoining portion of the Sonepat tehsil and Delhi. They are, say some scholars, probably the Dahim of Alexander's chronicles. Earlier their headquarters is Bhatgaon in Sonepat. In old records the Dahiyas are not found on friendly footings with the former clan, the Gathwalas. Earlier, they used to fight with each other, sometimes dividing the whole tract into two factions formed behind them. This factional fight showed its ugly head during the uprising of 1857 and even after it on a number of occasions. It has, however, subsided now.[26]

Another important clan is of the Gulias. They declare that they were originally Brahmanas who lost caste by inadvertently drinking liquor in a large vessel (*gol* and hence Gulia).[27] The Phogats are another important clan in Jind and Bhiwani and have spread into the neighbouring portions of Gurgaon and Rohtak. They do not intermarry with the Deshwals—the reason for this is not explained,[28] however. The Poonias are found in Rohtak, Sirsa, Jind and curiously enough in Ambala too. They are not a numerous clan.[29] The Beniwals are found chiefly in Hisar and Sirsa. In the fifteenth century the Beniwals held one of the six cantons into which Bikaner was then divided. At present their position is not so strong, however; their number is small. And so is the case with the Nains who are chiefly found in Bhiwani but of late have spread into Hisar and Sirsa also. Unlike them, however, the Rathis are a numerous clan. The word Rath is said to mean 'strong handed' or 'zabardast'. Their stronghold is Rohtak and they are among the oldest inhabitants of the tract.[30]

The Sahrawats are almost confined to Delhi, Gurgaon, and Rohtak where their settlements date from some 25 generations back.[31] Then there are Ahlawats who came from Jaipur some 30 generations ago and are settled in Rohtak, Sonepat and Karnal. The Deshwals or 'men of the country' are, as already stated, from the same stock as the Dalals. They are most numerous in Rohtak, Karnal and Gurgaon.[32] Other important clans are the Jakhars and Sangwans. They are believed to have come 20 generations back from Bikaner. They have common origin with Biru and Kadian clans. The Sangwans are most numerous in Jind and Hisar, though there is a small settlement of them in Rohtak also; while the Jakhar are almost confined to Gurgaon and adjoining Jhajjar tehsil of Rohtak; the Biru and Kadians are scattered in Rohtak.[33] Another important clan is of Dhankars who, as already noted, are of the same stock as the Rathis. They are almost confined to Jhajjar and Rohtak.[34] The Khatris, Dagars, Rawats, Chauhans, Lambas and Tanwars are also clans of some importance, though their numbers are small.[35]

The Jats are 'a bold peasantry accustomed to handle the ploughshare and wield the sword with equal readiness and success, second to no other race in industry and courage'. They are agriculturists and call themselves proudly *zamindars* (husbandmen). In the social hierarchy they occupy the same position as is claimed by other cultivating castes, such as Ahirs, Gujars, Rajputs, Rors. They eat and smoke with all these castes without any reservations.

Next come the Ahirs (popularly known as Abhiras in history). They are for the most part concentrated in the region around Rewari and

Narnaul, which because of their preponderance has come to be known as Ahirwal or the 'Abode of Ahirs'. In the districts of Sonepat, Rohtak, Hisar, Bhiwani, Kaithal, Kurukshetra and Karnal they number only a few thousand.

The Ahirs are divided into three sub-castes: (i) the Nandavanshis, who call themselves the offspring of Nanda, the foster-father of Lord Krishna; (ii) the Yuduvanshis who claim to be descendants of Yadu, the son of great Arya king Yayati; and (iii) the Gwalvanshis, who claim to have descended from the *gwala* friends of Lord Krishna. Except for a negligible minority, all the Ahirs in Haryana are Yaduvanshis and they call themselves 'Yadavas'. The Ahirs are not clanish like Jats, but have *gotras* all right. For all practical purposes, they stand as one 'clan'.

We cannot say for certain when were the Ahirs settled in Haryana. The *Mahabharata* places them here with another tribe called Shudra. Obviously, it is on the basis of such evidences that V.V. Mirashi has suggested that probably the original habitat of the Abhiras (Ahirs) was the region between the Sutlej and the Yamuna. From here some of them migrated beyond Mathura in the east and Maharashtra in the south. Tall, wiry and smart, the Ahirs make first rate agriculturists. The early British writers have spoken very highly of them as farmers—'Ahir-Kheti ki tadbir' (Ahirs are well versed in the art of agriculture). They are all Hindus. They chiefly worship Lord Krishna. Their birth, death and marriage ceremonies resemble those of the Jats, Gujars and Rors. Like them they practise Karewa, but the elder brother does not marry the widow of the younger. They eat uncooked and cooked food with all Brahmanas and Banias, but the latter do not eat uncooked food with them. They eat, and smoke with Rajputs, Jats, Gujars, Sunars and Barhis.[36]

Like Ahirs, the Gujars also constitute important segment of population. Being a pastoral tribe their settlements are mostly found in the riverine low lands along the Aravali hills in the south and the Shivaliks in the north. The region around Jagadhri and Buria where they lived in large numbers, was called 'Gujarat'[37] until recently. They are fine people who have had always been lovers of free living and hence always in revolt against the rulers of Delhi. Denzil Ibbetson perhaps means to say the same thing in different words: 'The Gujars have been turbulent throughout the history. They were constant thorns in the side of Delhi Emperors and are still ever-ready to take advantage of the loosening of the bonds of discipline.'

The Gujars also have many clans of which the four, Rawals, Chhokars, Chauhans and Kalisans are the principal ones. Other genets are Cheharwal or Deharwal, Bokan and Poswal in Gurgaon, Faridabad, and the neighbourhood of Delhi, Bhonkari and Bhodwal in Ambala; Karhawal in Rohtak; Bang and Khatana in Karnal and Gurgaon; Khari in Sirsa; Chauri in Hansi; and Garsi in Kurukshetra. Professionally, the Haryana Gujars have been, as referred to earlier, a pastoral caste. But now they are by and large agriculturists. The theory of their aboriginal descent which has sometimes been pronounced stands conclusively negatived by their cast or countenance. They are of the same social standing as the Jat, Ahir, Ror, etc., all eating and drinking in common without any scruple. An old proverb says: 'The Jat, Gujar, Ahir, and Golas are all four hail fellows, well met.'[38]

Slightly fewer in number than the Gujars are the Rajputs.[39] They are found scattered throughout the state. Like other castes, they are also divided into many clans, the chief among whom are the Tanwars. It is supposed that they are the original inhabitants of the region and in the early medieval times they ruled over here for a pretty long time from Delhi. This is the reason that the Tanwars are found here in a large number. Then come the Chauhans. They ruled over Ajmer, Sakambhari, etc., for a pretty long time and occupied Haryana in the early medieval times about 22 generations ago, probably in the time of Bahlol Lodi. They occupied the fertile tract in Ambala, Kurukshetra, Karnal and Jind, by driving out their original occupants, the Pundirs across the Yamuna. The next important clan is of the Mandhars. They are confined to the Nardak of Karnal, Kurukshetra and Ambala. In the early medieval time, they came from Ayodhya to Jind. They drove the Chandel and Bara Rajputs who occupied the tract near the Siwaliks and across the Ghaggar respectively. They fixed their capital at Kalayat (Kaithal) with minor centres at Safidon in Jind and Asandh in Karnal. But they have in more recent times spread down into Karnal district, with Gharaund as their local centre.[40]

The Pundirs, another important clan, were the local rulers in the early medieval times, with capitals at Pundri, Ramba, Habri and Pundrak; but they were dispossessed by the Chauhans under Rana Har Rai. They fled beyond the Yamuna. Some of them lived back, however; and their descendants are still found in the Indri pargana and some parts of Karnal, Kurukshetra and Ambala. The Bargujars,[41] another clan, are in small numbers in Gurgaon whence they came from Punjab about the fifteenth century. The Jatus,[42] another important clan, are believed to be Tanwars who once held almost the whole of Hisar district, and are still most numerous in that district and the neighbouring portions of Rohtak,

Bhiwani and Jind. The Rathors, Rawats and Gaurawas are also met with in some other districts but their number is extremely small.

The above account would indicate that in the early medieval times most of the Rajput clans occupied very important position in Haryana. Later they took to agriculture, the only respectable calling they could think of. But although in possession of large holdings, want of industry and false pride (looking down upon manual labour as degrading) made them poor farmers.[43] But now the position has changed. The Rajputs have taken to agriculture in all seriousness and they are good farmers. Besides, a large number of them are serving in the armed forces and police. They make first rate soldiers.

The other important peasant castes are of the Rors and Sainis. The former are settled in Kurukshetra, Kaithal and Karnal where they have their 84 (*chaurasi*) villages. Amin, a small village near Kurukshetra, is their headquarters.[44] The Rors are good farmers and stand on the same social footing as the Jats, Ahirs, Rajputs and Gujars.[45] The Sainis, enjoy the same social status and occupy almost the same tract as occupied by Rors. Their number is small.[46]

The artisan castes, Sunars, Barhis, Lohars and Kumhars, occupy the next position in the caste hierarchy.[47] The Scheduled Castes, Chamars, Dhanaks, Balmikis come last of all.[48] Until recently they were treated as untouchables by the so-called *swarnas*, but now the situation has changed. The plague of untouchability has been checked to some extent, although not wiped off in full.[49]

The Muslim Castes

Although Islam does not permit casteism,[50] in actual practice it is there. The Muslim society is broadly speaking stratified into two divisions:[52] (i) *ashraf* (comprising the higher castes), and (ii) *ajlaf* (consisting of the lower castes). The *ashrafs* are the Sayeds, Sheikhs, Mughals, Pathans and Rajputs, the *ajlafs* comprise the rest of the castes.[53]

The Sayeds occupy the highest place in the society. They were found almost everywhere, towns being their favourite abode, before 1947 when they migrated to Pakistan. For the most part they belonged to the Zaidi branch.[54] Besides being priests, the Sayeds held land and did farming. But in the latter profession they were bad. To quote Sir Denzil Ibbetson: 'The Sayed is emphatically the worst cultivator I know. Lazy, thriftless and intensely ignorant and unconcerned.'[55]

After the Sayeds came the Sheikhs. They were of two types: (i) the

Sheikhs proper, who claimed to be the original inhabitants of Arabia, like the Qureshis, Ansaris and Muhajarins and (ii) the Sheikhs of Indian origin (later converts to Islam), who despite conversion retained their old *gotras* and many customs. Besides these some low caste people who were converted to Islam in the medieval ages also called themselves Sheikhs. Whatever their origin, the social aspirations of Sheikhs have been always high. There is a Persian proverb which substantiates this: 'The first year I was a weaver (*julaha*), the next year a Sheikh. This year if prices rose I shall be a Sayed.'[56] Like Sayeds, the Sheikhs of Haryana have also gone to Pakistan.

After the priestly castes came the Mughals who were scattered all over the region, before 1947, although their favourite places were big towns. Although most of them were in services, some did take to agriculture also. They were not a very orderly lot: equipped with false pride of racial superiority, they quarrelled so often on trivial matters. They joined the army and police services, too, and made good soldiers and policemen.[57]

The Pathans, too, like the Mughals were, prior to their immigration to Pakistan (1947) scattered all over the region. Most of them seemed to have come here during the Sultanate period. Though socially important, they were not a numerous castes.[58] Another important Muslim caste was of the Rajputs. Before 1947, they were also scattered all over the region, though they hardly commanded any important socio-political status anywhere except in Sirsa and Hisar.[59] Like their Hindu counterparts, they were bold people, mostly engaged in agricultural pursuits.[60] Interestingly, though these people had given up the religion of their forefathers long ago, they still retained, like Meos, most of their age-old customs and rituals. They avoided *sagotra* marriages, celebrated many Hindu festivals, like Holi, Diwali and Dushera and both men and women donned Hindu style garments. The Brahmana *purohitas* conducted most of their social and religious ceremonies.[61]

The Ranghars, though no more here, were also an important Muslim caste before 1947. They were Rajputs who had embraced Islam during the medieval times. They lived in large villages in the districts of Rohtak, Hisar and Karnal. Financially, they were throughout in bad shape. Poor and needy, they took to anti-social activities almost everywhere.[62]

The Muslim Gujars, who were also an important caste before 1947, were settled in the low-lying lands along the Yamuna. They were financially poor and were mostly cattle grazers. Some of them who took to agriculture made poor farmers. They loved thieving and stealing.[63]

The Meos are another important caste who are for the most part settled in the present districts of Faridabad and Gurgaon. Because of their preponderance, the tract where they live is styled as Mewat. The Meos are a happy combination of Hinduism and Islam. Their village deities are the same as those of Hindus. They celebrate several Hindu festivals—'the Holi is with Meos a season of rough play, and is considered as important a festival as the Moharram, Id and Shabrat'. They celebrate Janmashtami, Dushera and Diwali. They often keep Brahmana priest to write the *pili chitthi* (note fixing the date of a marriage). On the day of *Amawasya*, Meos, in common with Hindu Ahirs, Gujars, etc., cease from labour; and when they make a well, the first proceeding is to erect a *chabutra* to Bhairon or Hanumana.[64]

The Meos are organized into twelve pals: Balant, Balawat, Darwal, Landawat, Chirklot, Dimrot, Dulot, Nai, Yunglot, Dahngat, Singal, and Kalesa or Kalsakhi.[65] The pals 'possess a strong feeling of unity and the power of corporate action'. They are further divided into *gotras*, which are 52 in number.[66] The major occupation of the Meos has been agriculture.

There is another important caste in Mewat of Khanzadas. The 'sons of Khans', they are precisely the Muslim equivalent to the Hindu Rajputs—'son of rajas'; and there can be little doubt that the Khanzadas are to the Meos what the Rajputs are to the Jats. They commonly say that 'they are Meos and this is their *gotra*'.[67]

Besides the above castes, there were many other minor Muslim castes, like Kumhars, Tarkhans, Telis, Awans, Chhimbas and Darzis before 1947. Their number was very small as compared to their Hindu counterparts. And same was the case with the lower castes, such as Mehtars, Julahas, Mirasis, Mochis, Qasabs, etc. Barring few, all of these people have gone to Pakistan.

The above discussion shows that like Hindus, the Muslims are also stratified into castes. Every caste is endogamous and has occupational specialization. The hierarchy is quite visible. But there is some difference, too, between the Hindu and Muslim caste systems. All Muslims, regardless of their social standings, pray together on Fridays and on other special occasions. They do not object to eating and smoking together whenever such an occasion arises and marriages can also take place in own castes, and so forth.[68]

THE SIKH CASTES

After Muslims came the Sikhs who, as noted earlier, had come to Haryana in the eighteenth century. They are mostly settled in some parts of Ambala, Kurukshetra, Kaithal, Panipat and Karnal. Later on, and especially after 1947, they moved into other districts also. Although Sikhism, like Islam, does not accept caste divisions, yet in practice these are there—very much as in Hinduism. Most of the Sikhs in the upper parts, who are agriculturists, are Jat Sikhs. There are some Gujars, Kambojs and Sainis, too, who are also peasants like the Jats. The town Sikhs, who are mostly in trade, commerce, business and services are Khatris and Aroras.[69] The artisan castes, the Kumhars, Lohars, Tarkhans and Darzis are also found in some numbers. And so is the strength of the so-called Majhabi Sikhs belonging to the so-called lower castes, such as Chamars, Chhimbas, Julahas, and Ramdasis.

The Castes in other Religions

Haryana, as noted above, had a large number of Jain population in ancient times. But now they form only 0.4 per cent of the population.[70] They are for the most part found in towns doing business or owning industries. They are mostly well-off. In social context they do not differ much from the Hindu Banias. Around Jind, however, there are a few villages of Jat Jains also who are mostly farmers.

There are some Buddhists also. They live in towns and have castes like others.[71] There are some Christians, too, who also live in towns. They, too, are divided into a number of castes—exactly like their Hindu counterparts.

The above account shows that Haryanavi society is divided into a number of castes. Their numerical strength is mentioned in Table 1. It was expected that the caste would lose its charm in the present times under the impact of modernism, education and democratic living. But unfortunately, it is not so. Barring Article 17 which abolished un-touchability, no provision is there in the Constitution which abolishes or intends to abolish the caste system. There is no law to the effect that caste being a retrograde thing should not be practised. There is no effect of modernization, education, etc., on this so-called 'hoary, relic of the past times'. Of course the purity-impurity aspect of the system is gone. Restrictions like no lower caste man could enter a temple or sit with *swarnas* in schools, etc., are hardly in vogue now. The rules relating to taking *roti* (inter-dining) with other castes stand relaxed. But not those of giving *beti* (inter-caste marriages) out of castes. There are some exceptions there no doubt but these are hardly liked by the concerned families and castemen of the 'violaters of the age-old custom'. In fact

TABLE 1: CASTE-WISE POPULATION IN HARYANA

High Castes	Percentage
Brahmana	7
Bania	5
Khatri/Arora, etc.	8
Jat	21
Rajput	3
Bishnoi	0.7
Ror	0.9
Others (Sikhs, etc.)	2.1
Total (1)	47.2
OBCs	
Ahir	5.6
Saini	3
Gujar	3
Meo	4
Others (Jangra Brahmana, Darzi, Nai, Sunar, Kumhar, etc., 66 castes)	16.75
Total (2)	32.65
Scheduled Castes	
Chamar, Balmiki, Dhanak, etc. 33 castes (3)	19.75
Others (4)	0.4
Grand Total (1) + (2) + (3) + (4)	100

Source: *Gurnam Singh Commission Report*, 1990; personal computation of Haryana population.

the caste has lost its ritualistic, religious and economic roles, but it has retained its social role and has taken up a new—political—role which has guaranteed its stay in the new situation.

THE CLASSES

The classes are yet another division of the society. Persons belonging to different castes, but having one specific type of economic interest, form a class, cutting across caste affiliations. To begin with, there were, as elsewhere, three classes—the upper, middle and lower—here. A number of *rajas*, *nawabs*, and *jagirdars* formed the first class; a few hundreds of their professional servants formed the middle classes; and the rest formed the lower classes. After some time, especially after the advent of the British (1803), the situation changed, however. Urbanization, industrialization, new education and some other such things had a serious impact on the social fabric. In the succeeding century some legislations, too, affected the position. Take for instance, the Land Alienation Act of 1900 which forbade the non-agriculturists from buying agriculturists' land. The Banias and moneylenders who were investing in land until the passage of the Act (1900) now diverted their wealth and usury towards cities. As a result, several industries like metal industry came at Jagadhari and Rewari, glass industries were started at Ambala and textile ones at Bhiwani and Hisar. This effected an increase in the urban middle classes and the working classes. In the rural areas the well-to-do peasants purchased the lands of the smaller, needy farmers on relatively easy terms owing to the absence of hard competition with the rich Banias and thus became owners of big holdings. As a result, a section of the middle classes also grew up in the villages among the peasants.[72]

Besides this, army service also did a lot of good to the village peasantry, for savings and *inams* of the soldiery bettered their financial position and pushed them from the lower classes to the middle classes.[73] Further, new members of the rural middle class sent their sons to colleges, and universities and many of them joined services and took to such professions as legal practice, etc., after their education. This was another addition to the new class.[74] The landless labourers and poor peasants, however, still remained in great numbers in their old lower (working) classes.[75]

The above account shows that the process of class formation on the modern lines had begun in this region after the British came on the scene. To begin with, this was a very feeble process. Subsequently—especially after the uprising of 1857—it received some impetus. Seriously speaking, the position was still far from satisfactory, however. The real class consciousness came to have hold on some sizable population only after the turn of of the nineteenth century in the wake of the nationalist movement.[76] In this period, the upper classes, forming a microscopic minority, became a non-entity. The middle classes gained in strength manifold. The working classes, however, still remained weak, though their number increased owing to setting up of new industries, especially after the First World War. The development of class consciousness did take place among them until the advent of independence.[77]

At present the middle classes are relatively numerous. And so is the case with the working classes. In the latter, the urban industry workers are organized and have a sort of class consciousness. In the rest the class consciousness is only skin-deep. They are torn between tradition and modernity—caste and class appeals.[78]

SOCIAL INSTITUTIONS

The Family

As elsewhere, family is the first social institution in Haryana also. It is the oldest institution. In the beginning, thousands of years ago, the families were quite large. In other words, they were of joint type, where several relations and even generations lived together under one roof. The head of the family was called *grihapati*. He was a kind and affectionate person, but if occasion demanded he would behave harshly. There was a great deal of mutual understanding among various members of the family, the elders being respected by the youngsters.[79] However, the system underwent change in modern times when the joint families gave way to nuclear ones. It began with the families among the non-peasants. But as the economy of the village diversified and changed from subsistence to cash, the joint families began to break up among the peasants also. Now hardly 30 per cent of families are, by a rough estimate, joint families in Haryana; and even these are under stress of further extinction.[80]

By this change, relations within the family have also undergone change. For instance, the break-up of joint families has effected the relationship between parents and sons. Earlier no son could dare stand and challenge a father's authority even if the latter was in the wrong. But now there are many cases where sons have done so, for a son can enjoy independence in economic terms now. Similarly, relationship between brothers has also changed. Earlier younger brothers showed 'great' respect to and even awed their elder brothers, but now it is not always so. As soon as the brothers grow they claim, at least in majority of the cases, equal status. In fact, economic reality finds expression in social behaviour of the brothers.[81] In the new circumstances, the fate of the joint families seems to be bleak. The new nuclear families have the future, for they create initiative, enterprise, spirit of hard work and industry so essential to cope with the changing situation among its members.[82]

Khandana

Next comes *khandana*. It is 'an aggregate of patrilineally related kinsmen who come from a common ancestor'. After some generations, a family grows to an almost unwieldy size and it breaks into four, five and sometimes even more families. These families comprise a *khandana.* When it becomes just unmanageable as a single social unit, a *khandana* also disintegrates and one *khandana* becomes two *khandanas*; and after sometime these two become three, four and so on.

Kinship behaviour between the members of a *khandana* is almost the same as within a joint family: the elders are treated with respect; they are addressed as in the family—for instance, father's brother is *kaka* and grandfather's son is also *kaka*. The cousins are treated as brothers and sisters. Earlier the kinship ties were very strong but in the changed circumstances these have become somewhat loose.

Thoka

The third institution is the *thoka*.[84] Several *khandanas* stemming from one root make this institution. The kinship behaviour in a *thoka* is almost the same as within the *khandana*. Head of the *thoka* is given the same respect by its members as the heads of other institutions command from theirs. The *thokas* have their specific names (usually after their ancestor), e.g. Thoka Ramuwala, Ratnawala, etc. The residential quarters of a *thoka* is called *pana*, which has been wrongly treated as a separate social unit by some sociologists/anthropologists. The relationship between different *thokas* is usually friendly. But if per chance disputes and differences occur they are settled sooner than they arise by the village elders. Some times these quarrels assume serious proportions and they are taken to courts. Such occasions are few and far between, however.

After the introduction of the panchayati raj, the *thokas* have got a new role and an important position as a political faction or a group in the village. The *thokas* form powerful political units and they function as pressure groups to get their 'own men' or 'men of their choice' got elected in the elections right from the village panchayat to the highest level. This has strengthened this social institution which was otherwise losing its importance.

The Village

After the *thoka* comes the village,[85] which, truly speaking, formed a very basic unit of social organization. It is difficult to give an exact date when this social organization came into being and which was the first village or the first few villages to be established in this region. We, however, know only this much that the villages came into existence, as noted elsewhere, thousands of years ago in the Chalcolithic Age. To begin with, their number was small but as time passed their number increased. The basis of a village are the peasant-proprietors, among whom there existed 'perfect equality, though some amongst them had more *bighas* of land and wealth than others'. In fact they inhabited the village for the first time. Then came the other inhabitants, the Brahmanas who conducted religious services and told the lucky or unlucky days for seed-time, harvest and for every other type of agricultural work; the carpenter, and the smith, who made and repaired agricultural implements; the potter, who made all the pottery of the village; the barber, who cut hair, and arranged marriages; the cobbler who provided with shoes and water-bags (*charsa*), whips, etc.; the mehtar, who performed the cleaning work; and others. Both these groups, the peasant-proprietors and other castes, were 'locked by economic and religious ties into an intimate inter-dependence', and they knew that neither would or could exist without the other, and, therefore, both cared for the existence and well-being of each other. That was the village community.[85]

In the works of the early British administrators, a great deal of disinformation is found about the village communities. Take, for instance, the following 'famous' statement of C.T. Metcalfe:

> The village communities are like little republics having nearly everything they want within themselves and almost independent of any foreign elations. They seem to last where nothing else lasts. Dynasty after dynasty tumbles down; revolution succeeds revolution. Hindu, Pathan, Mughal, Marhatta, Sikh, English are masters in turn; but the village communities remain the same. In times of troubles they arm and fortify themselves; a hostile army passes through the country, the village community collects their cattle within their walls and let the army pass unprovoked; if plunder and devastation be directed against themselves and the force employed be irresistible, they flee to friendly village at a distance, but when the storm has passed over they return and resume their occupation. If a country remains for a series of years the scene of continual pillage and massacre so that the villages cannot be inhabited, the villagers, nevertheless return whenever the power of peaceable possession revives; a generation may pass away but the succeeding generation will return. The sons will take the place of their fathers, the same site for the village, the same position for the houses, the same lands would be occupied by the descendants of those who were driven out when the village was depopulated; and it is not the trifling matter that will drive them out, for they will often maintain their post through times of disturbance and

oppression and acquire strength sufficient to resist pillage and oppression with success.[86]

This statement of Metcalfe has been quoted *ad infinitum* by scholars of rural history. When put to scrutiny, however, the statement is found to be misleading. The Haryana villages were never like 'little republics'. At no point in time, sovereignty was vested in the people; they had no say in economic matters—they were not consulted in fixing the revenues, imposing taxes, and other allied subjects; they had nothing to do with the framing of laws; even their tacit will was not ascertained in legal matters which directly affected their lives. They had no fundamental rights; they could not ask the state for even things like schools or dispensaries. The sovereigns or their officials could make any interference in any aspect of village life. It was, to be sure, government's indifference to the villages which Metcalfe has confused with the republicanism enjoyed by the villagers.[87]

In the second place, Metcalfe's theory of the village self-sufficiency is also incorrect. In his days, the villages were far from self-sufficient. Most of the villages did not produce commodities needed by them in their daily use. Even such article as salt eaten by one and all, was not locally available here. In most cases, rice, sugar, metallic vessels, cattle-seeds (like cotton-seed, etc.), cotton, and many other things of daily use were also 'imported'. Every village did not have blacksmiths, or carpenters. A goldsmith who was needed for making ornaments was also a rare species: he was usually found in big villages only. The same was true of the weavers. Even in fodder and grains, the villages were not always self-sufficient as is usually believed.

Nor were the villages 'independent of any foreign relations'. The imperial authority, the provincial *haqims* and the local official had 'relation' with the village, and if these were severed at some moment, the element of force was used to rehabilitate them. Nor were the villages insulated against political changes taking place at the centre. In fact, every political change had some influence on the villages and, therefore, we find the villages taking congnizance of these changes. With every change, the rules and regulations changed, new leaders were 'born', and a new administrative system came into existence, which affected almost every aspect of the village life.[88] Even in such matters as what crops were to be sown, the 'foreign' influence played a vital role. The peasant was to a great extent forced by his creditor to grow the type of crops which were in demand in the outside market with which he (creditor) was linked. The rate of the peasant's produce was also decided by outsiders.

In sum, the economic life was also regulated from outside the village.

It may be interesting to examine how Metcalfe arrived at such incorrect conclusions. But this question falls outside the scope of this work. It might be sufficient for our purpose here to point out that such documents should be used with utmost care, for they have tended to distort the perspective of the studies of Indian village life even when these were carried out by such celebrities of dazzling brilliance and scientific approach as Marx. Surely, but for his reliance on such documents, the master of historical dialectics would not have said:

> We must not forget that these idylic village communities, inoffensive though they may appear, had always been the solid foundation of Oriental despotism, that they restrained the human mind within the smallest possible compass, making it the unresisting book of superstition, enslaving it beneath traditional rules, depriving it of all grandeur and historical energies. We must not forget the barbarian egotism which, concentrating on some miserable patch of land, had quietly witnessed the ruin of empires, the perpetration of unspeakable cruelties, the massacre of the population of large towns, with no other consideration bestowed upon them than on natural events, itself the helpless prey of any aggressor who deigned to notice at all. We must not forget that thin, undignified, stagnatory and vegetative life that this passive sort of existence evoked on the other part in contradistinction; wild, aimless, unbounded forces of destruction and rendered murder itself a religious rite in Hindustan. We must not forget that these little communities were contaminated by distinctions of caste and by slavery; that they subjugated man to external circumstances, instead of elevating man to be the sovereign of circumstances; that they transformed a self-developing social state into never-changing natural destiny, and thus brought about a brutalizing worship of nature, exhibiting its degradation in the fact that man, the sovereign of nature, fell down on his knees. England, it is true, is causing a social revolution in Hindustan.[89]

When taken seriously, hardly any of these statements can stand close scrutiny. For instance, it is difficult to agree that the social structure or the functioning of the villages in Haryana had any touch of despotism on account of which it could serve as a base for oriental despotism of the state. Neglected by the powers that be the villagers managed their own affairs but not despotically. Their heads were the *muqaddams*, 'the rustic philosopher kings', who were chosen by the villagers themselves. These posts could not be purchased by wealth, influence or pressure. Neither poverty, nor low birth could debar a person from them. Conversely, the *muqaddams* here 'frequently suffered for affluence and material strength; they possessed at times but a small comparative property'. They were not autocrats. Any abuse of power could disqualify them from holding the office. In effect, they could not afford to be 'Venetian Council of Ten' even if they so desired.[90] Social oppression, economic exploitation and disturbances found negligible place in the village life. Says Fortescue (1810):

> No instances occur of a proprietor being driven from the village by oppression or violence, on the contrary, it is observable that they tender each other the most friendly and essential aids when in distress. They will supply cattle, till the lands themselves, contribute money when a sharer has been really unfortunate and they will assist him in disposal of his produce in providing seeds, bullocks and implements, should they be satisfied with him. This feeling is extended to the widow and necessituous family of a deceased sharer and its effects scarcely surpassed.[91]

The artisans, menials, and other inhabitants of the village also received a similar treatment. But if some one violated the rules or tried to harm or hurt some one, the panchayats, the classical tribunals, intervened and dispensed with justice. Their principle of equity and fair play had full say. To quote Fortescue again:

> Injustice or partiality are not charged to these tribunals, . . . and it is no weak proof in their favour that we found a perfect equality amongst the people in rank and fortune.[92]

Likewise, the villages were not just the 'stagnatory and vegetative' entities always clinging to false tradition, 'not changing even when they ought to change'. By this I do not mean to suggest that the villages in the period under study, were not in a bad shape. No doubt superstitions, devotion to ignorance and wrong traditional values had hampered the pace of progress. The economic development was rather slow and the agencies of social change were not active. But our scholars, unfortunately, miss the real point, that even in this wretched condition, the people, or at least some of them, were alive to the situation. Not only that. They also made attempts to develop some sort of mechanism for bringing about change in existing stagnant life. Voices were raised and movements started against ignorance, superstitions, empty rituals and social evils by villagers. For instance, the Satnami movement (sixteenth century) had its origin at Bijeshwar, a small village near Narnaul; the Garibdasi movement (eighteenth century) had its birth in a village named Chhudani, near Jhajjar and the Nangi movement (eighteenth century) took its roots in the soil of Dhansra, a small village in Mahendragarh.[93] The followers of these movements who gave up orthodox and traditional mode of social behaviour and adopted new, liberal ideas lived for the most part not in towns or big cities but in villages. Does it not speak of a progressive attitude on the part of villagers that they were ready to accept change in the context of the changing times?

Likewise, the meek and wretched portrait of the villages drawn above is also not correct. The people living in hamlets were never a helpless multitude sitting on bended knees in their mud houses or in narrow streets crying and praying for mercy to the invaders. They were, in fact, just the opposite, as has been rightly pointed out by Fortescue:

> They were able singly to resist ordinary attacks. By inter-marriages and the necessity of a common cause the interests of several villages were identified, and thus leagued, they were strong enough to oppose more regular and formidable foes. We know consequently of individual villages having frequently repulsed assaults from the local troops of the Amil and Faujdar, and of the forces of many villages united by the *Rooka* (or particular loud cry of the voice) to have been equal to the complete defeat of the best appointed and most numerous forces that the State could send against them: such was the union spirit and desperate bravery of the people.[94]

Another important question: Were the villages managed poorly before the advent of the British? Most of the British writers who have written about this period give such an impression. This is obviously due to one reason: image-building of the colonial rule. Fortescue is, however, an exception in this regard. His treatment is a great deal objective and he does not remain oblivious of the virtues of the traditional village life and management. Nor does he forget to point out the flaws in his own system introduced here. 'Our public officers and police,' says he, 'have muddled with the villages. They do not seem to be wanted in them.'[95] Similarly, the British courts, in his estimate, were no match when compared with the village panchayats. He rated the panchs, the rustic Ciceros and Demosthenes, who composed these panchayats, a great deal better than the judges in British courts.[96] A few illustrations to bring home this truth may not be irrelevant. Metcalfe, who served here in the period in question as a judge punished offenders without weighing their guilt. He sentenced a policeman, Roshan Khan, to life imprisonment with hard labour for stealing seven pounds of thread. Another man, Ramdiya was imprisoned for seven years, in 1815, on a similar charge of theft. His attempts to escape from jail thrice eventually increased his sentence to 56 years.[97] Another man, Makhan Singh was sentenced to seven years rigorous imprisonment for forging Metcalfe's signatures. In some cases Metcalfe passed judgement on the absentee offenders without giving them any chance of defence. In fact, in many cases no trials were held and judgements were passed privately. Matcalfe was, however, reprimanded for these lapses. Another official, Henry Middleton, the superintendent of the Delhi territory, apparently gave his assistants the power of granting solitary confinement for life. Even death penalties were awarded without printed regulations.[98]

The village communities languished and people suffered[99] in ways more than once until India attained freedom (1947). Now, however, the situation is different: the people have become masters of their own destiny in their villages—at least that is what the Constitution says.

Thapa

After village came the *thapa*. A tribal community having obtained possession of a tract experienced, says Sir Denzil Ibbetson, in course of time that it was inconvenient for them all to live together, and a part of the community would found a new village. This process would be repeated, till the tract became dotted over with villages, all springing originally from one parent village. The group of villages so bound together by common descent formed a *thapa*. The original village, however small or reduced in circumstances, is always acknowledged as the head village (*tika*), and the *chaudhari* of the parent village is considered as a *chaudhari* of the whole *thapa*. When a headman dies the villages of the *thapa* assemble to instal his heir, and the *pagri* (turban) of *chaudhrayat* (headship) is tied on his head by each village. In olden days the subordinate villages used to pay some small *chaudhrayat* tax, too, to the head village on the day of Diwali, but now the system is discontinued.

During the medieval times, the *thapas* 'based upon tribal organization' were adopted as convenient revenue units by the rulers. The revenue assessment was fixed for a whole *thapa*, and then distributed over the constituent villages by the headmen of the villages, presided over by the head of the *tika* or chief village. The revenue was primarily assessed and collected by the local *amil*, an official, but he worked principally through the *chaudharis* or local heads of the *thapas*. For this service, the *chaudharis* of the *thapas* were rewarded. Nowadays *thapas* do not carry any such authority.

Other Organizations

After *thapa* several other organizations are referred to in historical and sociological works. Of these the two *khanpa* and *sarvakhanpa* are taken to be important. *Khanpa* is usually an aggregate of several *thapas* and *sarvakhanpa* of various *khanpas*. They assemble from time to time to decide the matters of common interest to their people. Excepting in a few Jat villages, both these organizations have now lost importance in the region.

In sum, a considerable social change has taken place in the society during the period under study under the impact of modernism. As a result, the religion has lost its medieval fanaticism and social institutions their backward, obscurantist outlook. The individual has begun to exert himself for gaining his dues of modern life—like freedom, dignity and social equality. But his path is not smooth and struggle is not easy. The medieval content in some institutions which still remain intact or are revived by vested interests in the recent past stand in the way. An example would help us get it: we have taken to democratic polity where the individual has unlimited power to exercise his vote the way he liked. But some families, *khandanas*, village panchayats, *thokas*, *thapas*, *khanpas* and *sarvakhanpas* take collective decision in medieval fashion to back this candidate or that man, thus depriving an individual of freedom to cast his vote the way he liked! Education, and modern awareness would, it is guessed, change the situation—and before long!

NOTES

1. According to 1991 census.
2. For details see *JHS*, vol. XVI, 1984, pp. 32-91.
3. Ibid.
4. Ibid.
5. Ibid.
6. Ibid.
7. Ibid.
8. Ibid.
9. Ibid.
10. Denzil Ibbetson, *The Punjab Castes* (hereafter *Castes*), p. 1.
11. *Rig*. X, 117.9.
12. Ibid., I, 113.6.
13. Ibid., pp. 2-20.
14. Ibid.
15. Ibid.
16. Ibid.
17. See Denzil Ibbetson, *Castes*, pp. 215-21; K.C. Yadav, *The Revolt*, pp. 4-9.
18. Ibid., p. 220.
19. Ibid.

20. Ibid., p. 179.
21. K.C. Yadav, *Revolt*, p. 4.
22. Denzil Ibbetson, *Castes*, pp. 247-50.
23. Ibid., pp. 250-2.
24. Ibid., pp. 126-31.
25. Ibid.
26. Ibid.
27. Ibid.
28. Ibid.
29. Ibid.
30. Ibid.
31. Ibid.
32. Ibid.
33. Ibid.
34. Ibid.
35. Ibid.
36. Ibid., H.A. Rose, *Glossary*, vol. II, pp. 4-7; K.C. Yadav, *Revolt*, p. 5.
37. K.C. Yadav, *Revolt*, pp. 5-6.
38. Ibid., p. 185.
39. Ibid., pp. 131-9.
40. Ibid.
41. Ibid.
42. Ibid.
43. Ibid., p. 6.
44. Ibid.
45. H.A. Rose, *Glossary*, vol. III, pp. 334-5.
46. K.C. Yadav, *Revolt*, p. 7.
47. Ibid.
48. Denzil Ibbetson has discussed this aspect very clearly in the *Settlement Report of Karnal.* The present account is based on that.
49. Ibid.
50. For instance, Quran, S. 49 (verse 13) gives in very clear-cut terms the following injunction on this point: 'O mankind! we have created you male and female, and appointed your races and tribes, that you may know one another.' See P.C. Aggarwal, 'The Meos of Rajasthan and Haryana', *Castes and Social Stratification among the Muslims* (ed. Imtiaz Ahmad), p. 21.
51. Some scholars, however, do not agree with this. For refutation of such views, see ibid., pp. xvii-xxxiv, 21-4.
52. For the above division, see ibid., pp. 21-2.
53. See Denzil Ibbetson, *Castes*, pp. 222-3.
54. Ibid.
55. Ibid.
56. H.A. Rose, *Glossary*, vol. III, p. 399.
57. Ibid.

58. Ibid.
59. Of all these clans, the Bhattis were by far the most important. In the later Mughal times they added to their power and prestige. Before moving into Haryana, they wielded political power in Rajasthan near Bhatner. But they were expelled from there by the Rathors of Bikaner in the eighteenth century. They settled in Haryana permanently in this period and founded two states here in Rania and Fatehabad which were confiscated by the British soon after they assumed power here.
60. The Pachhadas were also an important clan. Though no more here, they occupied important position before 1947. The word 'pachhada' is a corrupt form of 'those coming from Paschima (west)'. They migrated in the later Mughal times from west and hence this name. They claimed Rajput descent and were divided into following principal tribes: Sohus, Sukheras, Hinjrasons, Chotias or Bhanekan. They were poor agriculturists and took to many anti-social activities.
61. K.C. Yadav, *Revolt*, p. 7.
62. Ibid., p. 8.
63. Ibid.
64. Besides these, there is a small sub-pal also called Pahat.
65. K.C. Yadav, *Revolt,* p. 7.
66. Ibid.
67. *Gurgaon District Gazetteer*, 1910, p. 61.
68. Imtiaz Ahmad, op. cit., p. 22.
69. This is against religious injunctions, however.
70. Figures of 1991 census.
71. Ibid.
72. K.C. Yadav, *Revolt*, pp. 8-10.
73. Denzil Ibbetson has described the social life in the *Settlement Report of Karnal* at length. I have borrowed from there.
74. Ibid.
75. *JHS*, vol. XVI (184), pp. 47-8.
76. Ibid.
77. Ibid.
78. Ibid.
79. Ibid., pp. 22-3.
80. Ibid.
81. Ibid.
82. Ibid.
83. The account is based on M.C. Pradhan, *The Political System of the Jats of Northern India*, pp. 57-66.
84. The account of *khandana* is also based on ibid.
85. See K.C. Yadav, *Revolt*, pp. 20-4.
86. Minute of the Board of Revenue, 17 November 1830.
87. K.C. Yadav (ed.), *Socio-Economic Life in Rural Haryana*, p. xi.

88. Ibid., p. xii.
89. See Karl Marx and F. Engles, *On Colonialism*, pp. 40-1.
90. K.C. Yadav, *Revolt*, pp. 20-4.
91. See Y.C. Yadav, *Socio-Economic Life in Rural Haryana*, p. 45.
92. Ibid.
93. Ibid., p. xiv.
94. Ibid., p. 38.
95. Ibid., p. 4.
96. See D.N. Panigrahi, *Charles Metcalfe in India*, pp. 149-51.
97. See K.C. Yadav, *Socio-Economic Life in Rural Haryana*, p. 51.
98. Ibid.
99. *Marx and India*, p. 18. Cf. Hiren Mukherjee, '1857', in *New Indology*, pp. 109-10: 'It is more likely that Indian advance in the contemporary world would have been after trials and tribulations, no doubt, more genuine and effective if foreign rule had not deeply disturbed and distorted the very perspective of the advance.'

18

Language, Learning and Literature

LANGUAGES

Haryana is a Hindi-speaking state. But some people do use other languages, too, as Table 1 indicates:

TABLE 1: LANGUAGES SPOKEN/USED IN HARYANA[1]

Language	Percentage of users
Hindi	89.42
Punjabi	8.34
Urdu	1.95
Others	0.29

In their ordinary conversation with each other the people here use six different dialects which have stemmed from the vedic Sanskrit (*chhandas*) in the manner as given in Table 2.

TABLE 2: DEVELOPMENT OF HARYANAVAI DIALECTS[2]

Before 1500 BC	*Chhandas*	
1500 BC-600 BC	*Udichya*	
600 BC-AD 200	*Sanskrit*	
AD 200-AD 600	*Prakrit*	
	Abhiri Apabhramsa	*Sauraseni Apabhramsa*
AD 600-1000	*Rajasthani (Eastern Hindi)*	
AD 100	*Ahirwati Mewati Bagri*	*Bangru Braja Ambalavi*

As given in Table 2 above, the dialects in vogue here are broadly classified into two categories:

(i) Western Hindi: Bangru, Braja and Ambalavi; and
(ii) Eastern Hindi: Ahirwati, Mewati and Bagri.

Bangru

This is an important dialect spoken by a large number of people.[3] Its area is bounded by the district of Ambala in the north, by Gurgaon in the south, by the Yamuna in the east, and the Bagri-speaking belt of the Hisar and Sirsa districts in the west. As noted above, it is a form of Western Hindi, influenced in its vocabulary by Khari Hindi, Urdu and at places even by Panjabi and strongly affected in its grammar by Ahirwati. It is known by several names according to locality and the castes of its speakers: in Hisar, Sirsa and Bhiwani it is called Deshwali, or Deshari; in Rohtak and Sonepat it is usually called Jatu; and in the rest of the area it is Bangru, the most popular designation.[4]

The dialects, it is said, change their forms after every eight *kos*. The Bangru is no exception. But in its general structures and content, the dialect remains the same throughout the region specified above. The following three specimens from three different localities will bear both the points. The first specimen is from Jind, the second from Karnal, and the third from Rohtak. The last specimen is taken to be a standard one for scientific study of the dialect.

Specimen 1

Ek Bahman tha ar ek Bahmani thi. Bahman chun mang-kai li-sya karda. Bahmani Kaihan laggi, 'Is nagri-mai rajja Bhoj sai. Yu slok Kauhakai Bahman-nai ek taka sona-ka de sai. Is rajja-kai tau bhi ja-kai slok kah. Bhaman Kaihan laggya, 'Mai slok ni janda.' Bhamani kaihn lagi, slok tanni mai sikhya dungi.'

Specimen 2

Ek manas kai do chhore the. Un-mai-tai chhote-ne bappu-tai kahya 'ak, bappu ho dhan-ka jaun-sa hissa mere bande awe-sai mannai de de'. Tau us-ne dhan unhai band-diya. Ar thore dina pachhai chhotta chhora sab kuchh kattha kar-ke challa gaya, ar urai apna dhan khote chalan-mai kho-diya.

Specimen 3

Ek Hir manda para tha. Us ka asna bera-len aya. Jis din us-ka asna aya us din tuk-tuk us-ko chain thi. Hir apne Bhai-se bola 'ak, yoh, chhora kau sai'? Us-ka bhai bola 'ak mhra asna sai'.

AMBALAVI

Ambalavi is spoken in the district of Ambala.[6] In the upper parts of the district the dialect has some influence of Panjabi on it and in the lower ones that of the Bangru. In its pure form, however, it is something like *Khaṛi-boli*. This will appear from the two specimens which are given below. The specimens are, one a portion of a version of the 'Parable of the Prodigal Son', and the other, a statement made in court by an accused person.

Specimen 1

Ek admi-ke do chhokre the. Un-mate chhote chhokre-ne apne bap-te kiha 'ki, man-nu jo hisas gar-ma-te-awe-he yo mera man-cu hand-de'. To ba-ne dona-nu band diya. Thoṛe dina pichchhe oh chhokra pardes chala-gaya. Waha us-ne apna sara rupya lauchpayna ma-kho-diya.

Specimen 2

Musammat Mehatabi mere ghar-wali nu tap chothya do sale-se ata tha. Gat-ma satya nahi rahi thi. Pher ek din musmamat Mahtabi ghar gasi kah-kar gir pari. Us ke gir kar chot lag-gai. Hatha chakki-ka or lakriya waha pari-thi. Me-ne mari nahi thi. Mere ghar-ki orat be. Pher Nanak-ne kedawat se thane-ma bol-rahe be. Pher meri orat-nu thane-ma bula liya. Meri orat-ne kah-diya ki, man-nu mara nahi, or no chheta be.

In these specimens we may note the influence of Panjabi in the use of kiha (for 'said'), *bandna* not *batna* ('to divide') and the use of *nu* or *no* (to indicate the dative). Among other local forms, we may note *or* or *hor, ma* (in) and the employment of an oblique plural in *a* not *o* in *dona-nu* (to both), etc.[7]

Brajabhasha

A form of western Hindi, it is spoken in a limited area of Palwal tehsil in the newly formed district of Faridabad. It is influenced by the Rajasthani and Ahirwati which are its neighbouring dialects.[8] The dialect as it is spoken here is shown in the following specimen from Palwal:

Specimen

Ek admi ka dwai beta he. Unte lalre-ne bap-te kahyo 'ki, Bhai hamare batke phissa hat diyo'. Jab-to woi-ku bat diyo, Thore din pichhe sab dhan le ke woho larika pardes chaldiyo. Aur wah apno mal khoti sangat men ura diyo.

A perusal of the specimen would show that the Braja spoken in Palwal area of Haryana is fairly pure, despite the impact of the two neighbouring dialects referred to earlier.

Ahirwati

Ahirwati is an important dialect. It is spoken in the districts of Rewari, Mahendragarh, a part of Gurgaon, and Faridabad and a small part of Bhiwani. It gets its name from the Ahira who are in preponderance in this locale. A specimen from Rewari will give an idea as to what type of dialect is this:

Specimen

Ek sakas-ke do beta tha. Un-mah-tai chhotno bap tai bolyo 'ak, bapu mai ko bat jo mu-ne dinu hoy so de-do'. Jab-u-ne wo mal-ke bat jis tarah kahyo-tho us-i-tarah bat-diyo. Thora din pichhe chhota beto sagla mal jama-kar-ke pardes-ne chalo-gayo Une wathai apnu dhan badchalni me kho-diyo.

In its grammar, Ahirwati does not differ much from Mewati. It is in fact a stepping stone between the Mewati and Bangru.[9]

Mewati

Mewati is also an important dialect.[10] It is spoken in those parts of district Faridabad and Gurgaon which recalled Mewat. It is bounded on the east by the Braja of Bharatpur and Faridabad and on the south by the Dang dialects of Jaipur. On its north it has the Ahirwati of Gurgaon and Faridabad, and on its south-east the Torwati form of Jaipur. On its north-west is the Ahirwati of Mahendragarh. It is in fact a border dialect which represents Rajasthani fading off into the Braj. There is some influence of Ahirwati, too, on it. The specimen of the dialect is as follows:

Specimen

Ek admi-ke dwai beta he. Unte lohre-ne bap-te koho 'ki, bhai hamare bat-ke-hissa de deyo. Sab dhan le-ke lohrro larika pardes-ku chal diyo. Aur wah apono mal khoti sangat me lira diyo.

Bagri

Bagri is not an extensively used dialect.[11] A form of Rajasthani, it is spoken in those parts of Hisar and Sirsa adjoining Rajasthan and some parts of Loharu and Dadri parganas of Bhiwani district. This dialect was brought here about the seventeenth and eighteenth centuries by Jats who migrated from Rajasthan. A specimen of the dialect is given below:

Specimen

Ek raja tho, Vi ek sahukar kane das-pach kror rupaiyo dekhi aur sunho. Vi raja-ke man-me esi-k ai ki, i-ra rupaiya khosna chahije, Esi tajwij su lena chahije ki-i-hu broo bi malum na deve.

The dialect is a great deal akin to the Rajasthani spoken in Bikaner district—difference being only a little due to the influence of the bangru and Panjabi on it.

In the beginning these dialects were used in both towns and villages. But nowadays, the townsfolk use standardized languages—Hindi (*Khari-boli*) in most of the cases, and Urdu and Panjabi in some. The villagers have not changed, however: they still use the dialects, though owing to the influence of the soldiers in the main and other service persons who had opportunity of remaining in multi-lingual societies, and school and college going students, as also owing to radio, television, etc., their vocabularies have changed a great deal. A large number of English words, like plate, cup, college, class, chalk, card, bank, table, bench, school, result, pass, fail, board, cheque, pencil, pen, pin, car, taxi, bus, rail, jeep, tractor, trolly, harrow, tube-well, motor, connection, switch, full, dim (supply), bolt, net, election, MLA, MP, parliament, member, minister, chief minister, secretary, Xen, SDO, BDO, vote, petition, promotion, rank, gun, pistol, fire, out, officer, wife, family have crept into the dialects. Earlier there was no word like *aap* in the dialects (*tu* was used for one and all). Now it is *aap* for elders, respectables. Similarly several other changes have also occurred.

EDUCATION

In the beginning of the modern period, i.e. the first quarter of the nineteenth century, education still continued to be taken as nothing more than the knowledge which would make a child proficient in the parental profession. Thus it meant differently to different sections of the people: to a priest's son education was the knowledge of a little Sanskrit for a Brahmana and that of Arabic for a Muslim; to a shop-keeper's son it was only some arithmetic and *mundiya*; to a clerk's son it was a little Persian or Urdu; and to a peasant's son it was only learning his father's job-mastering details of its execution. Education in the real sense of the term was, according to the peasant, of no use to him and he, therefore, did not send his child to a school.[12]

This was precisely the reason that in the nineteenth century we do not come across any schools worth the name in rural Haryana where the peasants lived in great majority. The schools were found only in big towns, and there, too, the position was far from satisfactory, as the following account shows:

> In the lower region, i.e. the districts of Rohtak, Hisar and Gurgaon there were 27 Muslim schools with 289 pupils and 24 teachers, and 70 Hindu schools with 886 pupils and 70 teachers. In the district of Delhi, there were 247 schools most of them being in the city itself. In the upper region, i.e. the districts of Karnal, etc., the position was equally bad. In pargana Sonepat, there were but three schools. In the town of Panipat, there were ill-supported and thinly attended schools. In the town of Karnal (20,000 inhabitants) there was only one school. Elsewhere in 18 mosque schools there were 227 pupils.[13]

The education in these schools was either gratis or the remuneration was provided by the scholar, except 'in the instance of one school of seven scholars (in Delhi) the master of which received Rs. 3/- per month from the King'. The teachers were mostly Brahmanas and *maulavis*. They were not trained for teaching and 'knew as much as they taught in their schools'. In spite of their low income, however, they were respected in the society.[14]

The courses of teaching in these schools were very elementary in type and extended up to four years or so. Since the need of the individual and the society were limited, the objectives of instruction were also limited. The curriculum comprised three R's. The admission age was not fixed (normally varying from 6 to 15 years). A pupil could join school at any time of the year. Academic sessions were flexible to suit the needs, capacities and abilities of the individual students. There were no formal examinations and pupils were promoted to the next higher class as and when found fit by the teacher. Methods of instruction were crude. Pupils were subjected to monotonous, repetitive oral drill and loud recitation for hours.[15]

The government hardly took any interest in the education of the people. In fact it was not a part of their official policy to do so. However, in 1813, they realized the inappropriateness of following such a policy and the Charter Act of that year put forth a positive provision in its educational clause that

> a sum of not less than one lakh of rupees in each year shall be set apart and applied to the revival and improvement of literature and the encouragement of the learning among the natives of India, and for the introduction and promotion of knowledge of the sciences among the inhabitants of the British territories in India.[16]

Despite this, however, no serious efforts were made for quite some time by the government to implement this clause of the Act and the money allocated for this purposes remained undisbursed.

The Fraser Experiment

Unlike the government, however, some individuals in the service of the Company made positive efforts to spread education. In Haryana such an individual was Fraser, an assistant. Unaided by any government or private agency, he started two schools in 1816, a third one in 1820, and fourth one in 1823 in the pargana of Sonepat on his own for the children of the peasants.[17] To run these schools Fraser followed a very peculiar method of paying both the teachers and the pupils, the former with the allowance of a rupee a month per boy and the latter with a seer of wheat flour per head per day. The reason for paying the students was that these schools were exclusively for the children of the peasants and without rations the parents would not send their children to be taught for the boy's 'labour is lost to the family and the ideal hand is not willingly supported by the rest'.[18]

In these schools, the knowledge of three R's, was imparted. But this type of instruction couzld hardly give satisfaction to Fraser. He, in fact, wanted to give much more useful knowledge than this through English, Persian, and Hindi and that, too, not to a limited number of students but as many as eighty boys in a hundred. But Fraser could not do this satisfactorily for his mean were totally inadequate.[19] The establishment of the General Committee of Public Instruction in 1823 with the function of taking charge of the government educational institutions and giving educational grants to others brought hope to Fraser. He promptly made an appeal to the Court of Directors and the Committee to patronize the schools started by him. Justifying his case he wrote:

> The establishment of schools in cities and towns is comparatively speaking of secondary consideration—the majority of children of the classes that inhabit cities and towns are educated by their parents. It is the children of the *zamindars* of the peasantry the mass of the people; thousands to one of the people that require this instruction.[20]

The appeal of Fraser failed to impress the people at the helm of affairs, however. On 29 November 1823, the General Committee of Public Instruction turned down his appeal with the remarks that such a measure would go contrary to their principle which was 'to assign funds only for the purpose of public education chiefly directed to the best means of improving the education of the more respectable members of the Indian society'.[21] The schools of Fraser were closed down.[22]

New Experiments

In the closing years of the 1920s, things started moving in the different direction. The government, under pressure from several quarters, began to give a serious thought to the problem of educating the Indian masses. But as far as Haryana was concerned, we find little being done even in the changed situation for a long time to come. It is surprising that even the administrative change in 1834 which made this region a separate division of the newly-formed North-Western Provinces, and the change of education from the central to provincial subject in 1840 did not improve matters at all.

In 1843, however, fortune smiled on the unlucky region when an energetic person sincerely devoted to the cause of spreading education, James Thomason (1843-53) became the lieutenant-governor of the province. He opposed the idea of giving educational facilities to the upper and better stratum of the Indian society only. He favoured the

TABLE 3: INDIGENOUS SCHOOLS IN HARYANA, 1980[23]

District	Schools in		Villages without
	towns	villages	schools
Panipat	56	50	416
Hisar	13	20	587
Delhi	297	24	386
Rohtak	22	24	275
Gurgaon	50	50	1230

kisans who formed the bulk of the population and whose plight was very sad. To begin with, the lieutenant-governor directed his attention towards the indigenous schools. He gave them attention and money. As a result, the situation improved, as shown in Table 3.

The lieutenant-governor sent a detailed report to the government on the subject (dated 18 November 1846), proposing that every village of a certain size (of about 200 houses) should have a school, provided the villagers agreed to make a grant of *jagheer* from 5 to 10 acres of land which gave a rental varying from Rs. 20 to 40 per annum for the maintenance of the school master. The government, he further observed, 'should give up its revenue from that land'.[24] The scheme as such was turned down by the authorities but he was asked to submit a revised plan (dated 19 April 1848) suggesting 'establishment of one government middle school (as a model school) in each tehsil (tehsildari schools).[24] The lieutenant-governor did it right at once and the scheme was approved by the Court of Directors (vide their dispatch dated 30 October 1849).

The new scheme was put into effect in eight districts on experimental basis (February 1850). The scheme proved to be a success. Unfortunately, it was not taken to any tehsil in Haryana. Here things stood as they were until the Education Despatch 1854 (popularly known as Wood's Despatch) came about. This solved the financial problem of opening new schools by offering grant-in-aid to even private institutions.[25] As a result, many tehsildari schools were opened in the districts of Delhi, Gurgaon and Rohtak in 1856, and in the remaining districts after some time.[26] These schools functioned well. The course of instruction in them consisted of

reading-writing, grammar, composition, arithmetic, mensuration, algebra up to quadratics, the first four books of Euclid, the history and geography of India, general geography, ancient history, the elements of political economy and plan-table surveying.[27]

The medium of instruction was 'either Hindi or Urdu and in some instances even both'.[28]

Some town schools were also opened at this point in time which were of middle standard. These schools were more or less like the tehsildari schools and were situated at Shahbad, Ladwa, Thanesar, Kaithal, Sadhaura and Ropar in Ambala; Sonepat in Delhi; Gurgaon and Palwal in Gurgaon; Panipat in Karnal; Hansi in Hisar: and Jhajjar and Bahadurgarh in Rohtak.[29] High schools were established at Karnal and Rohtak in 1856 and at Bhiwani, Rewari, Delhi and Jagadhari in 1857.[30]

The educational activities suffered serious setback owing to the uprising of 1857. But the situation improved after petering out of the uprising when the region was transferred from the North-Western Provinces to Punjab in February 1858. A scheme which envisaged improvement of indigenous schools and the establishment of a school at the centre of six villages[31] was launched. Since no time limit was fixed

TABLE 4: EXPANSION OF SCHOOL EDUCATION (1871-1901)[32]

District	Year	Total no. of schools	Area in sq. miles covered by one school	Children of school-going age in each district	No. of children going to schools in each district
Ambala	1870-71	73	–	86290	4929
	1880-81	97	–	72062	8319
	1890-91	–	–	–	–
	1900-01	180	10	67994	9133
Karnal	1870-71	52	–	50910	139
	1880-81	42	75	68337	2694
	1890-91	69	46	71763	2483
	1900-01	203	15	73602	5393
Rohtak	1870-71	34	–	44746	1791
	1880-81	40	45	46134	3562
	1890-91	82	22	49206	2286
	1900-01	98	18	52556	5097
Hisar	1870-71	27	–	57956	1846
	1880-81	51	102	56047	4189
	1890-91	112	46	64667	3636
	1900-01	105	49	65143	5085
Gurgaon	1870-71	34	–	58054	2224
	1880-81	82	24	53487	3807
	1890-91	116	17	55744	4693
	1900-01	128	15	62184	5139

for completion of this highly useful project, it moved at a very slow pace till 1870. But after 1870, owing to certain changes in policy, we find it acquiring greater speed and proportions as Table 4 shows.

In this situatiuon, Ambala district occupied good position as compared to other districts. By the end of the century under review it had one school for every 10 sq. miles of its area. Karnal and Gurgaon had one school for every 15 sq. miles. Rohtak had one school after 18 sq. miles. Hisar was the most backward district in this respect: it had one school for 49 sq. miles.

The rate of progress in opening new schools was the highest for the Karnal district. It had 52 schools in 1870-1 and in 1900-1 the number went to 203. District Rohtak occupied the second place, from 34 in 1870-1 to 98 in 1900-1. The district of Hisar was poor in 1870-1 when it had only 27 schools, but it caught up effectively with other districts as time went by—in 1900-1 it had 105 schools.[33]

The extent of literacy was, however, discouraging. A large number of children who ought to have gone to schools remained at home and received no education at all. The reason for this were many. The villagers had no interest in education.[34] For it was of little use for them in their daily life. It was expensive and they could not afford it. There was a lapse on the part of the government, too, for it did not advertise the advantages of education.

A word about female education. Indigenous instruction was provided to the girls in the city of Delhi by well-to-do families especially of the Muslims. Elsewhere it was next to nothing. The government was aware of the seriousness of the problem but we find them taking initiative in this direction only after 1890 when they opened some schools. But these

TABLE 5: FEMALE EDUCATION, 1871-91[35]

District		1870-1	1880-1	1890-1	1900-1
Ambala	Schools	9	–	–	4
	Scholars	203	–	–	232
Rohtak	Schools	1	–	–	5
	Scholars	16	–	124	29
Karnal	Schools	10	2	1	4
	Scholars	17	88	97	87
Hisar	Schools	4	–	1	5
	Scholars	133	–	–	197
Gurgaon	Schools	9	4	8	11
	Scholars	188	105	188	243

schools could not serve any useful purpose, because the people did not respond favourably as Table 5 indicates.

The above table shows that the girls' education was not popular during the period under consideration. For instance, in Ambala the number of schools decreased from 9 in 1870-1 to 4 in 1900-1, and in Karnal from 10 in 1870-1 to 4 in 1900-1. Gurgaon, Rohtak and Hisar showed slight improvement over the 1870-1 situation at the end of the century, however. But this was negligible. All these girls' schools, it may be pointed out, were of the primary standard only. There were no middle or high schools for the girls throughout Haryana up to 1900.

The position of higher studies was equally bad, if not worse. There was no college in Haryana during the period under study. A few students who wanted to pursue higher studies had to go to Delhi or Lahore.

In sum the position of education in the region in the nineteenth century was far from satisfactory. A small number of institutions imparted education to a few people and the bulk of the population remained uneducated. On the other hand, the picture of the Punjabi-speaking region seems to be comparatively better. There were more schools and colleges there. In consequence, the people there were quite ahead in the matter of literacy of their counterparts in the Haryana region.

Pertinently, a question is relevant here: Why did the government adopt such an attitude towards the Haryanavis? There were several reasons for it. First, they were neglected out of vengeance, for they had played a great role against the British in the uprising of 1857. Secondly, the poverty of the people here which the government did little to eradicate, stood in the way of the people educating their children. *The Punjab Education Report*, for 1887-8 confirms this fact. In the Delhi Circle, it says, the attendance has been affected by an unusually sickly season and also due to enhanced rates of schools fees.[37] Secondly, ignorant and poor, the peoples here did not understand the usefulness of education. In the rural areas one could frequently hear people discouraging the persons going to schools by reciting such sayings as 'It is only the fate which decides everything in life. Education as such cannot be of any use. Even highly educated people, i.e. well versed in Persian, can be seen selling oil in the streets.' Worse, the village communities which managed village affairs did not seem to have played any substantial role in spreading education. Nor did individuals, unlike other parts of the Punjab,[38] come forward to play a role of private munificence in education. Says a government report for 1887-8 in this regard: 'The number of native gentlemen who are really interested in educational matters and are anxious to found new schools or improve the old ones is very small.'[39]

As a result, the people of Haryana became backward in the field of education.[40]

Fortunately, the situation improved to some extent in the succeeding century. It all began with the primary education.

Primary Education

The government replaced the *zamindari* schools which were being run in the villages since 1856 by village schools[41] to be managed by district boards.[42] The scheme received further impetus in 1919 when, following the guidelines of the Government of India Act, 1919, the Punjab government passed the Punjab Primary Education Act, 7, making provision for compulsory and free primary education for the children between 6 and 11 years of age. Rohtak was the first district to have been covered under this scheme. Subsequently, it was taken to other districts. Table 6 indicates in brief the results of the venture covering 1922-35.

A strange phenomenon is noted in Table 6: it shows that there was a fall in the number of schools from 1931-2 onwards. This was obviously owing to the economic depression experienced not only in this region or Punjab, but in the whole of the country and even outside it at this time. Meantime, an Education Commission made the recommendations that haphazard growth of primary education was not good and that it led to a great deal of waste. To substantiate the latter point the Commission submitted that out of every one hundred students who joined the primary class only 18 remained there to complete education up to the 4th class. In view of this, the Commission suggested that instead of opening a large number of schools, the standard of education should be improved. The Punjab government accepted the suggestions and in consequence, schools which were not doing well were closed.[43]

A change in this situation occurred, however, after 1937. After the provincial elections (1937), the Punjab, like other provinces, got a responsible government of the Unionists which paid great attention to the

TABLE 6: PROGRESS OF PRIMARY EDUCATION, 1922-35[44]

Year	New schools in Urban Areas	New schools in Rural Areas
1922-3	–	6
1926-7	6	148
1931-2	20	900
1934-5	24	880

TABLE 7: PROGRESS OF PRIMARY EDUCATION, 1947-66[45]

Year	Schools
1947-8	1564
1950-1	1775
1953-4	2637
1956-7	3958
1959-60	4005
1962-3	5532
1965-6	4458

extension of primary education. It opened a large number of schools in the backward region of Haryana, 1175 in 1937-8, 1270 in 1940-1, and 1498 in 1946-7.

The position had, in certain sense, improved. But it was not ideal in any way: a good deal was done, but still much remained to be done. Fortunately, the deficiency was made good after independence, or to be more appropriate, after 1950, when a new Act making primary education compulsory and free for every child up to 14 years of age was passed, as is evident from Table 7. This means that after independence the increase was 100 per cent during the first five-year plan which went up to 105.2 per cent during the second five-year plan. The line went still higher on the graph in the third plan when every big village came to have a primary school. It was indeed a great achievement.[46]

Secondary Education

A word about secondary education. As compared to the primary education, its progress was not so satisfactory during the period under study. The not-so-good condition of education at this stage was primarily owing to the fact that the government did not pay much attention to it. Nor do we find private agencies coming forward to make good the neglect. How bad was the state of secondary education in the region until 1947 can be seen from Table 8.

The table clearly shows that progress in respect of opening new secondary schools was slow and unsatisfactory during this period. Nor was the public response insofar as sending of pupils to these schools was concerned good. After 1921, however, we notice some change in this respect. This was obviously due to the initiative of the military personnel from this region who during their visit to different places in and outside India during the War became aware of the usefulness of education. They

TABLE 8: PROGRESS OF SECONDARY EDUCATION, 1911-46[47]

District	Schools	1911	1921	1931	1941	1946-7
Gurgaon	High	1	4	6	10	12
	Middle	6	10	10	20	21
Karnal	High	1	7	10	15	18
	Middle	8	9	16	21	24
Ambala	High	7	9	12	16	18
	Middle	9	8	13	20	23
Hisar	High	1	4	8	10	16
	Middle	1	7	16	20	23
Rohtak	High	1	7	16	20	23
	Middle	8	12	21	28	20

sent their sons and even daughters to schools. Secondly, the societies like the Arya Samaj, Sanatan Dharma Sabha, etc., propagated in favour of education. Several caste organizations, like the Jat Mahasabha, Ahir Mahasabha, Vaishya Mahasabha, Gaur Sabha, etc., also popularized education among their castemen. Thirdly, the national consciousness aroused in the wake of freedom struggle also encouraged the people to go for education.[48]

Despite all these factors, however, the progress of secondary education as compared with Punjab proper, was far from satisfactory. Such a situation continued to prevail until 1947 when independence came.[49] The new government made substantial endeavours to change the situation. To begin with, a large portion of the state budget was allotted for education for the backward region of Haryana. For example, in 1951-3, it made a provision of Rs. 40.47 lakh in the budget for secondary education. After the expiry of the first-five year plan, the amount was increased to Rs. 115.93 lakh. During the second five-year plan, the amount was Rs. 476.82 lakh. In the third five-year plan it was a lot more. Besides this, schools being run by private bodies were also given handsome grants-in-aid by the government.[50]As a result, more schools came up.[51] The exact position as it was during the period 1951-66 can be seen in Table 9.

Higher Education

A word about Higher Education. In the beginning of the present century higher education was in a pretty bad shape. There was no college here before 1927. The students, who wished to go for higher education beyond matriculation had to, as noted above, either go to Delhi or to

TABLE 9: SPREAD OF SECONDARY EDUCATION, 1951-66

District		Schools 1951		1961		1966	
		Middle	High/Hr. Sec.	Middle	High/Hr. Sec.	Middle	High/Hr. Sec.
Ambala	Boys	75 (14545)	73 (6415)	75 (14545)	73 (42203)	61 (16852)	58 (10265)
	Girls	27 (42203)	38 (20256)	27 (6415)	38 (20256)	16 (37604)	28 (18831)
Karnal	Boys	26 (–)	24 (–)	82 (20870)	61 (28633)	105 (26636)	80 (437777)
	Girls	x	x	17 (4695)	18 (11019)	18 (10482)	19 (15404)
Gurgaon	Boys	99 (18415)	31 (121137)	34 (7930)	69 (2741)	102 (22551)	69 (34279)
	Girls	7 (1594)	1 (22)	16 (26613)	11 (4608)	14 (13405)	13 (8786)
Rohtak	Boys	102 (23413)	43 (19155)	84 (9997)	74 (39929)	118 (47685)	94 (57221)
	Girls	47 (2739)	3 (1103)	33 (7135)	14 (7531)	30 (17220)	23 (18685)
Hisar	Boys	47 (–)	18 (–)	89 (14982)	66 (24353)	111 (28491)	85 (37229)
	Girls	x	x	22 (4705)	9 (4540)	28 (11208)	10 (11209)
Mahendragarh	Boys	46 (–)	11 (–)	48 (8569)	31 (12758)	74 (18234)	38 (21801)
	Girls	x	x	x	5 (1445)	3 (3125)	5 (3964)
Jind	Boys	71 (2193)	22 (13599)	57 (10144)	69 (34297)	38 (9020)	23 (15168)
	Girls	7 (859)	12 (696)	6 (–)	14 (6633)	2 (1414)	3 (2617)

Lahore. It was only in 1927, that an intermediate college was established at Rohtak. Eleven years later, a degree college, S.A. Jain College which imparted education up to B.A. classes, was established at Ambala. In 1941 the Intermediate College, Rohtak was upgraded to B.A. level. In 1944, Rohtak had another degree college—All India Jat Heroes Memorial College. The Agrawala Mahasabha established Vaishya College, Bhiwani in the same year. In 1945, Yadav Mahasabha opened the Ahir College at Rewari. In 1946, Vaishya community founded another Vaishya College at Rohtak. In all, there were six colleges in Haryana before independence, whereas Punjab had over 48 colleges. And surprisingly most of the Haryana colleges were arts colleges where the students could study for English, Persian, Urdu, Hindi, Sanskrit, History, Economic, Political Science, Geography, etc. Arrangements for teaching sciences as Chemistry, Physics and Mathematics were very limited. The medium of instruction was English.

After independence, as already noted, the government took interest in higher education. As a result, there was some progress, as indicated in Table 10.

Indeed the expansion was encouraging: from 6 colleges in 1947 to 40 in 1966. The strength of the students also increased about seven times. Female education also received a fillip: out of the 40 colleges in (1966) nine were exclusively meant for girls. Besides, the Haryana region also got its first University at Kurukshetra in 1956. Initially the University was meant to promote the study of Sanskrit. Later on (1961), however, the University became a multi-faculty university.

TABLE 10: SPREAD OF HIGHER EDUCATION, 1947-66[52]

	Colleges				
District	1947	1951	1956	1961	1966
Ambala	1	4	6	9	9
Gurgaon	1	2	3	4	6
Hisar	1	3	5	6	6
Jind	–	–	–	1	1
Karnal	–	1	3	8	8
Mahendragarh	–	–	1	1	1
Rohtak	3	4	5	7	9
Total	6	14	24	36	40

TABLE 11: TECHNICAL EDUCATION, 1965-6[53]

Types of Colleges	Number
Medical College	1
Engineering College	2
Agriculture College	2
Veterinary College	1
College of Technology	1
Dairy Science College	1
Total Colleges	7

TECHNICAL EDUCATION

A word about technical education. Unfortunately, this important aspect of education started receiving attention very late. Before independence, there was no institution for technical education, barring a few small insignificant schools in a few cities. The situation changed after 1947 a great deal and a network of institutions giving technical education were established to meet the demand of the public as Table 11 indicates.

Besides these, there were five Colleges of Education. There was, however, no provision for the study of higher courses in Law, Commerce, Architecture, Home Science, etc.

In sum, despite great expansion, the position of higher education was far from satisfactory during the period under study, especially so if we compare it with what was obtaining in Punjab. The population of non-Haryanavi area (in Punjab) was about 38 per cent, but it had only 28 per cent of the total colleges in Punjab. The difference in the number of students going for higher education was more than 60 per cent. The government spent less than 30 per cent of the total education budget on Haryana. The situation improved, however, after the formation of Haryana as a separate state when greater attention was focused on the subject.

LITERATURE

Despite unsatisfactory state of education during the period under study, it is heartening to note that litterateurs from Haryana continued to make some contribution to different aspects of Indian literature, as the following account shows.

SANSKRIT LITERATURE

As compared to the olden times, the contribution to Sanskrit literature during the modern period was far from satisfactory. This was owing to the fact that in the preceding period, as also in the nineteenth century, the study of the language was badly neglected. However, after the advent of the Arya Samaj in the present century it was again revived through *gurukula* system of education and we find a positive difference.

Nischal Das (1791-1863) a great Sanskrit scholar stands at the top of the list of contributors to Sanskrit literature in the period. A Jat of Dhanana village in Hisar, this gem among scholars was a product of the old Sanatanist school. He is reported to have written brilliant commentaries on *Ishopanishad*, *Kathopanishad*, *Mahabharata* and many other original works, like *Vritavivaranas* and *Vritidipika*.[54] Unfortunately, none of these works are available in full today. In the later part of the nineteenth century, Shridhar of village Densa (Kurukshetra) wrote a scholarly commentary on *Bhagvadgita*. Hardwari Lal, again of Kurukshetra, did an equally scholarly commentary in two volumes on *Shukraniti*. Hardwari Lal's contemporary Swami Hiradasa of the Dadu sect from Bhiwani wrote a *mahakavya* named *Daduramudaya* in 14 cantos which described, in poetic style, the life and teachings of the well-known saint Dadu. Almost at the same time Sita Ram Shastri, again of Bhiwani, did a good commentary on the Yashka's *Nirukta* in three volumes. His two other works entitled *Sahityoddesha* and *Sahityasidhantasara* are learned exposition of the subjects concerned.[55]

In the present century a large number of scholars wrote on various aspects of literature. Of these scholars, Chhajuram Shastri (popularly called *Vidyasagara*) of Ratauli (Jind) tops the list of honour. His earliest work is a *kavya* (in five cantos) entitled *Sultanacharitam* on the life history of a king Mahipala, son of Mahendrapala of Chittor (popularly known as Suratana = Sultan). His play *Durgabhayudayana* in seven acts has for its theme the pauranic story relating to the encounter of goddess Durga with demon Mahisa and his destruction at her hands. It is a scholarly work of merit. His another equally great play is *Chajjuramayanam*. It tells the story of Rama in seven acts. Among his other publications are *Kurukshetramahatmyam*, *Karmakandapaddhati* and *Sahityabinduh*. He has also done commentaries in Sanskrit on old texts, like *Mulachandrika* on the *Vyasihantamuktavali*, *Sarala* on the *Nyayadarshana*, *Sarvabodhini* on the *Vedantasara*, *Pariksha* on the first two parts of the *Mahabhashya*, *Sarabodhini* on the five *adhyayas* of the

Nirukta, *Sadhana* on the *Laghusiddhantakaumudi* and *Pariksha* or *Vidyasagari* on the *Kavyaprakasha*. Besides these works, Chhajuram has also done a history of Sanskrit literature, *Vibudharatnawali* in verse which seeks to refute many a well-known theory of Western scholars, and *Shivakathamritam* on the Shiva legends in the *Puranas*.[56]

Madhavacharya Shastri, a contemporary of Chhajuram, is another great Sanskrit scholar. He has also written many works of which *Kabir-charitam* and *Paratatvadigdarshanama* are well-known. Vidyavidhir Shastri of Satana (Panipat), another great scholar, has also authored several works. Of these *Vyavaharabhanu*, *Shridayananda-rishicharitam, Suktisangraha*, *Maitrayanisamhita* and an epic on Arya Samaj and its founder Dayananda Saraswati are prominent. Vidyadhar Shastri Gaur of Sirsa Khedi (Jind), another famous scholar, has published comment-aries on the *Katyayanasrautasutravritti* and *Sulvasutravrtti* which are remarkable for their clear exposition. Shastri has also published a monograph on *Nityakarmaprayogaha* on the daily rituals and other ceremonies like *Devayajnikapaddhati, Sraddha, Smartoprabhu, Shila-nyasapaddhati, Vivahapaddhati* and *Upanayanpaddhati*.[57]

Another Sanskrit scholar, Satyadeva Vashitha of Bhiwani, has published three learned works, *Satyagrahanitikavyam, Satyabhuayam* commentary in four volumes on the *Visnusaharanama* and *Naditatvadarshanam* a work on *Ayurveda*. Shivanarayana Shastri of village Gotoli (Jind), who has specialized in Philosophy, has written a good commentary *Chhatrabodhini* on the *Tarkasamgraha.* Bhikshu Gaurishankar of Bawani Khera is a great lexicographer and his work *Sarvatantrasidh-Antapadertalakhasnasamgrah* is a famous work on the subject. Kokila-nand Sharma of Bhiwani's *Mahayajna*; Shridatta's *Kenopanishad*; Radhakrishan Shastri's *Hariyanavaibhavam*; and Shivanarayan Shastri's *Niruktamimansa* are also learned works on the respective subjects.[58]

Urdu Literature

Haryana is regarded as the birth place of Urdu. It is, therefore, in the fitness of things that state has produced a large number of Urdu lit-terateurs who have enriched the language and literature a great deal. Of these great men of letters Mir Mehadi Majruh (1833-1902) of Panipat was very famous. He was a pupil of Mirza Ghalib and that is why his couplets resemble those of his teacher in content, language and style. His letters, which he wrote to the Mirza are also invaluable, having a great deal of literary taste. Slightly later, another great litterateur came on the scene—Altaf Hussain Hali (1837-1914). A highly gifted scholar of Urdu,

Persian, and Arabic, he wrote several scholarly works in prose as well as poetry. Of these works the famous ones are: *Mazamin-i-Hali* (1881), *Makatib-i-Hali, Maqalat-i-Hali, Mawtabat-i-Hali* (2 vols.), *Musaddas-i-Hali* (1879), *Hayat-i-Sadi* (1884), *Muqaddima-i-Sher-o-Shairi* (1893), and *Yadgar-i-Ghalib* (1897). All these works are fine pieces of scholarship. But the masterpiece is *muqaddima-i-Sher-o-Shairi*. It is truly an epoch-making work, wherein a little over two hundred pages Hali has elaborately discussed the art of poetry as understood in the East and West and has summed up the essentials of good poetry.[59] Hali has set an example to others by composing poetry on modern lines discarding the old, stale and vulgar style hitherto followed by many Urdu poets. And thus rightly earned the title of 'the father of modern Urdu poetry'.[60]

Another literary giant from Panipat, and a contemporary of Hali, was Khawaja Jafar Hasan Ansari (1837-1915). A disciple of Mirza Ghalib, he was also a great scholar of Urdu, Persian and Arabic like Hali. Some of his famous works like *Diwan-i-Jafar*, *Ramuza Sakhun Kilida*, *Hikmar*, etc., have been published from Ambala.[61] Vahid-ud-din Salim (1867-1928), disciple of both Hali and Hasan, was also a great man of letters. He was private secretary to Sir Sayed Ahmed Khan for sometime. Later he took to journalism. He edited many famous papers, like *Aligarh Gazette, Muslim Gazette* (Lucknow) and *Zamindar* (Lahore). He wrote several books of which *Vaza-i-Istlahat* is famous. His critical essays *Ifadate Slim*[62] also make good reading.

Vishambar Das Garma Panipati, a contemporary of Hali, was also a famous Urdu poet and dramatist. His first contribution of *ghazals* was published in 1912. Later he published several plays which were staged in different cities of Haryana, and elsewhere.[63] Shugan Chand Roshan (1896-1958), again of Panipat, was also an equally famous scholar. he was a great patriot and that is why in his works we come across a trio of patriotism, romanticism and philosophy. His famous works are *Kalam-i-Roshan, Diwani-Roshan*, *Tofan-i-Dil*, *Nara-i-Qaum*, *Ghazaliat-i-Roshan*. His prominent plays include *Kaumi Farishta* and *Nurjahan*.

Another Urdu poet of the period was Anup Chand Aftab (1897-1968), again from Panipat. He was also a great nationalist poet. Lal Chand Falak, the famous Urudu poet of Punjab had influenced his writings a great deal. His works include *Jalva-i-Aftab*, *Khyalat-i-Aftab*, *Zakhmi Vatan*, *Josh-i-Vatan*, *Kaumi Talwar*, *Jalvat-i-Aftab*, *Shamshir-i-Vatan* and *Gam-i-Roshan* (all poetry) and *Rishi Ka Bolbala*, *Drama Sati Anjana*, *Hindustani Shurma* and *Kaumi An*[64] (all prose.) Other nationalist poets of this period, Rampat Yadav (1890-42), Islam Ahmad Hadi Rohtak (1898-?), Gaurdhan Das Shakir Khadri (1898-?), Navbahar

Singh Sabir Tohanavi (1907-84), have also contributed a great deal to Urdu literature through their stirring poems.

Khwaja Ahmed Abbas (1914-80) from Panipat, was a versatile scholar. He wrote his first story 'Ababil' in 1936 which has been translated into 16 different languages of the world. He wrote more than 20 books of which *Ek Larki*, *Musafir ki Diary*, *Jafran ke Phool*, *Chirag Tale Andhera* and *Andhera-Ujala*[65] are well-known. Of the many living writers Balkrishan Muztar (Kurukshetra) and Kashmiri Lal Zakir (Chandigarh) are making very substantial contribution to Urdu literature.

Hindi Literature

The earliest writers of Hindi (of the period under study) was Nischaldas of Dhanana (Hisar). A great scholar of his times, he was real master of *Sankhya Nyaya*, *Vyakarana*, *Vedas*, etc. He was a Dadupanthi. Remarkable for his creative genius, he wrote a number of monumental works in prose and poetry (Hindi) of which *Vicharasagra* is very famous. It has been translated and published in English, Bengali and Urdu. Swami Vivekananda has rated this work as 'the greatest work on *Vedanta* written in any Indian language within the last three centuries'.[66] His two other works *Yuktiprakasha* and *Vritprabhakara* are also quite well known. These are also masterly expositions of advaita philosophy.[67]

Balmukund Gupta (1865-1907) of Gudiani (district Rewari) was another great litterateur. A versatile linguist, proficient in Hindi, Sanskrit, Urdu, Persian, Bangla, he wrote in almost all these languages. His contribution to Hindi journalism and literature is unique, however. Possessing a powerful pen, this master of beautiful prose wrote thousands of learned essays. Among his books *Shivasambhu-Ke-Chitthe aur Khat*, *Dilli Bhasha*, *Khilona*, *Khel-Tamasha* are well known. Gupta was a great nationalist. Through his stirring essays, he aroused political consciousness and national awareness among millions of his readers. Father of Hindi prose, creator of Hindi journalism, he was also a pioneer who paved the way for *swarajya*.[68]

Like Balmukund, another great Hindi scholar of Haryana of this period was Madhava Prasad Mishra (1871-1907). He also made great contribution to Hindi prose and journalism. Born at Kungar (district Hisar), he edited a number of papers and periodicals, chief among them being *Sudarshana*, *Vaishyopakaraka* and *Brahmana*. Besides that, he wrote learned essays on various political, social, economic and religious themes. All these essays of Mishra are published in the *Madhavaprasad Nibandhavali*.[69]

Kehari Kripan (1886-1974) of Bhiwani was also a good writer of this age. His works *Shishupalavadha* is well known. Viswambharnath Kaushik (1891-1945) from Ambala, author of *Man Bhikharani*, *Bhishma*, *Galpamanadir*, *Chirsala*, etc., was also a great writer.[70] Bhadant Ananda Kaushalayana, also of Ambala, and author of *Buddhavachana*, *Bhikshu ke Patra*, *Buddha aur Uske Anuchara*, *Jataka* (2 parts) has also made significant contribution to Hindi.[71] Unlike the present times, Hindi was not popular in Haryana before independence. Urdu was a sort of official language in the region. Hindi was confined to only a few persons who took to it either under the influence of the national movement or just by chance. Hence this insufficient literary output. We see substantial change in the position after independence. A great deal of contribution is being made to different aspects of Hindi literature by the present day writers.

The above picture is not rosy. As a matter of fact, it could not have been so for two obvious reasons: (i) the state of education was far from satisfactory here during the period under study; and (ii) there was no powerful tradition or legacy of literary activity here because of disturbed conditions in the medieval ages that this region experience on account of its typical location. In view of this, whatever grew up in the barren land should be taken as satisfactory.

NOTES

1. *Statistical Abstracts, Haryana*, 1986-7, p. 54.
2. The chronology has been adopted from T. Nara, *Avahattha and Comparative Vocabulary of New Indian Aryan Languages*, Tokyo, 1979.
3. For details see E. Joseph's 'Jatu', *JASB* (n.s.), vol. VI (1910) pp. 693-872.
4. For details see George Grierson, *The Linguistic Survey of India*, part I, vol. IX, pp. 66-8.
5. Ibid., pp. 252-64.
6. For details see ibid., pp. 240-4.
7. Ibid.
8. Ibid, pp. 323-50.
9. Ibid., pp. 49-52, 233-370.
10. Ibid., pp. 44-7.
11. Ibid., p. 159.
12. William Fraser, a British official, who served here in those days, says in this

regard: 'The peasant would not send his son to the school for the boy's labour is lost to the family and the idle hand is not willingly supported by the rest.' Vide Sharp, *Selections from Educational Records*, vol. I, pp. 13-15.

13. *Reports* for the years, 1926 and 1927 vide ibid., pp. 189-90.
14. Ibid. Karna Singh, 'Education in Haryana in the nineteenth century', *HRJ*, vol. I (1966), pp. 19-24.
15. Ibid., pp. 21-2.
16. K.C. Yadav, 'A Brief History of the Development of Education in Haryana', *JHS*, vol. I, no. 2 (1969), p. 7.
17. Sharp, op. cit., vol. I, p. 107.
18. Ibid., pp. 13-15.
19. Ibid. He said, 'I find that monthly expense of about Rs. 200/- is too heavy for me to support.'
20. Ibid., pp. 13-15.
21. Ibid.
22. Ibid.
23. See Thornton, *Memoirs on the Statistics of Indigenous Education in the NW Provinces*, pp. 18-19; Leitner, *History of Indigenous Education in the Punjab*, p. 18; Richey, *Selections from the Educational Records*, part II, pp. 240-2; NAI, Home Public Proceedings, no. 11, 5 Dec. 1846.
24. Thomason, *Despatch*, vol. II, pp. 397-405; Richey, op. cit., vol. II, pp. 243-5.
25. *Report of the Select Committee* (House of Lords), 1952-3, vol. 32, Question no. 597, quoted by Dharma, Bhanu, *History and Administration of the N.W.P.,* p. 365.
26. Richey, op. cit., vol. II, pp. 269-70.
27. Ibid., pp. 249-50; *Report on the State of Education in the NWP*, 1859-60, p. 36.
28. Ibid.
29. Ibid.
30. Ibid.
31. *JHS*, vol. I, no. 2 (1969), pp. 14-15.
32. NAI, Foreign Miscellaneous, no. 365. Richey, op. cit., vol. II, p. 305.
33. Ibid.
34. Ibid.
35. Ibid., vol. I, no. 2 (1969), p. 156. See K.C. Yadav, *Haryana: Studies*, pp. 94-5.
37. Ibid., pp. 14-15.
38. The inspector of schools, Jullundur division says in this regard: 'The year under report has been of marked activity in respect of the private enterprise in education.' See ibid., p. 17.
39. Ibid., p. 16.
40. See *Report of the Haryana Development Committee*, 1966, pp. 136-50.
41. See K.C. Yadav, *Haryana*, vol. II, pp. 283-311.

42. Ibid.
43. Ibid.
44. Ibid.
45. Ibid.
46. Ibid.
47. Ibid.
48. Ibid.
49. Ibid.
50. Ibid.
51. Ibid.
52. Ibid.
53. Ibid.
54. This section is based on the survey of Dr. Satyavarta (of Delhi University). Some information was also supplied by Dr. Amar Singh (of Kurukshetra University). I am thankful to both these scholars.
55. Ibid.
56. Ibid.
57. Ibid.
58. Ibid.
59. Latiff, *Influence of English Literature on Urdu Literature*, p. 10.
60. R.C. Majumdar calls him the innovator of the modern spirit in Urdu poetry. *British Paramountcy*, vol. IX, part II, p. 215.
61. Bishambar Das Garma, *Diwani-Garma*, pp. 87-8.
62. S.A.S. Dehalvi, *Tassurat*, pp. 39-40.
63. See K.C. Yadav, *Haryana: Swatantrata Andolana Mein Kaviyon, Shairon, Bhajnopadeshakon Ka Yogadana*, Delhi, 1989.
64. Ibid.
65. For details see his *Autobiography,* entitled *I am not an Island.*
66. Vivekananda, *Collected Works*, vol. IV, p. 280.
67. *JHS*, vol. XIV (1982), p. 59.
68. Ibid., p. 60.
69. Ibid.
70. Ibid.
71. Ibid.

19

Economic Development

The economic condition of the people of Haryana in the ages gone by—ancient and medieval—was by and large good. They had enough to eat and spare. It deteriorated, however, in the modern times—when actually it should have improved still further. This was so because of the exploitative colonial rule which bled the people white.[1]

The Company Rule, 1803-1857

The economic colonial policy of the British East India Company hit almost every sector of the Haryana economy very hard, the worst sufferer being agriculture on which about 90 per cent of the population depended, directly or indirectly. Thomas Fortescue, a middle rung bureaucrat serving in Haryana in the beginning of the Company rule, has given a graphic description of the condition of the Haryana agriculture and the attitude and policy of the old and new rulers towards it in one of his write-ups dated 1820. According to him there was 'no person in Haryana so elevated as to be styled a *raja* or a *taluqdar*. Nor did such a thing exist in this territory as a plurality of villages comprising the *zamindari* of an individual, nor of a single village. . . .' There were village communities instead which held the entire village land in common. The *muqaddams*, 'the managers and leaders of the village land in common decided the quota of each sharer and collected the government's share and deposited it in the government treasury through the agency of the *qanungo*, the lowest government official deputed to collect revenues of a *pargana*.'[2]

How much was the government's share of the revenue which the *muqaddams* collected? This is a very difficult question to answer with exactitude, for the rates of revenue varied from place to place and from time to time. But in any case, the government assessment (*jama*) never exceeded from 1/6 to 1/4 of the gross produce.[3] We are informed that at many times, especially during the Mughal rule, the collections (*hasil*) made were far less than the rates of revenue. Bayazid tells us that in Akbar's reign the *hasil* of a *jagir* in Sunam (Hisar) was many times less than its *jama*.[4] In the next reign, says Pelsaert, 'in many regions only half the nominal assessment was generally realized'.[5] During the reigns of Shahjahan and Aurangzeb the same practice was followed and no attempt was made by either sovereign to make the *jama* correspond exactly to the *hasil*.

On the other hand, says Irfan Habib, the difference between them was recognized for a fact and the annually changing ratio between the receipts and the standing assessment was marked out for each mahal and expressed in terms of month-proportions (mahawar).[6]

Thus where the current *hasil* equalled half *jama*, the *jagir* was styled six monthly (*shahmaha*), where it was one-fourth, three-monthly (*sihmaha*) and so on.[7] After the death of Aurangzeb even this practice could not continue and the people hardly paid any revenue at all unless forced to do so militarily.[8] The situation, however, changed after the advent of the British. The new rulers started on a happy note (?). They declared:

From the earliest times to the present period the public assessment upon land has never been fixed, and according to established usage and custom, the rulers have exercised a discretionary and despotic authority. The tenants and cultivators of the soil have been exposed to rapacity and oppression. The government had, therefore, decided in order to induce the cultivators to feel secure to make a three year settlement with them, to be followed by a second for the same period and then by one of four years.[9]

This, to be sure, must have pleased the agricultural classes, the peasant-cultivators, tenants-at-will, cropsharers, and agricultural labourers. But their happiness must have proved short-lived. The zealous settlement officers rushed to their lands,[10] and instead of giving any relief to the peasants, fixed government revenue at more than 50 per cent of the gross produce without consulting or taking consent of the peasants in any way. On the other hand, they tended to use compulsion in their dealings. The testimony of the late settlement officers suggests that when the settlements were made by these early zealous officials, the headmen (of the villages) were imprisoned till they agreed to the terms offered and having accepted them till they furnished security for payment.[11]

The contemporary records indicate that in spite of applying coercion of the worst type, the government could not collect their full dues

(Table 1). This clearly implies that the rates fixed were exorbitant.

For many poor farmer the cumulative revenue arrears proved, even when they had good harvests, an unbearable burden. Consequently, they became defaulters and had to visit jails four to five times in the space of a few years.[13] After some time, however, when the settlement officers gained notoriety for their high-handedness and their work began to be adversely criticized even in their own circles, some changes were effected in the revenue system. As a result, the settlements began to be conducted somewhat thoughtfully. But despite these modifications, the settlements continued to be harsh.[14]

The mode of collection of land revenue was as extortionate as the assessment was oppressive. The collections were made in February and September, long before the harvest. It was but natural that people should have made some protests against such mistimed collections when they had practically nothing with them in cash or kind. The government, however, did not realize their mistake and made their collections with the help of a large force kept everywhere for this purpose. For instance, in a small tract in Karnal, 136 horsemen were deployed for collecting land revenue, while 22 sufficed for police duties for this area.[15]

The ultimate outcome of such a revenue policy should be obvious. It completely shattered the peasants' economy, and quite a few of them deserted their villages. A settlement officer of Karnal district tells us that in his district the inhabitants of some villages had abandoned their lands and homes and migrated to distant parts en masse to escape ruination.[16] Equally painful is the picture of the people of Sonepat *pargana* as drawn in the *Settlement Report* of the Delhi district: the nine villages of Pasara, Chidy Yusufpur, Chasanali, Chyaspur, Sunpara, Panava, Patti Brahmanan and Bengha, settled in 1826, were completely deserted in 1842. A similar tale of over-assessment and ruin by previous settlement is mentioned in

TABLE 1: ACCUMULATED REVENUE DEBT[17]

Year	Land assessment			outstanding balances		
	Rs.	As.	Ps.	Rs.	As.	Ps.
1811-12	987,030	11	6	10,073	6	11
1812-13	10,39,560	0	0	60,304	15	6
1813-14	12,56,502	12	0	17,967	2	1
1814-15	12,15,470	13	6	34,215	8	3
1815-16	13,88,978	0	0	95,913	3	0
1816-17	17,01,663	0	0	1,24,318	0	0
1817-18	17,23,691	0	0	2,68,797	0	0

John Lawrence's report of the Rewari pargana which he assessed in 1836. Though he effected a reduction in revenue, the over-oppressed peasantry did not feel relieved.[18] Rohtak district also had the same sad tale to tell. A later settlement report observes that 'the injudiciously heavy revenue have greatly retarded the progress of the district.'[19] The *District Gazetteer* of Hisar gives interesting details about that district:

The demand of the first settlement from 1815-1825 was so high that it exceeded by almost 20 per cent the revenue which has in 1890 been fixed for the same villages; but high though it was and though the actual collections came to have decreased, the demand was increased in the second and third settlements to such an extent that the assessment fixed of the same tract in 1890 is 32 per cent less than the average demand for the last five years of the third settlement, viz Rs. 4,88,609.[20]

In short, the colonial government charged very high revenues which caused great hardship to the Haryana peasantry. The situation was further worsened by the sharp decline in the prices, especially after the forties (Table 2).

Thus between 1851 and 1856 the prices of wheat and corn (maize, jowar, etc.) declined practically by 50 per cent. This made the condition of the peasants still worse. Their produce in most of the cases could not fetch enough money to pay even their revenues. In these circumstances, the hard-hit peasantry felt compelled to go to the village Bania, the money lender, to borrow money to pay their land revenue. The shrewd money lender charged an exorbitant rate of interest, which despite being paid by the poor borrower at every harvest by selling him (the money-lender) his produce and other belongings, at times even the ornaments of his wife at throw away prices, never got cleared off. And when the poor peasant went to the British courts, to seek redress, against the Shylock, he was in most of the cases a loser, for the Shylock, in the words of

TABLE 2: FALL IN PRICES OF AGRICULTURAL PRODUCTS[21]

Years	Price of wheat per maund			Price of Indian corn per maund		
	Rs.	As.	Ps.	Rs.	As.	Ps.
1841-51	2	0	0	1	11	16
1851-2	1	0	0	0	14	16
1852-3	1	3	16	1	1	16
1853-4	1	3	16	1	2	16
1854-5	1	0	0	0	13	16
1855-6	1	1	16	0	14	16

Denzil Ibbetson, was 'a necessity, for he shall receive the produce of the fields (of the peasants) in exchange for the hard cash in which alone government will receive its revenue'. He seemed to his masters an air chamber in a fire engine. They could never think of destroying him.[22]

All these measures struck heavy blow at the Haryana peasantry with the result that many of them were obliged to leave, as noted above, their hearths and homes. This explains why we come across such remarks in the contemporary revenue records as 'this village is entirely abandoned', 'half the villagers of this village have run away', 'only five families are left in this village' and son on.[23]

The ruination of the Haryana peasantry had a very adverse effect on the village artisans and menials, too, for both these classes were not commodity producers and depended entirely upon the peasantry for their subsistence. When the *kisan* (their masters) suffered, they were also bound to suffer. In short the new rulers' economic policy reduced about 90 per cent of the Haryana population to a precarious and wretched condition.

Like their village counterparts, the townsmen broadly following four major professions, namely (i) services, (ii) trade, (iii) crafts and industries, and (iv) labour, also became victims of the British exploitation. In the absence of sufficient contemporary records, it is not possible to paint a full picture of these people's sufferings. We only know this much that by destroying many old states and reducing the job-opportunities in the rest, as also by importing personnel from the Bengal Presidency, the new rulers rendered hundreds of townsmen jobless. By encouraging their own men to monopolize trade of every type, they destroyed the lcoal trade and by flooding market with cheap machine-made goods, they ruined the indigenous craftsmen and the labourers whose lot was intimately connected with them.[24]

As a result of the ruinous economic policy the once beautiful, populous Haryana towns became dirty, deserted places, as the following two statements would show:

(i) Thomas Fortescue's description of Haryana towns (1820)

The brick built towns; the numerous stone edifices of ornaments and worship; the numerous, the spacious walled gardens; the costly and airy pleasure houses; the expensive and lasting masonry of deep walls, reservoirs and lengthened conduits; the large safe and convenient *sarais* with the *kosminars* for accommodation and ease of travellers and above all perhaps the bold and stupendous undertaking of several rand aqueducts which utilized many thousand of bighas and brought crores into the public treasury—are amongst the infragable demonstration of former abundance, population security, wealth and happiness.[25]

(ii) And after ten years one of these towns (Karnal) was visited by Jacuemont (1831). It was in this condition:

. . . The interior, an infamous sink, a heap of uncleanliness winding paths scarcely passable for horses, and having here and there a few miserable huts, I have seen nothing so bad in India, and it is fit to mention that amongst the native its filth is proverbial.[26]

Indeed, the British economic policy brought about the systematic ruin of the Haryana towns and their dwellers.

Like the servicemen, traders and artisans in the towns, a large number of feudal chiefs were also ruined by either biting off large portions of their ancestral estates (Table 3) or in some cases by taking over their possessions entirely (Table 4).

TABLE 3: ESTATES SUBJECTED TO PARTIAL REDUCTION[27]

Name of the Estate	Year of reduction	Reason of reduction
1. Rewari	1805	Not helping the British in the Anglo-Maratha war-1803
2. Farrukhnagar	1805	–do–
3. Ballabhgarh	1805	–do–

TABLE 4: ESTATES PERMANENTLY CONFISCATED[28]

Name of the Estate	date of forfeiture	Cause of forfeiture
Rania	1818	Revolt of Nawab Zabita Khan
Chhachhrauli	1818	Rani Ram Kaur's 'failure' to give good government and Jodh Singh's interference
Ambala	1824	Death of Sardarni Dia Kaur, widow of Dulcha Singh
Dialgarh (shares of Daya Kaur)	1829	Death of Mai Daya Kaur, widow of Bhagwan Singh
Thanesar (2/5 shares of Bhag Singh)	1832	Death of Sardar Jamait Singh without male heirs
Kaithal	1843	Death of Bhai Udey Singh without male heirs

Bubbeal	1838	Death of Sardar Harnam Singh without male heirs
Chalaundhi	1844	Death of Sardarni Ram Kaur, widow of Bhagal Singh
Ladwa	1845	Revolt of Raja Ajit Singh
Thanesar (3/5 share of Bhanga Singh)	1850	Death of Rani Chand Kaur, widow of Fateh Singh
Halladhar	1850	Death of Sardar Fateh Singh, without make heirs
Dialgarh (1 share of Mai Sukhan)	1851	Death of Mai Sukhan, widow of Bhagwan Singh

The dispossessed chiefs, their descendants, officials, *panditas*, or *ulema* and a host of other retainers, who enjoyed their patronage, became jobless.[29]

UNDER THE CROWN, 1858-1947

The above situation changed a little after the region came under the British crown (1858-1947). The progress made during the period could in no way be called satisfactory, however. Substantiation: the peasants worked hard, as is shown in Table 5 which relates to a holding of 7.72 acres, all the twelve months a year, but got very little in return:

TABLE 5: WORK PUT IN BY A PEASANT FAMILY IN A YEAR[30]

Month	Nature of work	No. of men employed	No. of working days	Average working hrs. per man at work
Beginning of June	Carting manure to fields	2	4	9
until the rains	Ploughing	1	10	7
(*Jeth-Har*)	Attending cattle	1	–	–
Beginning of rains to	Ploughing and sowing			
mid-August	cotton	2	2	10
(*Har-Savan*)	Maize	2	2	9
	Rice	2	2	12
	Chari	2	4	12
	Other crops	2	2	10
	Repairing	1	3	5
	Fencing fields	2	2	10

	Ploughing at intervals	1	5	8
	Hoeing and weeding cotton and maize	2	5	12
	Attending cattle	1		
August to mid-Sept. (*Bhadon*)	Middle of Hoeing and weeding cotton and maize	–	–	–
	Taking out grass from rice	2	2	7
	Ploughing at intervals			
	Sowing gram and sarson	–	–	–
	Bringing grass from fields	2	30	5
	Harvesting chana	2	1	7
	Atteding cattle	1	1	7
Middle of Sept. to mid-Oct. (*Asoj*)	Harvesting maize	–	–	–
	Harvesting rice	1	7	11
	Ploughing and working sohaga	1	22	8
	Sowing gram and sarson	–	–	–
	Cutting chari fodder and bringing home for cattle	2	30	6
	Attending cattle	1		
Middle of Oct. to mid-Nov. (*Katak*)	Ploughing and working sohaga	1	6	10
	Sowing wheat	–	–	–
	Sowing berra and sarson	–	–	–
	Cutting chari fodder and bringing home for cattle	1	30	6
	Attending cattle	1		
Middle of Nov. to mid-Dec. (*Magh*)	Ploughing and working sohaga, sowing wheat	2	10	6
	Fencing fields	–	–	–
	Cutting chari fodder and bringing home for cattle	2	7	9
	Threshing rice, jawar and maize	2	5	9
	Attending cattle	1		
Middle of Dec. to mid-Jan. (*Poh*)	Fencing fields	1	–	–
	Collecting and stacking fodder	2	–	–
	Attending cattle	1	–	–
	Ploughing	1	10	–
Middle of Jan. to mid-Feb.	Plying gadda on hire	1	13	–
	Labour on working other than cultivation	–	–	–

(*Phagh*)	Bringing fodder from fields	1	30	–
	Attending cattle	1		
Middle of Feb. to mid-March (*Phag*)	Plying gadda on hire	1	–	–
	Labour other than cultivation	–	–	–
	Bringing fodder from fields	1	–	6
	Attending cattle	1	–	–
Middle of March to mid-April (*Chet*)	Harvesting gram	2	7	9
	Harvesting sarson	1	2	6
	Bringing fodder from fields	1	15	8
	Attending cattle	1	–	–
Middle of April to mid-May (*Baisakh*)	Harvesting wheat and other crops	3	10	13
	Threshing wheat, etc.,	3	10	10
	Attending cattle	1	–	–
Middle to end of May (half *Jeth*)	Threshing wheat, etc., collecting and stacking *bhusa*	2	3	11
	Collecting and stacking *bhusa*	2	3	11
	Carting wheat and *bhusa*	2	10	–
	Attending cattle	1		

The above Table (5) obliges us to ask a question: How come that a Haryana peasant who put in so much effort all through the twelve months a year remained poor? His returns were negligible. There were a four main reasons for this: (i) high rate of revenue, (ii) traditional mode of agriculture, (iii) inadequate means of irrigation, and (iv) rampant illiteracy and ignorance among the people.

There is no denying the fact that powers that be did make some efforts to improve the situation by various means, of which strengthening of the irrigational systems was the main (Table 6).

Additional water changed agricultural scenario in Karnal, Hisar and a part of Gurgaon. A good acreage came under cash crops—cotton, sugarcane, and oil seed. The double-cropped area also increased a little. Besides this, the peasants were also given some education to make use of good manure, good seeds, good pesticides and good improved implements. But because of the campaign, the peasants being ignorant the efforts did not seem to have made any appreciable impact.

TABLE 6: IRRIGATIONAL FACILITIES IN HARYANA[31]

Canal	CCA	Total areas irrigated (*in lakhs of acres*)
Western Yamuna Canal	26.14	
Ghaggar Canal	· 0.73	11.82
Saraswati Canal	1.55	
Agra Canal	–	2.25

To fight the menace of indebtedness, the Government established cooperative credit societies and cooperative mortgage banks after 1904 and 1920 respectively, which lent money to farmers at low rates of interest from 8 per cent to 9 per cent per annum.[32] Cooperative credit societies were also started about this time with a view to helping the farmers to improve the breeds of their cattle. A number of acts were passed to give relief to the debtors.[33]

Steps were also taken in 1920 to check the fragmentation of land holdings which posed a big problem to the farmers and check the *thugee* and looting of the farmers by vested interests in *mandis* and bazars by passing several *mandi* acts.[34] The Punjab peasant was benefited a great deal by these measures. But in the backward region of Haryana the ignorant, poor peasant could derive anything but negligible benefits.

In the field of industry, the picture was still more dismal. The government tried to give some incentives, especially during and after the first world war (1914-18) to develop some industries. As a result, textile industries came up at Bhiwani, some shoe-making units sprang up at Karnal and brass, copper utensils manufacturies developed at Rewari, Panipat and Jagadhari.[35]

In sum, however, the development of industries was not up to the mark. There were several reason for this. In the first place, raw material necessary for the industries was not available in abundance. It had to be 'imported' from outside at big price. Secondly, the region being backward, adequate capital was not available. In the third place, the people lacked technical know-how. And fourthly, the colonial government's support to the industries was not to develop them for the good of the people concerned or the country, but for meeting their own selfish needs.

In the beginning, the position of trade and commerce was also unsatisfactory. But it was not to remain so for long. For soon after the development of means of communication, which the government had to undertake for serving its own selfish ends after 1880,[36] the trade and commercial activity increased here to some extent.

As noted elsewhere, the government had banged the doors of government services on the people of this region. During the first world war, however, when it was in dire need of able-bodied men for its armed forces, a shift was effected in this policy. As a result, about 84,000 youth, especially from rural areas, joined the armed forces.[37] This had a positive effect on the rural economy in the region, for soon after a regular flow of cash money started taking place here.[38] In the changed circumstances after the war, some other jobs were also given in the civil sector.

The long and short of the story is that economy during the period 1803-1947 was far from satisfactory. In the presence of the colonial exploitative order at the helm of affairs, it could not have been anything but that.

Independence and After

After independence, the situation changed and with stupendous speed. The new Government took keen interest in removing the age-old backwardness in the economy which had come about as a result of the colonial distortions. Agriculture, obviously, received the first priority. The obscurantist practice, like *zamindari* system, etc., were done away with. A large number of legislations to effect improvement in the agricultural sector were passed. Loans were given on easy interest rates to the peasantry to effect improvement in their operations. Consolidations of holdings were done. Measures were taken 'to educate farmers' to go for insecticides, pesticides, etc., and tractors and all that. More water was given to the thirsty lands. The Western Yamuna Canal was strengthened by various measures. After a while another big canal—the Bhakra Canal—came. For the locales where canal water could not be supplied public tube-wells were set up. These measures quenched the thirst of the vast strethces of the unwatered lands. Because of this the cropping culture changed, as Table 7 shows.

As a result, the area under cash crops increased a great deal. Even in respect of food grains, a shift was taken towards the superior cereals, like paddy, wheat and maize. The people did away with the sowing of inferior crops. The low yielding crops, like bajra, jawar, barley, etc., went down.

Equipped with new knowledge, blessed with new facilities—water, electricity, etc.—and with renewed enthusiasm to get more and more from the Mother Earth, the peasant was successful to some extent, as Table 8 indicates.

TABLE 7: CHANGE IN CROPPING CULTURE[39]

Crops	1950-1	1960-1	1963-4	Per cent increase/ decrease in 1963-4 over 1950-1
Food Crops				
1. Paddy	181	380	382	+111
2. Wheat	902	1,544	1,682	+86
3. Maize	76	258	281	+269
4. Jawar, bajra and barley	3,265	3,017	2,605	+20
5. Gram	2,163	3,808	3,436	+58
6. Massar, and moong moth	145	156	112	-23
Total	6,732	9,163	8,498	+126
Cash Crops				
7. Cotton American	7.6	132.0	251.5	+3,209
8. Cotton Desi	126.4	96.7	180.6	+43
9. Sugarcane	137.0	317.0	280.0	+104
10. Oilseeds	275.0	393.0	562.0	-104
Total	546.0	939.2	1274.1	+133

TABLE 8: AVERAGE YIELD PER ACRE IN HARYANA[40]

Crops	1950-1 (*in lbs*)	Average 1961-4	Percentage increase/ decrease
1. Paddy	773	1,586	105
2. Wheat	720	116	55
3. Maize	354	826	133
4. Jawar, bajra and barley	321	312	-3
5. Gram	400	537	34
6. Cotton	167	253	51
7. Sugarcane	2,927	3,337	114
8. Oilseeds	295	534	81

As in agriculture, so in industry, there was improvement in the post-independence era. The government, besides taking to a number of its own large and medium scale projects, gave inducement to private entrepreneurs for setting up small to large industries. As a result, a large number of industries came up, as shown in Table 9, by 1965-6, in big cities, especially in the statellite towns around Delhi, like Faridabad,

TABLE 9: INDUSTRIES IN HARYANA[41]

District	Total no. of registered industries	Industries per lakh of population
Hisar	152	9.9
Rohtak	146	10.3
Gurgaon	280	22.6
Karnal	197	12.2
Mahendragarh	7	1.3
Ambala	324	39.4
Jind	18	3.9

Ballabhgarh, Gurgaon, Badarpur, Palwal, Aurangpur, Bahadurgarh, Sonepat, Ganaur, Dharuhera, etc.

The above table shows good improvement over the pre-1947 position when industries were almost non-existent in the region.

As in the agricultural and industrial sectors, so in the sphere of trade and commerce, there was marked progress in the post-independence period (1947-66).

In sum, the Haryana region made substantial progress in agriculture, industry, trade and commerce after independence. But the level of development was still far from satisfactory, especially so when compared with the position obtaining in other parts of Punjab. This was one of the main reasons for the people of Haryana to ask for a separate state.

NOTES

1. For exploitative role of the British, see R.C. Dutt, *Economic History of India*, pp. 329-30.
2. *Delhi Residency and Agency Records* (hereafter *Delhi Residency*), vol. I, pp. 82-6.
3. For a detailed discussion on the nature of revenue system in vogue before the advent of the British, see besides Irfan Habib, *Agrarian System of Mughal India*; Baden Powell, *The Land System of British India*, vol. II.
4. Irfan Habib, op. cit., p. 264.
5. Ibid.
6. Ibid.
7. Ibid.
8. *Delhi Residency*, vol. I, p. 115.
9. The early settlement officers believed in collecting the best price from their subjects. They enhanced revenue on every settlement without much rhyme or reason. As a result, the farmers became over-assessed. The evil was,

unfortunately, increased by the difficult, dutiful zeal of the public officers to obtain full dues of government at every settlement. Quoted in D.N. Panigrahi, *Charles Metcalfe in India*, p. 47.

10. *Settlement Report*, p. 46.
11. D.N. Panigrahi, op. cit., p. 47.
12. *Settlement Report*, p. 47.
13. Despite effecting reduction, the revenue charged was still heavy. After 1857, however the government seems to have given a serious thought to the problem and made substantial reduction, as the following table comparing to revenues of the pre-Revolt and post-Revolt days of the Hisar district would show:

Tehsils	Pre-revolt revenue	Post-revolt revenue
Bhiwani	81,181	73,206
Hansi	1,60,209	1,42,739
Hisar	2,01,204	56,438
Barwala	63,743	69,438
Fatehabad	79,066	69,438

It is pertinent to point out here that area of the tehsils in both the periods under study was the same. But of course, the cultivated area in the post-Revolt period had increased by over 33 per cent. In view of this there is all the more reason now to feel that the earlier settlements were really ruinous, See *Hisar District Gazetteer*, p. 255.

14. *Settlement Report, Karnal*, p. 47.
15. Ibid.
16. *Settlement Report, Delhi*, p. 141.
17. Douvie, *The Punjab Settlement Manual*, p. 10.
18. *Settlement Report, Rohtak*, p. 139.
19. *Hisar District Gazetteer*, pp. 236-7.
20. *Selections from the Records of the Govt. of India*, no. XVIII, p. 28.
21. Ibbetson, *Settlement Report*, pp. 111-12.
22. Ibid., p. 48.
23. For economic interdependence of the village artisans and craftsmen of the peasants, see K.M. Ashraf, *Life and Conditions of the People of Hindustan*, pp. 113-63.
24. See K.C. Yadav, *Revolt*, pp. 29-30.
25. *Delhi Residency*, vol. I, p. 114.
26. Quoted by Ibbetson, *Settlement Report*, p. 221.
27. See K.C. Yadav, *Revolt*, pp. 24-30.
28. *Assessment Report of Pipli Tehsil* (1888), pp. 31-2; *Hisar District Gazetteer*, p. 34, (for Rania); Cunningham, *History of the Sikhs*, p. 127; Hamilton, *Statistical*, vol. I, p. 464.
29. For a specimen of the feelings of the dispossessed dynasts, see NAI, Mutiny Papers, Box no. 34, Document no. 12 (1857).

30. See the Board of Economic Enquiry Punjab, *An Economic Survey of Naggal (Ambala)*, (1933) pp. 30-1.
31. For details see *Haryana Development Committee Report*, pp. 42-82.
32. For instance the debt had gone up to Rs. 90 crores in 1921 which worked out to be Rs. 31 per cultivated acre or Rs. 76 per head of the agricultural population.
33. Eg. The Punjab Relief of Indebtedness Act, 1934; The Punjab Debts Protection Act, 1936, etc.
34. Called the Punjab Agricultural Producers Act, 1939.
35. For details see, *District Gazetteers* of different districts in Haryana.
36. The means of communication were improved as follows:

Railway lines	Year of start
Ambala-Meerut	1869
Ambala-Ludhiana	1869
Delhi-Rewari	1873
Rewari-Hisar	1883
Hisar-Sirsa	1884
Rewari-Bhatinda	1889
Gurgaon-Farrukhnagar	–
Delhi-Ambala-Kalka	1890
Narwana-Kaithal	1900
Delhi-Palwal-Mathura	–
Roads	
Delhi-Ambala	1870
Delhi-Sirsa	1970
Sirsa-Ambala	1870
Ambala-Jagadhari	1870
Delhi-Rewari	–

37. According to M.S. Leigh, *Punjab and the War*, the Haryana region supplied about 84,000 jawans during the war (1914-18).
38. Besides this, ex-soldiers received substantial amount by way of pensions as the following figures from 1928-9 show:

District	Amount received in pensions (*in lakh*)
Ambala	Rs. 2.62
Hisar	Rs. 7.51
Karnal	Rs. 0.53
Rohtak	Rs. 7.61
Gurgaon	Rs. 6.65

The Punjab Provincial Banking Enquiry Report, 1930, p. 362.

39. Ibid.
40. Ibid., p. 19.
41. Ibid., p. 85.

20

Art and Architecture

The Art

Peace, tranquillity and freedom are the basic requirements for the proper growth and development of fine arts. Unfortunately, the Haryana region remained, because of its situation, the worst sufferer in all the three respects, as seen elsewhere, in the eighteenth century, the so-called 'times of great-trouble'. Unfortunately, things did not improve even after the advent of the British, for, though the new-comers restored law and order to some extent, the other most important thing, namely the freedom remained absent. This explains why fine arts could not develop here properly during the period under study.

Painting

The art of painting was the worst sufferer. Despite best efforts, we could not lay our hands on any standard paintings belonging to the nineteenth century, except for the one portrait of a feudal chief—nawab of Jhajjar (of 1840s or 1850s) and some miniatures in a *Bhagavatapurana* (of almost the same time). The former depicts the chief and his two sons in a sitting pose in his royal palace. The latter portray Lord Krishna in different poses and some other deities in rhythmical lines. Some of the pictures, if not all, are in beautiful, bright colours and bear masterly touches. It is an irony, however, that we do not know the names of the artists who have done these paintings.[1]

The position is a little better, when we come to murals. These are of two types—paintings and folk drawings. In the former, the painters follow tradition and their popular themes are historical and mythological heroes, beautiful dance scenes, and depiction of hunting expeditions, wrestling bouts, cock and ram fights, troops on the march and engagements, and wildlife. Such paintings, says Lieutenant William Bart who accompanied Lt. Col. C.M. Wade in a Mission to Kabul in 1840s were found almost in every town and big villages in the preceding century. 'The houses of the richer *baboos*', he says, 'are plastered with the finest *chunam,* decorated with paintings of various devices in much better taste than is usually displayed on such occasion'.[2] Some old *havelis* in Pehowa, Pundri, Beri, Dadri, Rewari, Bawal, and Narnaul also give evidence of the presence of a lot of murals there. Unfortunately, not enough care is being taken to preserve them. For instance, beautiful murals at the Mansa Devi Temple near Panchkula are partly damaged in the process of renovation. The same is true of the paintings in the Rang Mahal at Buria and in the Jain Temple at Sonepat.

Luckily, the murals found in a private mansion at Dadri are in good shape. Chandrasen, a high official of Nawab Bahadurjang Khan of this place had an excellent taste in art and literature, and he got over two dozen paintings done in his *Diwankhana* in 1854-5.[3] These murals have for their themes gods and goddesses, important contemporary and historical persons, scenes from classical literature and animals and birds.[4] Who were the artists who did these murals, is a question which cannot be answered now. The guess is that some unknown court artist has done it with the help of some local artists from town/countryside. For instance, the paintings of the forefathers of the nawab, the ceiling painted in geometrical designs in lively colours are the works of the former but the lower portions of the ceilings and walls having portraits of soldiers in standing pose and horses, princes smoking *hookah* and floral designs are the works of the latter. They are simple and do not have masterly touch.[5]

Birla Temple at Thanesar (Kurukshetra) and Kirorimal Temple at Bhiwani also have rich paintings. Done by modern artists, these pictures portray gods and goddesses, sages, seers and depict scenes from *puranas*, etc.

Besides the works of professional artists, the laymen who, too, have artists in them also did this work. The folk murals on the whitened walls in black, red and blue colours, and special ritualistic decorations and auspicious paintings during the festivals at the time of marriage, child birth and such like occasions, like the *sathias*, *mandanas*, *sanjhi*, etc., are their works. Though crude and simple in forms, some of these paintings have a capacity for abstraction.[6]

Music

Like painting, music, too, presented not so encouraging a picture in Haryana during the period under study. There was no institution which could give boost to the waning art. But, fortunately, individuals were there who somehow kept it alive. Kallan Khan and his sons Hafiz Khan and Basir Khan of Gudiani, a small village near Kosli in district Rewari contributed, for instance, a great deal to the form of *khayal*. Kallan, a disciple of Hoddu Khan (d. 1870), the greatest singer of the Gwalior House, sang lyrical *khayals*.[7] Kallan's son Hafiz Khan (d. 1920) was even greater than his father. His fame had reached even beyond the Vindhayas—south India, to be precise. He was invited by the king of Mysore to adore his court. He won laurels there. Subsequently, he was employed at the court of Indore.[8] Basir Khan, his brother was in certain respects taller than Hafiz. Educated by two music giants of his age, Umrao Khan of the Delhi House, and Inayat Hussain of Sahaswan, he shaped into a master artist. His fame as a great *khayal* singer reached far and wide like his brother's. He was, however, a man of independent disposition who would not stay at one place for more time. He left one court after the other. Mysore, Bhavanagar, Indore, etc., were some of these courts that he visited and stayed at. He got recognition for his musical excellence.[9]

Mian Achapal was another great musician of this time. It is an irony that we do not know the real name of this great master artist: we simply know his *takhallus*. And same is the case with his birth place: we only know that he came from some village in Haryana.[10] He was a great singer and a great musician who had acquired unparalleled mastery over a number of styles, *khyal*, *tarana*, *trivata*, *chturanga* and *saragama*.[11] His compositions are famous even to this date and many great musicians sing them. Achapal had a large number of disciples of whom the most famous was Tarnas Khan, a big name in the history of Indian music.[12]

A pertinent question may arise here: How come music which had strong tradition here declined during this period? There were several reasons for this like: (i) there was the absence of local feudal courts, like those of Rajasthan and U.P. where classical music was patronized. A few courts which existed here were for the most part of north-western frontiersmen who had no taste for anything like music; (ii) extreme poverty of the people owing to exploitative colonial rule made the general public indifferent to such pursuits.[13] In the 1930s, however, under the influence of the national renaissance, some activites to revive the classical music were taken seriously. As a result, some classical vocalists came to the fore. Among these celebrities one who stands apart as a giant is Jasraj (b. 1930) who hails from Hisar. He was trained in the tradition of *Mewati gharana* especially by his elder brother Mani Ram. Popularly called *swara-samrata* he has exhibited a perfect harmony between the *svara* and *laya*.[14] Jasraj's son Sharangadev is also a chip of the old block. He is shaping to be a good classical vocalist.[15]

Like the vocal, instrumental music, too, which had fallen on bad days in the beginning of this period, was revived after some time somehow by folk artists, like the *jogis*, *mirasis*, *bhats*, *sangis* and *bhajnopadeshakas*. Some 'brown *nawabs*' (British officials) also took interest in it. As a result, harmonium, violin, piano and what is called 'western orchestra' were introduced. In big towns, especially among the westernized elite, this form became popular.[16]

However, unlike the classical music, its folk countrpart, remained in as flourishing a state as it ever was in both its forms, vocal as well as instrumental. To the accompaniment of *dholaka*, *ghara*, *khartala*, *chimta*, etc., the simple, rustic folks continued to sing their folk songs—the songs of the body and the soul containing wishful aspiration of love, appreciation of beauty, the pangs of separation, the joys of festivals, child-birth, marriage, harvest and sorrows that nature bestowed upon man as her pranks, in as simple a way as the rain drops fell from the clouds.[17]

Dance

A word about dance. For the reasons given above, the classical dance did not flourish here during the period under study. But folk dance did. The folk dance was of two types: (i) social dances, and (ii) ritualistic dances. In the former, which were many a time more in number than the latter, there was expression of great feeling of the joy of a festival, the pleasure after a harvest, or the happiness that comes on the occasion of ceremonies, like marriage, birth of a son, etc. These were usually group dances, naive and simple in technique. The second type of dances were performed on the occasion of some religious festivals. Of both the types of dances the important ones were as follows:[18]

Chhathi Dance: This dance full of excitement and thrill, is performed by womenfolk with the accompaniment of folk songs on the sixth day of the birth of a boy. The *domani* or any other woman of the village who has a little knowledge of musical instruments, like *dholaka* or *matka*, etc., gives a *tala* to the dance. After the dance and *bankalis* or boiled gram and wheat are distributed.

Khoria Dance: It is performed on the occasion of the marriage of a son. After the *barat* (marriage party) consisting of menfolk of the *mohalla* or village is gone to the bride's village the womenfolk rejoice by dancing and singing at night, again on the *tala* of *dholaka* or a *matka*. The *bankalis* are distributed among the women after the dance.

Teej Dance: It is performed on the occasion of the Teej festival. Young girls in bright new garments gather in a circle or in two rows holding each other dance and sing songs at dusk in the village *gaura* (outskirts).

Phag Dance (Ladies): It is performed in the month of *Phalgun* about fifteen days before the Holi festival. In the night the womenfolk assemble at some village *chauk* (open space) where there is ample privacy and dance to the accompaniment of folk songs. Some talented ladies also do mono-acting and take to *swanga* of different types on this occasion.

Phag Dance (Males): Like their women, the men also perform a dance called *dhap* dance or *dhamal* during the Holi days. In the evening they assemble in some number and dance and sing 'holi' (songs) to the accompaniment of *dhap* (a circular drum with one flap), or *nagara* (a big drum). It is a big entertainment.

Loor Dance: This is not a common dance. It is performed only in the areas adjoining Rajasthan. Like other dances, it is also performed in the night. The dancers form two rows holding each others' hands like two opposing teams on a sports ground and sing songs which usually contain taunts for their opponents. The more talented side wins the contest which, however, remains unacknowledged by the losing side.

Chhari Dance: The people here have great reverence for Guga Pir. He is specially worshipped on the day following the Janamashtami in *Bhadon*. The *bhakatas* (devotees) of the *pir* make a *chhari* or the *pir's* standard—a long bamboo covered with red cloth having *gota* decorations, peacock feathers, hand-made fans and such like things; take it to an open ground, and after performing puja (worship) start dancing and singing around it. Initially, dancing is of very common nature, but as the time passes, the rhythm picks up and the devotees shake their bodies in a terrific manner. Around the midnight a *sadhaka* (staunch devotee) takes iron chains and hits them on his back. That is the climax. This dance is performed exclusively by men.

RAMALILA

Besides folk dances, several types of folk dramas have also been in vogue in this period. Of these (i) the *Ramalila* and (ii) the *swang* deserve special mention. The former is a dramatic performance of the story of Rama for about fourteen days around Dushera (during September-

October). Usually the local talent is used in it but occasionally performance is also given by some professionals from outside the village. The male actors play both the male and female roles. The dialogues and songs are in most of the cases taken from the *Ramayana*[19] of Jaswant Singh, a talented folk poet from Tohana, a small town in district Hisar.

Swang

The other performance, that is *swang* or *sang* (as it is locally called) is much more popular than *Ramalila*. It is difficult to give an exact history of the development of this great folk performance, but some clues found in the old literature here and there indicate that it was used for folk entertainment even in very old days. For instance, there are references to such entertaining performances in the *Harshacharita* of Bana.[20] But the *swang* in its present form is of very late origin, its first performance being staged about 1700.[21] A local genius Krishna Lal Bhat is said to be its originator.[22]

In its initial stages, the *swang* had to compete with several professional performances, like the ones by the *nakkals* and the *vaishyas*. But since the entertainment by the *nakkals* was not very lively, colourful and rich and that of the *vaishyas* was very costly and to some extent amoral also (or at least some people thought it to be so), the *swang* gained popularity over them, and in due course of time say about 1930s it made them obsolete. And since then, it became, thanks to the efforts of great masters, like Deep Chand, Hardeva, Lakshmi Chand, Mange Ram, Ramkishan,[23] a very popular performance.

The *swangs* are performed by professional troupes comprising about ten persons. They recited the story in verses called *raginis* or sweet melodies to the accompaniment of *sarangi*, *tabla*, *khartal*, *chimta*, *dholaka*, harmonium, etc. The stage for the performance is usually set in an open field (*maidan*) near the village pond, or in some *chauk* (open space) in the village itself. The audience sit around it on all the sides (women sit separately at a distance or on roofs of the nearby houses).[24]

The first artist to have started the *swangs* was, as noted above, Krishan Lal Bhat who lived about 1700. He was the first artist to employ a *mandali* (troupe), make stage and give a *swang* performance. The male characters did not dance, only the female characters did. This practice is followed even today. His orchestra was very simple, a *sarangi* and a *dholaka*. His *raginis* were in *chaubaulas*.[25] After some time came Deep Chand, from Khanda Kheri, a village in district Hisar. The early part of the present century is credited to be his time (*Deep Chand-Yuga*). He was a learned man who changed the *swang* a great deal; he enlarged the troupe to 8 to 10 actors, and employed a comprehensive orchestra consisting of modern instruments, like *tabla*, harmonium, etc.; and introduced sweet *raginis* in the *kafia chhanda* instead of *chaubolas*.[26] Hardeva, a disciple of Deep Chand, introduced the present day *raginis* in place of *Kafia chhandas* of his *guru.*

Of all the *sangis* of the past and present, Lakhmi Chand was, however, the greatest. He hailed from Janti a small village in district Sonepat. His guru was a blind, illiterate preacher named Man Singh, who moving from village to village recited simple, but impressive poetry for the simple village folks. Lakhmi Chand was deeply influenced by him and became interested in his poetry. Later on he joined Sohan Kundalwala and learnt the art of dancing and singing as also composing *raginis*, etc., by taking vigorous exercises. As a result, he became a very famous *sangi*.[27]

Lakhmi Chand's famous *swangs* are *Harish Chandra-Taramati, Nala-Damayanti*, *Satyavana-Savitri*, etc., based on Hindu religious and epic literature, and *Meerabai*, *Padmavati*, *Nautanki*, *Jani Chor*, *Raja Bhoj* and *Shahi Lakarhara* based on history and legends. In the *swangs,* he used the simplest and the most effective vocabulary touching different aspects of life. His songs were sweet and dance rhythmic, though lacking sophistication. In short, what can best be found in the Haryana *swang* at present is Lakhmi Chand's giving.[28]

Many *sangis* came after him, like Ram Kishan Vyas, Chandra Bedi, etc. They could not keep up the tempo of the folk opera however. This was owing to the strong influence of cinema, television, etc. In the changed circumstances, the *swangs* still engaged in the traditional trade have started deserting their own rich musical heritage in favour of film songs and tunes. In a way the past is being crushed thoughtlessly.

To avoid the destruction of this traditional art, however, the *swang* has to change with the changing time. More than that, it has to stand against the forces which seem to destroy its very fabric. It should transform itself into a modern folk opera that suits the modern time and taste.[29]

The Architecture

A word about architecture now, which, for the convenience of study, can be divided into two broad categories: (i) secular architecture and (ii) religious architecture.

TABLE 1: CLASSIFICATION OF ARCHITECTURE

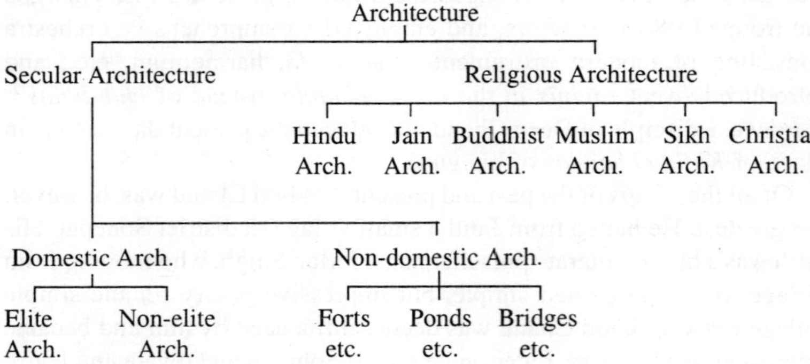

Secular Architecture

With the advent of the British (1803), new townships came into existence in our region. In these townships new buildings were mostly planned on European lines. Karnal, as far as the records show, can claim the honour to be the first modern town with such buildings in 1806. It was the British authorities established their cantonment here and constructed simple, but modern houses, barracks, and shopping centres. Of all these buildings, the two, Ochterlony House and Adams House are still in existence. These are palatial mansions with architectural merit.[30] Almost of the same period is the civil station of Gurgaon. A large number of European type houses were built here also. Of these, one built by Cavendish (the first administrator of the place), locally called Ghamandi Sahib's House, and a Sarai are fine pieces of architecture.[31] In 1837, Major Thereby, Superintendent of Bhatiana, founded yet another modern town at Sirsa. There also many impressive buildings, such as the Dak Bangalow and the '*Sahib logon ke bangle*', were worth seeing.

Ten years later, the Ambala cantonment was laid (1843). Covering 7,220 acres, this oblong-shaped township running from north-east to south-west was definitely an improvement on other attempts in town planning and architecture. Here the streets were wide and straight and the impressive bungalows and houses. There were wide roads and straight street and the bungalows and houses. There were many good public buildings, such as the Mosonic Hall, the Sirhind Club, the Town Hall, Government School, Wards' Institute, Lepers' Asylum, Public Library, Post Office, Dak Bungalow and Commissioner's Kutchery.[32]

Modern buildings were constructed at other important towns also, such as Rohtak and Hisar. Most of these buildings had architectural make-up to suit tropical climate. They had spacious rooms, good ventilation, high ceiling and in many cases double roofs. These buildings were surrounded by well-laid out grassy lawns, ornamented with fine shady trees.[35]

The elite are copied by the masses who have means, especially, the town dwellers. This happened in our region also. The people with some means built *kothis* or bungalows, as these were called, after the European fashion. This is not to suggest, however, that the old architectural style was replaced by the new. The businessmen, the traditional classes still clung to the old *havelis* which were often multi-storeyed. After independence, however, these *havelis* have been replaced by new structures, spacious living room, 2-3 bed rooms, wide verandahs, kitchen, bathroom, lavatory and lawns, usually both in the front and back.[34]

The poor people in the towns still live in the old types of houses which are in most of the cases of three types: (i) small *pucca* houses with one or two rooms, a kitchen, and a bathroom and a lavatory in congested areas, ordinarily lacking fresh air, open yards, etc., (ii) small, but newly constructed *pucca* houses in new colonies, like the first type, but with open space and plenty of fresh air and light, and (iii) semi-*pucca* or *kachcha* houses with one or two rooms with no bath or lavatory facilities. These are occupied by a large number of working classes. Some people live in *jhuggis* and *jhonpris* also.[35]

The houses of the village poor differ a great deal from what we have in the towns in their architectural plan, materials used, and other factors, such as comfortability, etc. Broadly, the houses can be divided into seven categories: (i) substantially roomy houses (*pucca*), (ii) substantially roomy house (*kachcha*), (iii) *chhapars*, (iv) *jhonpris*, (v) *gher*, (vi) *gatwar*, and (vii) *baithaks*. The first two types of houses have identical planning as far as their architecture goes. They only differ in material used in their construction. The first is made of *pucca* bricks, either with lime or cement, and the second of mud-bricks. Their plan of construction is usually as follows: main gate, big room, called *poli* or *deodhi*; then courtyard (*angan*) with a small kitchen (*rasoi*) at one end and often cattle shed or open *than* on the other; then there is the *dalan* or open verandah after which come the sleeping and living rooms (*kothas*). The cattle are generally penned at night either in the *angan* or in the *poli* and fodder is often stacked on the mud roofs. Now-a-days this practice has changed in some cases: the cattle are penned in *gher* (a small house built away from the residential quarters and the fodder is also stacked either in the *gher* or in the *gatwara* (thorny enclosure outside the village-*basti*). Some rich persons, especially those belonging to the middle classes, have constructed *baithaks*, too, in their *ghers*. The poor have usually one-room houses of mud-bricks and thatched roofs. These are called *chhappars* or *chhans*. Those who are extremely poor live in still humbler dwellings than the *chhappars*, namely *jhonpris* having small mud walls and inferior thatched roofs. Around them is put a thorny enclosure *(bar)*.[36]

A large number of modern public buildings of architectural beauty like those of schools, and colleges, offices of different institutions, hospitals, rest houses, etc., have also come up recently at every district headquarters and important places. These buildings are built in modern style for the most part with bricks and cement. The use of iron is quite profuse in these buildings. Some buildings, at least some of these, give majestic look. Some private agencies and persons have also built such buildings in several towns for schools, colleges, hospitals, *dharmashalas*, etc.[37]

Religious Architecture

There are religious buildings of the period which have some architectural importance of these. The earliest is the church of St. James at Karnal (1806). Though simple in structure, it is impressive. It is having a spacious hall, and about 100 feet high tower supporting large ornamental cross.[38] Subsequently, two more churches were built here: (i) St. Emanuel's Church, and the Scension Church. Though not as impressive as the former, both these churches are also structures of some merit.

There are some churches at Ambala as well, which were built slightly later than the Karnal churches. Of these, the St. Paul's Church is of great architectural importance. It is a handsome, semi-gothic structure capable of accommodating more than a thousand persons. Unfortunately, this grand building was destroyed in 1871 during air raids by Pakistan.[40] The two other churches, Holy Red Church and Emersy Church (1905) are average structures. The Sadar Bazar Church is a humble construction.[41] There is a Methodist Church at Sonepat. The same is true of the Baptist Church at Palwal made of red brick and grey stone. The church at Rewari, built by the S.P.G. Mission in 1890s is, however, an attractive construction—a spacious good building.[42]

There are some good mosques, too, of some architectural importance. Of these the most important is one at Gurgaon—Aliwardi Masjid.

Situated about 2 km. north of the old tehsil office, it was built about 150 years ago. There is a tomb nearby, probably of the builder of the mosque (Nawab Aliwardi) with an artistic trelis screen of red-stone. The Jama Masjid at Ferozepur Jhirka is equally impressive. It was built by Ahmed Baksh, the nawab of the place. It is 80 feet in length and 72 feet in breadth, and has a bath 29 feet x 26 feet inside. It has the later-Mughal touch. The central mosque at Palwal, the Bayarwali mosque at Jhajjar and the Nai Mosque at Panipat are also good specimens of the religious architecture of this period.[43]

Many Sikh gurudwaras, specially at Ambala (Manji Sahib), Kurukshetra (Chhathi Padshahi), Lakhan Majra (Rohtak) (Manji Sahib) and Jind (Ninth Padshahi) are of some architectural importance. They have gilded domes and artistic interior make-up.

Some Jain temples, especially at Ambala, Bhiwani, Gurgaon, Rewari, built during this period are also impressive. They are for the most part built of marble and have elegant interior decoration.[44]

There are several Hindu temples also which have architectural merit. Of these Shiva Temple at Sirsa, built by Siryonath Jogi in Rajasthani style depicts good architectural beauty.[45] Murli Manohar Temple at Bahadurgarh (Rohtak) is also impressive. It has five-foot long idols of Radha and Krishna.[46] At Asthal Bohar (Rohtak) there is an important monastery of the jogis (*kanaphatas*). A part of the huge architecture over here is no doubt old (of the pre-medieval and medieval times), but most of its buildings belong to modern times. The Dhuni Chauranginath and Kala Mahal occupy pride of place in the whole complex.[47] At Beri, a small distance from Rohtak, there are many temples of which the one dedicated to goddess Bhimeshwari built in Rajasthani *haveli* style is very impressive.[48] Several temples have also been built at Kurukshetra in modern times. But of these, only two deserve special mention: (i) the Lakshmi Narayan Temple built on the banks of the Sannahit Tank is a magnificent building; it has *chaula* touch which indicates that either the builder or the craftsmen belonged to South India;[49] and (ii) a very recent temple built by G.D. Birla (called Birla Mandir) is also quite an elegant structure, standing amidst a verdant grassy enclosure with a spacious hall floored with marble; it is built in old Orissan style.[50]

The most beautiful of all the temples built during the period under study, is, however, the Gauri-Shankara temple at Bhiwani (Kirori Mal Temple). The multi-storeyed shrine is a magnificent piece of architecture. The entrance is an imposing structure. The shrine has three sub-temples, of Gauri and Shankara in the the middle, and of Laxmi and Vishnu and of Radha and Krishna on the right and left sides respectively. The life-size marble idols of the deities are placed in each sub-temple. Carving of various scenes from epics and *puranas* are configured on the walls, pillars. This adds to the grandeur of the building. The top of the temple is a long pyramidal structure bearing a golden *kalasha* with a trident on the apex. The building is indeed a magnificent structure.[51]

Haryana had made substantial contribution to art and architecture, in the ancient and medieval times. But in the modern age, as seen above, there were certain impediments which stood in the way of the growth and development of these finer aspects of life. Happily the situation has changed after independence. This explains why some positive activity is witnessed in this field in the period from 1947 through 1966.

NOTES

1. It is not unlikely that if a serious search is made some more works of this type may be available.
2. William Bart, *Journey of the March from Delhi to Kabul*, p. 10.
3. The painter was some Wazeer Khan of the Oudh school.
4. *The Tribune*, 10 April 1980.
5. Ibid.
6. *The Marg*, vol. XXIX (1974), no. 1.
7. See S.K. Chaube, *Sangita Ke Gharanaun Ki Charcha*, pp. 92-3.
8. Ibid.
9. Ibid.
10. He belonged to some village in the present district of Sonepat.
11. S.K. Chaube, op. cit., pp. 134-5.
12. Ibid.
13. *JHS*, vol. XV (1983), pp. 21-55.
14. Ibid.
15. Ibid.
16. Ibid.
17. Ibid.
18. Ibid.
19. Ibid.
20. See V.S. Agarwala, *Deeds of Harsha*, for details.
21. Raja Ram Shastri, *Haryana Loka Mancha Ki Kahanian*, Introduction.
22. Ibid.
23. Ibid., pp. 1-8.
24. For details pertaining to these persons and their contributions see ibid., pp. 8-9.
25. *JHS*, vol. XV (1983), pp. 21-55.
26. Ibid.
27. Ibid.

28. For details see K.C. Sharma, *The Life and Works of Lakhmi Chand.*
29. Recently we have seen an experiment performed in this direction by a famous folk artist Mr. Habib Tanvir. The experiment has been quite successful. The *swangs*, *Shahi Lakarahara* and *Jani Chor* of Lakhmi Chand were chosen by him. He retained the original form (the same type of stage, the same type of male actors) but changed the presentation. The atmo-sphere was made natural. The time limit of presentation was reduced from 4-5 hours to 2 hours. The slow going-on of the *swang* was raised and the orchestra improved to suit the performance.
30. K.C. Yadav, *Sketches: Geographical and Historical*, pp. 9-10.
31. Ibid., pp. 26-7.
32. Ibid., p. 37.
33. *JHS*, vol. XV (1983), pp. 25-30.
34. Ibid.
35. Ibid.
36. Ibid.
37. Ibid.
38. The Church was dismantled after the cantonment was shifted from here to Ambala (1843). Now only a part of this tower stands.
39. C.H. Buck, *The Annals of Karnal*, pp. 34-41.
40. K.C. Yadav, *Sketches*, pp. 1-2.
41. Ibid.
42. The account is based on K.C. Yadav, *Freak with the Past: A survey of the Historical Monuments in Haryana*, and personal survey.
43. Ibid.
44. Ibid.
45. Ibid.
46. Ibid.
47. Ibid.
48. Ibid.
49. Ibid.
50. Ibid.
51. Ibid.

Postface

This is the end of the first part of our story—the story which began on 30 December 1803, when Haryana passed under the British control and finished at 1 November 1966, when it became a full-fledged separate state. It is by and large a painful story. For about 143 years, the British exploited the region to the fullest extent to satisfy their colonial greed and imperial designs in literally hundred odd ways. They maltreated the people and spared no weapon in their armoury to break their brave spirit and down their manly morale.

Hearteningly, our people withstood these shocks and injuries right heroically. Not only that, whenever and wherever they could find an opportunity, they tried to undo the oppressive knots of poverty, hunger and dependence. It was thus a long-drawn struggle that they were, like their country-men elsewhere at that time, fated to wage against their rulers.

The struggles, no matter how bloody and long, do have their ends. The one in which the people of Haryana were engaged also terminated on 15 August 1947. As the clock struck 12 at mid night, the Union Jack came down and the Tri-colour took its place. And India became free! The people of Haryana, like their fellow countrymen elsewhere, became masters of their destiny!

The new found freedom, it was hoped, and rightly of course, would change *everything* for the people. Admittedly, the situation did improve. But *everything* did not change. The dreams that the over-exploited backward people of Haryana had seen in the pre-1947 days, were not fulfilled to their satisfaction. Their hopes, aspirations, and needs were not cared for, as they ought to have been in swaraj.

The main reason for this state of affairs was Haryana's being tagged with Punjab. Socially, culturally, linguistically, the two regions—Punjab and Haryana—were different and the elder brother did not look after the interests of the younger one with care and concern. Haryana did not get enough water for its thirsty fields. There was inadequate supply of credit, advisory services and so forth. As a result, the farmers did not get the fruits of hours of patience, care and upkeep of the soil. There was hardly any incentive available here for setting up industry, trade and commerce. There were no adequate facilities for education. No serious concern for health and other welfare activities.

The sufferers felt bad, unhappy and annoyed. They lodged strong protest against the step-motherly treatment meted out to them and demanded their separate state.

There was struggle and strife for a while. Eventually, the separate state of Haryana came into being on 1 November 1966. The people were mighty pleased. And why not?—after all they had become the masters of their destiny in the real sense of the term after a pretty long time.

This is all that we have discussed at length in the present volume.

II

The new state was awfully backward in almost every sphere of life. Small wonder, then, that the newly born became a fashionable object of gloom for many a future teller. This economically unviable thing will not last long, they said. And there seemed to be some sense in their pessimism. Understandably, with no water, minerals and other resources, no experienced managers and leadership, the state was a natural candidate for being doomed sooner than expected. But amazingly, it did not happen. The future tellers, the prophets of doom, were proved wrong. The state not only survived but made great progress in agriculture, trade, commerce, industry and so forth in no time. One of the richest and healthiest states in the country today, it is a synonym of action, affluence and excellence. Every coin, they say, has two sides. Haryana, too, has its bright and black sides. It is materially rich but culturally backward. The intellectual field is infertile. Political awareness is skin-dip. The leadership—a crowd of 'Aya Rams-Gaya Rams'—is immature and untrustworthy. The 'subject culture' where people look towards the powers that be as '*maibaap*' still thrives. They have hardly any taste for mass mobilization for securing rights and privileges.

Why, one might ask, a state, which is so forward-looking, rich and healthy in one field is so backward, old and sick in the other. Answers to this and other such complex questions will be sought in the second volume.

Part Four

BIBLIOGRAPHY

Bibliography

Primary Sources

A. Unpublished Records

I. NATIONAL ARCHIVES OF INDIA, NEW DELHI

(i) *Pre-Mutiny Records*

Finance Department, 1810-59
Foreign Department, 1757-1859
Home Department, 1704-1859
Legislative Department, 1777-1859
Military Department, 1801-81
Public Works Department, 1850-9
Thaggi and Dakaiti Department, 1830-1904

(ii) *Post-Mutiny Records*

Department of Commerce and Industry,1905-20
Department of Commerce, 1920-47
Ministry of Commerce, 1947 onwards
Department of Education, Health, Lands, 1923 onwards
Home Department, 1860 onwards
Public Works Department, 1860 onwards
Reforms Office Records, 1919-47

(iii) *The Punjab Government Records*

Commissioner Ambala Division, 1867-1935
Confidential Files, Native States, 1897-1931
Financial Commissioner, Punjab, Excise Cases, 1888-1918

General and Judicial Departments Proceedings, 1849-60
Native States Proceedings, 1931
Pataudi State Special Bundle, 1881-1900
Miscellaneous Files (Pol. Dept.)
Revenue & Agriculture Files, 1849 onwards

(iv) *Newspapers*

Punjab, 1864-1911, 1920-6.

2. HARYANA STATE ARCHIVES, PANCHKULA

(i) *Ambala Division Records*

Principal Matters, 1822-94
Non-Press listed
(a) All Departments, 1822-55
(b) Judicial Department, 1849-61
(c) Judicial Department, 1846-1984
(d) General & Political Department 1856-84
(e) Military Department, 1881-3
(f) Public Works Department, 1883-4
Press Listed
(a) General & Political Department, 1857-80
(b) Revenue Department, 1856-80
(c) Judicial Department, 1857-64
(d) Military Department, 1857-73
(e) Public Works Department, 1864-85

(ii) *Delhi Division Records*

Principal Matters, 1849-1907
Miscellaneous Records, 1863-1909
Press Listed
(a) Political Department, 1857-64
(b) Revenue Department, 1857-80
(c) General Department, 1857-80
(d) Judicial Department, 1857-73
(e) Military Department, 1857-9
(f) Education Department, 1861-3
(g) Public Works Department, 1862-73
(h) Diary & Despatch Registers, 1861-73
(i) Haqikat-i-Hal-i-Delhi Suba, 6 volumes
(j) Karnal District Urdu Records, 1822-58

(iii) *Hisar Division Records*

Principal Matters, 1855-99
Diary & Despatch Registers, 1878-84

(iv) *Commissionary Records*

AMBALA
English Records, 1920-78
Confidential Records, 1920-53

Hisar

Confidential Records, 1909-47

(v) *District Records*

(a) *D.C. Offices Records*

AMBALA
English Records, 1920-61
Confidential Records, 1889-1956
Secret Records.

GURGAON
English Records, 1857-80
Confidential Records, 1912-69

HISAR
English Records, 1901-57
Confidential Records, 1897-1964

KARNAL
English Records, 1850-1954
Confidential Records, 1878-1967

ROHTAK
English Records, 1910-58
Confidential Records, 1910-63

SONEPAT
Revenue Records, 1912-1900

(b) *Supdt. Police Offices Records*

AMBALA

Confidential Records, 1918-62

GURGAON

Confidential Records, 1913-64
English Records, 1857-1953

ROHTAK

Confidential Records

B. Private Papers

HARYANA STATE ARCHIVES

Habibullah Khan Collection, 1954-63
Praja Mandal Papers, 1945-75
Smt. Shanti Devi Mathur Collection, 1943-69
Ram Bhagat Garg Collection, 1938-67
Harihar Lal Bhargava Collection, 1921-53
Radha Krishan Verma Collection, 1936-55
Mohan Krishan Vaid Collection, 1937-56
Smt. Shakuntla Shukla Collection, 1912-72
Abdul Gaffar Khan Papers, 1962-73

K.C. YADAV COLLECTION

Babu Murlidhar Papers
Sir Chhotu Ram Papers
Zaildar Ghasi Ram Papers
Satypal (Rohtak) Papers
Master Nanhu Ram Papers
Aryanand Sharma Papers
Praja Mandal Papers

C. Newspapers and Journals

Civil & Military Gazettee, Lahore
Grama Sevaka, Hisar

Haryana Review, Chandigarh
Haryana Samvad, Chandigarh
Haryana Tilak, Rohtak
Haryana Research Journal, Rewari
Hindustan Times, Delhi
Journal of Indian History, Trivandrum
Journal of Haryana Studies, Kurukshetra.
Jat Gazette, Rohtak
Praja Shakti, Bhiwani
Punjab Past and Present, Patiala
Punjab History Conference Proceedings, Patiala
The Tribune, Lahore/Ambala/Chandigarh
Young India, Ahmedabad.

The following publications are very useful for our understanding of the history of Haryana:

1. INSTITUTIONAL/GOVERNMENT PUBLICATIONS

All India States Peoples' Conference Bulletin, New Delhi, 1940-7
Census of India (Punjab and Delhi), 1881, 1891, 1901, 1911, 1921, 1931, 1941, 1951, 1961, Lahore, Chandigarh, d.d.
Congress Bulletins, issued by the office of AICC, to 1947.
Evidence taken before the Disorder Inquiry Committee (Hunter Committee), 6 vols., Calcutta, 1920.
District Gazetteers
Ambala District Gazetteer, 1883-4, 1892-3, 1910, 1988
Gurgaon District Gazetteer, 1983-4, 1910, 1988
Hisar District Gazetteer, 1883-4, 1892, 1904, 1988
Karnal District Gazetteer, 1883-4, 1890, 1918, 1976
Rohtak District Gazetteer, 1883-4, 1910, 1976
Mahendragarh District Gazetteer, 1988
Imperial Gazetteer of India, Provincial Series, Punjab, 2 vols., Lahore 1908
Parliamentary Papers, Return of Elections, 1920-37
Report of Punjab Disturbances, April 1919, vol. XIV, Comd. no. 534
Punjab Administration Reports, 1900-35, Lahore, d.d.
Punjab Legislative Council Proceedings, 1920-36, Lahore, d.d.

Punjab Legislative Assembly Proceeding, 1937-66, Lahore, Chandigarh (after 1947), d.d.

Sedition Committee Report (Rowlatt Report), 1918, Calcutta, 1918.

2. NON-INSTITUTIONAL/NON-GOVERNMENTAL PUBLICATIONS/BOOKS

Aggarwal, P.C.: *Caste, Religion and Power*, Delhi, 1971.

Andrew, C.F. and K. Mookerji Girija: *The Rise and Growth of the Congress in India*, 1885-1920, Meerut, 1947.

Argov, Daniel: *Extremists in the Indian National Movement, 1885-1920*, Bombay, 1967.

Bajaj, Y.P.: 'Sir Chhotu Ram', Ph.D. Thesis, Kurukshetra, 1969.

Bakhtawar Singh: *The Social and Economic History of the Punjab,* 1901-39, Delhi, 1971.

Bomford, P.C.: *Histories of the Non-Cooperation and Khilafat Movements*, Delhi, 1974.

Barua, R.J.K.: *Turya Ke Naad, Shankh Ke Swara* (Hindi), Calcutta, 1966.

Barrier, Norman Gerald: 'The Punjab Politics and the Disturbances of 1907', Duke University, Ph.D. thesis, 1966.

———: *The Punjab Alienation of Land Bill of 1900,* Duke University, 1966.

Besant, Mrs. Annie: *How India Wrought for Freedom*, Madras, 1913.

Bhagwan Dev, Acharya: *Balidan* (Hindi), Jhajjar, 1958.

———: *Veer Bhumi Haryana: Nam aur Seema* (Hindi), Jhajjar, 1965.

Bhagwan Josh: *Communist Movement in Punjab*, 1926-47, Delhi, 1979.

Brayne, F.L.: *An Economic Survey of Bhadas* (Gurgaon), Lahore, 1936.

Buddha Parkash: *Haryana Through the Ages*, Kurukshetra, 1966.

Buddha Parkash (ed): *Glimpses of Hariyana*, Kurukshetra, 1967.

Calvert, H.: *Wealth and Welfare of the Punjab*, Lahore, 1922.

Cave-Brown, J.: *Punjab and Delhi in 1857*, 2 vols., Patiala, 1970.

Chhabra, G.S.: *Social and Economic History of the Punjab, 1849-1901,* Jullundur, 1962.

Chhib, S.S.: *The Beautiful India: Haryana*, Delhi, 1977.

Chirol, Valentine: *Indian Unrest*, London, 1910.

Crooke, W.: *Tribes and Castes of the North Western Provinces and Oudh*, 4 vols., Calcutta, 1896.

Cunningham, Allexander: *Archaeological Survey of India, Reports*, 1862-65, Simla, 1871.

Darling, M.L.: *The Punjab Peasant in Prosperity and Debt*, London, 1925.

———: *Wisdom and Waste in the Punjab Villages,* London, 1928.
Desai, A.R.: *Social Background of Indian Nationalism*, London, 1948.
Deol, G.S.: *The Role of the Ghadar Party in the National Movement,* Delhi, 1969.
Dungen, P.H.M. Vanden: *The Punjab Tradition*, London, 1972.
Duni Chand: *The Ulster of India*, Lahore, 1936.
Elliot, M.: *Memoies on the History, Folklore and Distribution of the Races of the North Western Provinces of India*, London, 1869.
Fauja Singh: *Eminent Freedom Fighters of Punjab*, Patiala, 1972.
———: *A Brief Account of Freedom Movement in the Punjab*, Delhi, 1972.
Gandhi, M.K.: *The Collected Works of Mahatma Gandhi*, 100 vols., Delhi, d.d.
Ghose, K.: *The Role of Honour*, Calcutta, 1965
Ghosh, K.K.: *The Indian National Army*, Meerut, 1969.
Griffin, L.H.: *Chiefs and Families of Note in the Punjab*, 2 vols., Lahore, 1909-40.
———: *The Rajas of the Punjab*, 2 vols., Lahore, 1890.
Gupta, Daulat Ram: *My Sixty Years Reminiscences*, Rohtak, 1974.
Gustafron, W.E. & Jones K.W. (eds.): *Sources on Punjab History*, Delhi, 1975.
Handa, R.L.: *History of Freedom Struggle in Princely States*, Delhi, 1968.
Hussain, Azim: *Fazl-i-Hussain—A Political Biography*, Bombay, 1946.
Hussain, Mohammad: *An Attack on the Police Administration of Punjab Native States*, Ambala, 1893.
Hussain, Mohammad Syed: *Tarikhe-i-Patiala* (Urdu), Amritsar, 1877.
Hutchins, Francis G.: *The Illusion of Permanence; British Imperialism in India*, New Jersey, 1967.
Ibbetson, Denzil: *Punjab Castes*, Lahore, 1916.
Jagdish Chandra: *Gandhiji and Haryana*, Delhi, 1977.
———: *Freedom Struggle in Haryana*, Kurukshetra, 1982.
Jones, K.W.: *Arya Dharam: Hindu Consciousness in the 19th Century Punjab*, Delhi, 1976.
———: *Lajpat Rai: Autobiographical Writings,* Delhi, 1965.
Joshi, V.C. (ed.): *Lajpat Rai: Writings and Speeches of Lajpat Rai,* Delhi, 1966.
Juneja, M.M.: *Neki Ram Sharma and the Freedom Movement*, Hisar, 1976.

———: *Eminent Freedom Fighters of Haryana,* Hisar, 1981.

Kapil Dev: *Bhagat Phool Singh* (Hindi), Bhainswaḷ, 1966.

Kaur, M.N.: *Role of Women in the Freedom Struggle, 1857-1947,* Delhi, 1968.

Kaye, Sir John: *History of the Sepoy War*, 3 vols, London, 1870.

Lajpat Rai: *History of the Arya Samaj*, Bombay, 1967.

Leigh, M.S.: *Punjab and the War*, Lahore, 1922.

Madan Gopal: *Sir Chhotu Ram: A Political Biography*, Delhi, 1977.

Majumdar, B.B. and B.P. Majumdar: *Congress and Congressmen in the Pre-Gandhian Era. 1885-1917*, Calcutta, 1957.

Majumdar, R.C.: *History of the Freedom Movement in India*, 3 vols., Calcutta, 1962-3.

Malhotra, S.L.: *Gandhi and the Punjab*, Chandigarh, 1970.

Malleson, J.B.: *History of the Indian Mutiny*, 3 vols., London, 1880.

Mitra, H.N. (ed.): *Punjab Unrest Before and After the Rowlatt Bills*, Calcutta, 1920.

Mitra, N.N. (ed.): *The Indian Annual Register, 1900-47*, Calcutta, d.d

Mittal, S.C.: *Freedom Struggle in Punjab, 1905-29*, Delhi, 1976.

Muztar, B.K.: *Kurukshetra: Political & Cultural,* Delhi, 1978.

Naidis, Mark: *The Punjab Disturbances of 1919: A Study in Nationalism*, Microfilm NMM & L.

Niemeijer, A.C.: *The Khilafat Movement in India, 1919-24*, The Hague, 1972.

O'Dwyer, Michael: *India as I Knew it, 1885-1925*, London, 1926.

Panigrahi, D.N.: *Charles Metchalfe in India*, Delhi, 1968.

Panikkar, K.N.: *British Diplomacy in Northern India*, Delhi, 1968.

Prabhakar, D.S.: *Swadheenta Sangram Aur Haryana* (Hindi), Delhi, 1976.

Pradhan, M.C.: *The Political System of the Jats of Northern India,* London, 1966.

Punjab: Economic Enquiry: *Village Survey, Naggal*, Lahore, 1933.

Punjab Govt.: *Punjab Govt. Records: Delhi, Residency & Agency* Records, vol. I, Lahore.

Qanungo, K.R.: *A History of the Jats*, vol. I, Calcutta, 1925.

Raghubir Singh: *Chaudhary Chhotu Ram* (Hindi), Rohtak, 1965.

Rai, Satya M.: *Partition of the Punjab*, Delhi, 1965.

Rajaram: *The Jallianwala Bagh Massacre: A Pre-mediated Plan,* Chandigarh, 1964.

Ranjit Singh: *Hariyana Mein Arya Samaj Ka Itihas* (Hindi), Rohtak, 1975.

———: *Ch. Chhotu Ram: Gaurava Gatha,* Rohtak, 1991.
Rao, M.S.A. (ed.): *Social Movements in India*, 2 vols., Delhi, 1979.
———: *Social Movements and Social Transformations*, Delhi, 1979.
Risley, Herbert; *The People of India*, Calcutta, 1915.
Ross, David: *The Land of the Five Rivers and Sindh*, London, 1883.
Rose, H.A : *A Glossary of the Tribes and Castes of the Punjab and North and North-Western Provinces*, 3 vols., Chandigarh, 1970.
Satya Pal, Parbodh Chandra: *Sixty Years of Congress*, Lahore, 1946.
Sangat Singh: *Freedom Movement in Delhi, 1885-1919*, Delhi, 1972.
Sen, N.B. (ed): *Punjab's Eminent Hindus*, Lahore, 1944.
Sen, S.P. (ed.): *Dictionary of National Biography*, 4 vols., Calcutta, 1972-74.
Shakir, Moin: *Khilafat to Partition,* New Delhi, 1970.
Sharma, Neki Ram: *Shasan Sudhar Praveshika*, Bhiwani, 1920.
Sharma, R.S.: *Haryana: Directory and Who's Who,* Ambala, 1968.
Sharma, Shri Ram: *Haryana Ka Itihas* (Hindi), Rohtak, 1977.
———: *Meri Apni Ram Kahani* (Hindi), Rohtak, 1977.
———: 'Haryana Men Congress Ki Tahreek' (Urdu), Rohtak (unpublished), 1935.
———: *Haryana Ke Swatantra Senani* (Hindi), Rohtak, 1973.
———: *Asaudha Ka Satyagraha* (Urdu), Rohtak, n.d.
Shukla, S.P.: *India's Freedom Struggle and the Role of Haryana*, Delhi, 1985.
Sitaramayya, B.P.: *The History of Indian National Congress*, 2 vols., Bombay, 1946-7
Spear, Percival: *Twilight of the Mughals*, London, 1951.
Sugla, Harda Rai: *Pt. Neki Ram Sharma—Abinandan Granth* (Hindi), Calcutta, 1953.
Tara Chand: *History of the Freedom Movement in India*, 4 vols., Delhi, 1967-72.
Tendulkar, D.G.: *Mahatma—Life of Mohandas Karam Chand Gandhi*, 1869-1948, 8 vols., Delhi, 1952-4.
Tika Ram: *Sir Chhotu Ram—An Apostle of Hindu-Muslim Unity,* Lahore, 1946.
Verma, D.C.: *Sir Chhotu Ram—Life and Times*, New Delhi, 1981.
Waheed Ahmad (ed.): *Diary and Notes of Mian Fazl-i-Hussain*, Lahore, 1977.
———: *Letters of Mian Fazl-i-Hussain*, Lahore, 1976.
Walia, Ramesh: *Praja Mandal Movement in East Punjab States*, Patiala, 1972.

Wallace, Paul: *Political Party System of Punjab States, India: A Study of Factionalism* (Microfilm NMM & L).

Yadav, J.N.S. (ed.): *Haryana: Studies in History & Politics*, Gurgaon, 1976.

Yadav, K.C.: *Rao Tula Ram: A Hero of 1857,* Rewari, 1966.

———: *Ahirwal Ka Itihas* (Hindi), Delhi, 1967.

——— (ed.) : *Haryana: Studies in History and Culture*, Kurukshetra, 1968.

———: *The Revolt of 1857 in Haryana,* Delhi, 1977.

——— (ed.) : *Autobiography of Dayananda Saraswati*, Delhi, 1977, 1979, 1988.

——— (tr. ed.) : *Bechara Kisan* (by Sir Chhotu Ram), Hisar, 1979.

——— (ed.): *Delhi in 1857: Trial of Bahadur Shah*, Delhi, 1979.

———: *History of Haryana*, 3 vols., Macmillans, 1981-2.

———: *History and Culture of Haryana: A Classified and Annotated Bibliography* (co-author), Delhi, 1981.

———: *The Builders of Our Nation,* vol. I, *Murlidhar*, Kurukshetra, 1987.

———: *The Builders of Our Nation*, vol. II, *Shri Ram Sharma,* Kurukshetra, 1991.

———: *Arya Samaj and Freedom Movement* (co-author), vol. I, 1988.

———: *Rao Raja Tula Ram* (Hindi), Kurukshetra, 1988, 1998.

———: *Haryana: Swatantra Andolana Mein Kaviyon, Shairon, Bhajnopadshakon Ka Yogadana*, Delhi, 1988.

———: *Haryana Ka Zabtashuda Rashtriya Sahitya*, Delhi, 1988.

———: *Haryana: Itihas Evam Sanskriti*, 2 vols., Delhi, 1994.

——— (ed.): *Crisis in India: Reflections of Sir Chhotu Ram*, Kurukshetra, 1996.

Index